The Mysterious Life of the Body

DATE DUE

2004

The Mysterious Life of the Body:
A New Look at Psychosomatics

Jennifer Bullington

Linköping Studies in Arts and Science

In the Faculty of Arts and Sciences at Linköping University research is pursued and research training given within six broad problem areas known as themes, in Swedish tema. These are: Child Studies, Gender Studies, Health and Society, Communication Studies, Technology and Social Change and Water and Environmental Studies. Each tema publishes its own series of scientific reports, but they also publish jointly the series Linköping Studies in Arts and Science.

Distributed by:

Almqvist & Wiksell International

Jennifer Bullington
The Mysterious Life of the Body: A New Look at Psychosomatics

ISBN 91 - 22 - 01844 - 1

Cover picture: Francis Bacon 1909-1992 British
    Study from the human body 1949
    oil on canvas
    147.0 x 134.2 cm
    Purchased, 1953
    National Gallery of Victoria, Melbourne, Australia

Cover design: Monika Thörnell
Typeset: Monika Thörnell
Printed by: Kanaltryckeriet i Motala AB, 1999

"When I see myself in the phenomena of existence, I never see my true self; my transcendence alone lends to all finite phenomena a weight they could not have as mere existence. I see transcendence and feel sure of being even if it does not speak to me, even as I defy it. When I do not see it anymore, I feel myself go down."

Karl Jaspers

Table of Contents

PART II: A Phenomenological Theory of Psychosomatics

Prefatory Note and Acknowledgements

Ever since I was a child I have wondered how this particular collection of skin and bones and blood and nerve cells could be *me*? Where am *I* in all of this stuff? Or, in a similar vein, how is it possible to *see* with these globes we have in our eye sockets? What does it really mean, to see? What happens when I want to scratch my head, and my arm magically rises towards the itch? How is it that I can begin to speak a sentence without knowing exactly how it will end? I found out later on in life that these kinds of questions were not so strange as I thought, in fact they are perfectly respectable philosophical questions, the kinds of things you can write about in a dissertation. Consequently, it is with great pleasure that I begin my investigation of something which has always fascinated me, something called "the mind-body problem" in philosophy.[1] This classical philosophical issue is not only vast and complex, but has been debated for thousands of years by philosophers, theologians, writers and the like. I humbly admit that my task in this dissertation must be to find a small niche where I can have something to say about this topic, without drowning in the immensity of the issue. I have decided to approach the mind-body problem (or mystery) through examining psychosomatic pathology. The reason I have chosen this area of investigation is that psychosomatic diseases/illnesses are in themselves witness to the peculiar double nature of man. We are both psyche and soma, although how these terms are to be understood, and how they relate to one another are questions which this dissertation must address.

---

[1] A modern formulation of the mind-body problem is, how can states of consciousness arise in human brains, and how are we to understand the nature of the relationship between brain states and conscious acts? In other words, how do neurological processes relate to thoughts and volitions?

Studying psychosomatic pathology gives us a special opportunity to examine the mystery that is *me*, the mind-body unity[2]. Psychosomatic questions are, for example, how can something we think, wish, fear, or desire result in disease? How can the mind "cause" (or contribute to) somatic dysfunction? How can an experience (e.g. bereavement, stress, conflict) get "translated" into body pathology? As we shall see, these questions are not just the musing of philosophers, but are in fact of central importance to the understanding of psychosomatic diseases/illnesses. Because more and more clinicians begin to understand that the biomedical model of disease is insufficient for understanding the complaints of many patients seeking health care today, it is of vital practical importance that we come to a satisfactory theoretical understanding of psychosomatic health problems.

It was first during my psychotherapeutical work with psychosomatic patients within psychiatric health care that I started to wonder professionally about the psychosomatic connection between mind and body, person and world, health and disease. Patients seemed to become cured of their bodily symptoms and diseases when they succeeded in getting a grip on their lives. How to understand this? It seemed obvious to me that the mind-body problem was the issue, although I had not seen in clinical literature any satisfactory theoretical explication of how the mind-body interaction (relation) should be understood. In terms of treatment strategy, the Freudians seemed happy enough with their conversion premise (see chapter 2) and understood their job in terms of helping patients become conscious of unconscious conflicts. The medical doctors concerned themselves for the most part with trying out new medications, adjusting dosage and so on. This is of course a bit of a caricature, but there is some truth in the maxims "it's all in your mind" or

---

2 Defenders of substance dualism would question the "unity" contention here, and maintain that personhood need not necessarily be embodied. The notion of a person depends rather upon the unity of consciousness over time. A person would be, then, a matter of consciousness rather than the body which happens to support consciousness. The position I will be taking is that human beings are always necessarily embodied consciousness.

"it's all in your body". I never felt at home in either of these camps. It seemed to me that what was needed was some way to understand how the mind-body unity expressed itself through the psychosomatic pathology. There is perhaps nothing novel or revolutionary about this idea, until one starts to problematize what mind *is*. What kind of body are we talking about? Why would someone want to communicate in this way? Can the body express and take up meaning? What would this level of meaning be? To answer these types of questions, we need to formulate the field in a new way.

Thanks to the research program at Tema H. I have been able to pursue these questions in depth and take part in the exciting intellectual work-place that is Tema. There are many people who have given me inspiration and companionship during these last 5 years. I would like to first of all thank my two dissertation supervisors Lennart Nordenfelt and Jan Willner. They have given me good advice and encouragment and have posed some hard questions which have all been of great help to me in writing this dissertation. Helge Malmgren was a very appreciated opponent at my final dissertation seminar. Many thanks as well to my doctoral group colleagues at Tema, Agneta Andersson, Anita Björklund, Motzi Eklöf, Rikard Eriksson, Fredrik Svenaeus and Sam Willner, for our first years together as doctoral students. Special thanks to Fredrik Svenaeus who has made valuable comments on earlier drafts of my work and with whom I have had interesting discussions. The Tema librarians Christina Brage, Rosmari Malmgård and Inger Agendal were a fantastic help in the course of this project. Thanks to Monika Thörnell for her careful work on the manuscript, and to Yvonne Blixt, Lena Hector, Anna Schenell and Kerstin Sonnesson for their patient and tireless assistance with all adminstrative tasks. Thanks also to Malcolm Forbes for careful proof- reading of the final manuscript.

Outside of Tema a number of people have been involved in my work and I would like to give special thanks to Olle Hellström for his interest, encouragment and enthusiasm. Birgitta Sören has also been a loyal supporter. You both made me feel like I had something important to say. The "study circle" group in philosophy meeting every other Sunday evening for the last 13 years has been a source of inspiration and fun, so thank you Gunnar Karlsson, Gloria Zeligman and Ulf Åkerström! Before coming to Tema I had the privlege of working at a fantastic out-patient clinic in Kista, and to my co-workers from those years I want to send very warm thanks for those days. Going even further back, I must mention two teachers at Duquesne who made an impression on me and opened up my interest in phenomenology, Andy Giorgi and Paul Richer. My parents have been very supportive and I thank you both. Last but not least, my husband Gunnar Karlsson has been a constant dialogue partner, critic, supporter and all -round light of my life. Thanks to you all!

Linköping, March 1999

PART I:

Analysis of Traditional Theories of Psychosomatics

CHAPTER 1

The mind-body problem and psychosomatic pathology

"We impute no mentality to sticks and stones because they never seem to move for the sake of anything, but always when pushed, and then indifferently and with no signs of choice. So we unhesitatingly call them senseless."

--William James

"We know that brains are the de-facto causal basis of consciousness, but we have, it seems, no understanding whatever of how this can be so. It strikes us as miraculous, eerie, even faintly comic. Somehow, we feel, the water of the physical brain is turned into the wine of consciousness, but we draw a total blank on the nature of this conversion."

--Colin McGinn

"You would not find out the limits of the psyche, even though you should travel every road, so deep a logos does it have."

--Heraclitus

Background

The relationship between the mind and the body has fascinated and confused thinkers for thousands of years. Unfortunately, modern advances in neuroscience do not make the problem any easier to understand. The question of how synapses and transmitter substances in the brain relate to subjective states, ideas and wishes of the person is just a sharper picture of the problem, not its solution. Our modern everyday understanding of ourselves is dualistic.[1] Mind-body dualism cleaves man into two parts, an immaterial mind, or soul, and a material body. Descartes usually gets blamed for mind-body dualism, although one can find dualistic conceptions of man as early as 3000 BC in Egyptian hieroglyphics, where the deceased is depicted in terms of a body, a soul (Ba) and a non-material representation of the body (Ka). In the Judeo-Christian tradition, the Old Testament view of man is usually considered to be holistic,[2] while dualism is said to have infiltrated Christian thinking with the writings of St. Paul and the influence of Neoplatonic philosophy on early Christian theologists, especially St. Augustine. Our modern dualism stems from the thinking of Descartes, who lived during the scientific revolution of the 1600s. A radical change in world view took place during this time. Due to the success of the science of physics, a new, "modern" way of thinking about nature and the world took form. Nature was no longer considered to be driven by an innate spirituality *(telos)*, but rather worked in accordance with mechanical laws and principles, which could be discovered and formed into a comprehensive sys-

---

1   The term "dualism" comes from the Latin *dualis* meaning two-fold. Dualism states that the world is made up of two kinds of essences, that which is spirit or mind (immaterial) and that which is material. The opposite of dualism is monism, which maintains that there is only one basic stuff in the universe. A monistic position on the mind-body problem would be that minds and brains are made up of the same substance. Although dualists are in agreement about the dual nature of reality, there are controversies among them regarding the nature of the relationship between the material and the immaterial, and their interdependence.

2   The terms used to conceptualize man in the Semitic Old Testament are somewhat foreign to our modern way of thinking. Man is described in (Hebraic) terms of *ruach, nefesch, basar, leb*, each referring to a different aspect of the whole human being. Ruach is a term also used to describe the wind, or breathing, and in terms of man it generally refers to the vitalistic idea of God's breath/life in human beings. Nefesch refers to the neck, or throat, and it symbolizes the aspect of man which is dependent upon God. Nefesch becomes "psyché" ("anima" in Latin) in the New Testament, coming close to our "soul". Basar is the Hebrew word for body, carrying connotations of sociality, indicating creatures who are dependent upon one another. Basar can *also* refer to feelings and thoughts, interestingly enough. Leb is the heart, and comes closest to what we moderns would call "the self." Leb is the center of man's will and freedom. All four of these terms refer to different aspects of an integrated whole. I am indebted to Ulf Jonsson, SJ, for this information.

tem. Descartes was inspired by the advances made in physics, and he himself wanted to work out a universal mechanism. In Descartes' system, the human body belonged to the realm of mechanized nature, which scientists were so successfully mapping out in causal, mathematical terms. Descartes is famous for his classification of man into two different substances, the material body (*res extensa*) and the immaterial soul (*res cogitans*). Scientists had relieved the world of its soul, and Descartes finished the job by getting rid of the life of the body. From this time onward, the body was considered to be a kind of machine, mechanized and obedient to the rules of physics, while the human soul was something *different* from the body. And how these two spheres could interact with each other became the core of the mind-body problem.

Dualism states that the mind does not depend upon the body for its existence. A dualist will have to say that a person *could* exist without his or her body. To support this, they may point out that we can imagine being disembodied, or that many people in fact claim to have experienced being disembodied in near-death experiences. However, dualists admit that *empirically* we understand human beings in terms of a self or person tied to a physical body. Minds and bodies somehow belong together, however this is to be understood. One of the biggest problems dualism has to face is that of mental causation. In other words, how can the mental, conceived of as non-spatial and immaterial, exert an influence on the material extended body? Daniel Dennett has criticized dualism by remarking that a "ghost in the machine"[3] is of no help to your theory unless it is a ghost who can move things around, but if it can do that, it's not really a ghost, is it? Modern dualists such as Karl Popper and J.C. Eccles[4] have argued that the notion of mental causation is no real problem. As soon as one abandons the mechanistic, physicalistic no-

---

[3] The "ghost in the machine" is Gilbert Ryle's somewhat derogatory characterization of dualistic conceptualizations of mind, coined in his book *The Concept of Mind* (1949). To imagine mind as a force or power steering the body like a captain in a ship is a myth, according to Ryle. All of these dualistic notions which we have about mind are simply erroneous ways of thinking and speaking. For a modern version of this argument, see Dennett (1991).

[4] Popper & Eccles (1977).

tion of causation inherited from Descartes,[5] and replaces it with more modern, sophisticated notions of causation, one can in fact understand the mysterious interaction between the mental and the physical. Popper's most recent theory of mind likens it to a force field.[6] The idea that fields of force can influence matter is not controversial. We have no trouble today imagining that electromagnetic fields, as intensities, can influence material bodies. For the modern defenders of dualism, the only mind-body problem is a pseudo issue, based upon the erroneous notion that we have to reconcile an immaterial mind with an outdated, mechanical, material conception of causation. Once we change our notion of causation, dualism becomes feasible.[7] However, we are still left with the puzzling question, what is influencing what, and how? It is one thing to state that the mental is not reducible to the physical, it is a far more complicated matter to explain the relationship between the two. According to Noam Chomsky, the mind-body problem is so baffling that we must seriously consider the possibility that it could be one of those things which simply exceed our power of understanding. Just as a chimpanzee cannot appreciate a painting by Cézanne, or solve mathematical problems, so are we incapable of thinking about or understanding the mind-body problem. We are simply not equipped with the understand-

---

5 For Descartes and his contemporaries, all causal influence was conceptualized in terms of physical, mechanical, spatial causality. Causality could thus only exist between spatially extended bodies.

6 See Lindahl & Århem (1994).

7 One example of this would be so-called "downward causation" (Campbell 1974), which refers to the way in which the whole, or macro-structure may act upon an elementary particle or part. This is the opposite of reductionism, where the whole is explained as the sum of the parts (upward causation). Downward causation entails causal chains from emergent mental phenomena acting *downwards* upon physiological neural functioning. An example of this is given in Levine (1991), where he relates a study by a Japanese researcher Tsunoda, who examined the way in which the brain registers various listening tasks. He found that the area of the brain where Japanese people registered certain sounds, such as laughter and crying, was not the same as the one where Westerners registered these same sounds in a different part of the brain. The interesting exception to this finding was in the cases where the Westerner had managed to master the Japanese language fluently. These individuals registered the sounds in the same part of the brain as the Japanese.

ing necessary to grasp the mystery of how neurological occurrences relate to our mental life. It remains one of those incomprehensible things that we have to learn to live with. Another possibility is that the mind-body issue is wrongly construed from the start, and that we need to reformulate the problem. Part II of this dissertation will be a step in this direction.

Most people can say what body is, but it is not quite as easy to say what mind is. What *is* mind, after all, this specifically human capacity[8] which causes such so much philosophical trouble? Traditionally, mind is characterized by qualities such as the subjective, private, non-spatial, qualitative, intentional, privileged access (known only to me).[9] Mind has to do with our thoughts, feelings, attitudes, consciousness, self-awareness and so on. It is the "inside" of our experienced life. The crux of the mind-body problem is that these mental qualities are characterized in direct opposition to physical ones, such as the objective, public, spatial, quantitative and mechanical. For the dualists, it is difficult to relate these two spheres of mutually exclusive terms to one another, but it is just as hard for monists to *identify* these qualities with one another, i.e. to say that pain (subjective) *is* a brain state (objective). The question is, what ontological status do we wish to give these kinds of mental things? If one believes that mind is real, unique and all-pervasive, one is a mentalist /idealist. If one accepts the idea that mind exists alongside of the material

---

8 As we shall see in a later discussion, animals also possess "mind" in various forms. However, when I speak of mind and meaning without qualification, I am referring to the specifically human capacity for symbolic language, self-consciousness, consciousness of death and so on. It is these "higher orders" of mind which are of interest for this dissertation.

9 An interesting curiosity regarding the development of the term "consciousness" is that it derives from the Latin *con* meaning "together with" and *scire* meaning "to know." The original Latin verb *conscius* meant literally "to share knowledge together with other people", a sharing which originally seemed to include anyone and everyone. During the Middle Ages, the knowledge which was shared became limited to "sharing with some people, but not others." Finally, the only one with whom one shared this knowledge was oneself, the one who was *conscious of* something. Thus, the concept of consciousness has been transformed from shared knowledge to intimate knowledge, to privileged access (in Humphrey (1992), pp. 101-102).

world, one is a <u>dualist</u>. If one believes that mind is ultimately the same kind of stuff as the material world, one is a <u>materialist</u>. Strict mentalism, which reduces the body to the mind, is no longer a viable position today. The modern line of demarcation runs between various dualistic conceptualizations of mind and matter on the one hand, and different forms of materialism on the other. Dualists must account for the interaction between mind and body, while materialists must show that we can ultimately and adequately understand the mental in terms of physical processes and behavior.[10] Since the 1950's, materialism has been the dominant orientation in the philosophy of mind.[11] Strict reductive materialism maintains that mind is nothing but certain neurophysiological processes. Reductive materialism is sometimes also called "radical materialism" or "eliminative physicalism" or "eliminative materialism" since it eliminates the psychical as a phenomenon in its own right. Other materialists, such as Feigl[12], allow the psychical a certain reality status (i.e. there *are* such things as mental processes and internal events), but claim that although these inner states really do exist, they are merely the "inner principle" of brain states. This version of materialism, sometimes called

---

[10] There are some compromise positions between these two poles, the best known being neutral monism, which rejects both dualism and materialism. There is neither mind nor matter, but some third thing to which both mind and matter can be reduced. Although mind is here considered to be of the same substance as the physical, it does nevertheless possess further, unique properties which go beyond physical properties. This position is monistic, since it says that there is only one substance in the universe, although this one substance has "double-aspects" which show themselves in different ways. Emergent theory (sometimes classified as a form of dualism) is a variation on this theme, allowing that consciousness and mental life, as real mental properties, spontaneously emerge from the material once it has reached a sufficiently complex state of organization. The mind is dependent upon the brain, but it transcends the material and cannot be reduced to physical/physiological processes. The mental must be understood holistically according to emergent theory, and as such it cannot be defined atomistically in terms of the sum of its parts. Lloyd Morgan (1852-1936) originally formulated the emergent theory, while R.W. Sperry is a modern proponent of this position.

[11] Well-known representatives of the materialist tradition in the philosophy of mind are D.M. Armstrong, H. Feigl, P.K. Feyerabend, U.T. Place, and J.J.C. Smart.

[12] See Feigl (1958).

the "identity-theory" or "central state theory" of mind, claims that the mind and the brain are really just two aspects of one and the same thing. We mean, or refer, to the same thing when we say "mental act" and "brain state." The different designations have to do with the different modes of access we have to this one entity. When we speak of mind and inner experiences, we are using introspection and describing how this referent (mind/brain) shows itself via subjective experience, seen from the "inside." When we speak of brain states, we are describing how this same referent shows itself to us via neurophysiological procedures, seen from the "outside." Critics of materialism contest the idea that there can ever be an identity between mental life and physiological occurrences. There will always be something left essentially unaccounted for if we try to say, for example, that the experience of pain *is* such and such a brain state. The phenomenal aspects of experienced events (what it is *like* to have a pain) are not captured in physicalistic descriptions. I don't have a brain state, I have a *headache.* Accordingly, the mental *as* mental cannot, in principle, be approximated in physiological terms.[13]

If one is a materialist, the basic question concerns demonstrating how mental life, if it exists at all, is comprehensible in terms of material/physicalistic descriptions. And if the mental sphere does exist, what is its relation to the physical? The only form of materialism which can avoid the interaction problem here (which all dualists must necessarily take on) is strict eliminative reductionism, that is, the conviction that there are no mental processes. A variety of both empirical and theoretical problems arise if one takes this eliminative position. Firstly, it denies at the outset something that is an empirical given, i.e. the existence of our inner life, which we all have access to in an immediate, intuitive way. It is absurdly counterintuitive to claim that there are no subjective, phenomenal features of mental life.[14] We can just decide to think it away,

---

[13] See Nagel, T. (1974).

[14] Nagel, T. (1986) puts the matter in the following way: "There are things about the world and life and ourselves that cannot be adequately understood from a maximally objective standpoint, however much it may extend our understanding beyond the point from which we started...and the attempt to give a complete account of the

but this is intellectually unsatisfying. Secondly, there are many phenomena in life which are simply incomprehensible in physicalistic terms, for example how can we understand the phenomenon of preference in terms of material causes? Putman[15] takes the example of the fact that one person prefers ice cream to cake in order to demonstrate that there cannot be any physical, chemical structure the possession of which is a necessary and sufficient condition for preferring A to B. There may be people who prefer ice cream to cake who have completely different neurophysiological make-ups. The disposition to prefer ice cream to cake is not logically defined by X neurons in the brain (the "is" of definition) but must be understood as a contingent, empirical fact, that is, this person P who has this particular physical-chemical make-up, happens to prefer ice cream (the "is" of constitution[16]). There are in fact a variety of phenomena from our everyday experience which intuitively go against the materialist contention that the subjective life can be adequately explained or understood in terms of physical, material processes.

If one rejects eliminative materialism and opts for some form of interaction (either dualism or one of the weaker forms of materialism which allow for the existence of the mental in one way or another), then there are the classical interaction problems to solve. Dualists have the hardest task, namely to understand: 1) the nature of the interaction between the mental and the physical, defined as mutually exclusive categories; 2) the notion of mental causation (efficacy from mind to body); 3) the evolutionary origin of consciousness.[17] As for the materialists, as soon

---

world in objective terms detached from these perspectives (the subjective, particular point of view) inevitably leads to false reductions or to outright denial that certain patently real phenomena exist at all" (p. 7).

15 Putnam (1976).

16 Putnam (ibid.) distinguishes between the "is" of definition, dealing with logical, necessary truths (the square *is* an equilateral rectangle), and the "is" of constitution, having to do with a relationship between contingent statements in need of empirical verification (her hat *is* a bundle of straw tied together with a string.)

17 This third problem only applies to the non-theistic dualists, who cannot point to God as the source of consciousness. The problem is to show why and how consciousness arose in terms of evolution.

as the mind and the brain are allowed to have different properties, which some materialists would admit, one has the difficulty of explaining their alleged identity, as well as the usual problems about the nature of causality from mind to body. Since the statement "the mind is the brain" is considered to be a contingent statement of identity rather than a logical truth, materialists who believe in mind as something real have to be able to give logically independent meanings to "mind" and "brain" which nevertheless avoid violating their materialism. If one takes the line of retreat that the only real difference between mind and brain concerns the two different *avenues of knowledge* used to approach the mind-brain entity (introspection vs. neural-chemical investigations), we still need to understand what introspection *is*. If introspection is itself a brain process, we have the peculiar situation where one part of the brain is somehow looking at other parts of the brain. If introspection is not a brain process, then we have discovered a mentalistic term at the heart of our materialistic theory, which needs to be accounted for. In conclusion, dualism saves the mental as mental, but at the price of generating a variety of philosophical problems concerning interaction and efficacy. Weaker forms of materialism are also tied up in conceptual problems, and although eliminative materialism avoids the mind-body conundrum, it has nothing to say about our actual experiences of mind and mental life.[18]

---

[18] The analytic philosophers Ryle and Wittgenstein also question the existence of "mind" as the term is used. There is no real referent for "mind." Accordingly, the mind-body problem springs from a language problem, a so-called "category mistake" (Ryle). Words we have for "inner states" such as "happy" or "sad" do not describe inner states, but are simply a part of our behavior. We have all learned various ways of speaking about ourselves which we erroneously ascribe to a private sphere. This is one of the central ideas in classical behaviorist psychology as well.

The mind-body problem in relation to psychosomatic pathology[19]: a general charactarization of the field of inquiry

Many theoreticians within psychiatry and psychosomatic medicine dislike the term "psychosomatic." It is said to emphasize a dichotomy between mind and body which specialists like to think has been resolved. However, the term is so entrenched in our thinking that it is not likely to disappear. The term "psychosomatic" was historically preceded by various combinations of *psyche* and *soma* such as "psycho-physical", "psycho-organic", and even "Psychical Medicine". An early use of the term psychosomatic has been dated to the year 1838, when Christian Friedriche Nasse and Maximilian Jacobi founded a new periodical, "Zeitschrift für die Beurtheilung und Heilung der krankhaften Seelenzustände", containing several articles which used the term *"psychisch-somatisch"* and even the reverse *"somatisch-psychischen"*.[20] The earliest printed use of the term *psychische-somatisch* is found in 1818, in Professor of Psychiatry Johan Christian Heinroth's *Lehrbuch der Störungen...*[21] where he used it to characterize insomnia. The idea being expressed in all of these hyphenated words is the understanding that the psyche as well as the body is somehow involved in the etiology of the conditions of disease and ill health being described. This is really no new insight. The psychosomatic concept is ancient. But that which is especially modern, and problematic, is that we have come to understand the psyche, or soul, or mental life, or consciousness, in terms of non-material processes. Because of this, we have a hard time understanding how mental processes such as

---

19 The term psychosomatic "pathology" comes from the medical tradition, and carries with it biomedical associations. Following traditional usage, the terms psychosomatic "pathology", "conditions," "diseases/illnesses" and "symptoms" will be used in the dissertation, referring to various aspects of the psychosomatic way of functioning. The terms "pathology" and "condition" will be used interchangeably, while "disease/illness" and "symptoms" refer to the nature of the condition and to the specific manifestation of the condition, respectively. I will also use the term psychosomatic "pathology" in the phenomenological section (part II), for lack of a better word, since I too find this functioning to be maladaptive, but for specific reasons which will be made clear in the development of the phenomenological theory.

20 Recounted in Margetts (1950).

21 See Heinroth (1818), p. 49.

thoughts, feelings and attitudes can influence the functioning and structure of the somatic, physical body. As will be soon seen, any theory of psychosomatic pathology must attempt to deal with this problem. For example, how do psychosomaticians understand and conceptualize meaning-constitution, intentionality, attention, understanding and subjective interpretation? How do they characterize psycho-social factors, which are said to be so important in the development of psychosomatic pathology? What are their ontological status, and what are the mechanisms by which they "cause" somatic dysfunction? The mind-body problem and psychosomatic theory are inextricably bound up with one another. As my analyses will show, although we may have an increased awareness today of some of the theoretical problems associated with psychosomatic theory, we do not have a satisfactory solution to the mind-body problem in any modern theory, nor any feasible alternative way of conceptualizing the field.

As the coming chapters will show, the traditional psychosomatic theories I will be examining in this dissertation are either dualistic or reductionistic/materialistic. We will find either an objective mechanical body in some inexplicable relationship to psycho-social factors, or a characterization of the human being as a complex functional system, a system which ultimately replaces the person with the workings of the brain.[22] The problem is that the dualistic theories do not shed light on that which was to be the specialty of psychosomatic theory, namely explicating the relationship between the functioning of the body and the

---

22 The main problem with functionalistic conceptions of man is that there is no one there to *experience* anything in the system. Functionalists such as Dennett would reply that this is exactly the strength of functionalism, that it works without an Ultimate Observer in the Cartesian Theater. There is no Privileged Spectator or Central Meaner, and there is no place where it all "comes together", it is just a system that works. But if we accept that there is an experiential "side" of human life, it is difficult to see how experience can be adequately understood in terms of e.g. multiple channels of specialist circuits in the brain (Dennett, 1991). Is it really the *brain* which wishes and desires, remembers or anticipates, mourns or is happy? The most difficult part of the mind-body problem is the relationship between the experiential (subjective) and the non-experiential (objective, third-person). To get rid of experience is one way to solve the problem, but not a satisfactory one.

realm of meaning called "psycho-social factors" in traditional theories. On the other hand, the materialistic theories are in essence no different from the ordinary biomedical paradigm, since they have done away with mind *as* mind, ignoring that which makes psychosomatic phenomena specifically *psycho*somatic. The alternative to these two problematic avenues is a holistic approach which will take meaning[23] seriously, as well as underline the mind-body unity. As human beings, we are not a curious mixture of a mechanical, physical thing tied to a mysterious soul, nor are we just a collection of physical processes. We are a mind/body presence which we always experience simultaneously with the meaningful upsurge of the world. This unity is what we primordially live, and all the distinctions that are made between mind and body and world are purely analytic ones. For the French phenomenologist Maurice Merleau-Ponty, the unity of the mind/body subject in the world is the starting point for his philosophical investigation. I will be using the work of Merleau-Ponty as a source of inspiration for my own phenomenological theory of psychosomatics to be presented in part II of this dissertation. The challenge is to find a way to avoid the insoluble mind-body interaction problem without losing sight of the specifically psychosomatic field of study. To briefly introduce the approach which will be presented in developed in part II, let me already here take up a distinction which will be useful in the coming analysis chapters as well, namely the distinction between the objective body and the lived body.[24]

---

23 When I speak of "meaning" I am not referring to the analytic tradition of Frege, Russell and Wittgenstein which focuses upon the relationship between language and reality. How words refer to what they stand for is not my interest here . By "meaning" I am referring to the intentional, contextualized expression and understanding of communally shared significance. We already know *how to look* and *how to speak* before we articulate the world with specific knowledge and language. Phenomenology and existentialism are the philosophical orientations which investigate "meaning" understood in this way.

24 The term "the lived body" or *le corps propre* comes from Merleau-Ponty. In French, the term also means "my body" the personal, contextualized life/body of the subject. See chapter 6 on the lived body.

The objective body and the lived body

We are all familiar with the objective body. It is that collection of bones and tissues and blood cells and organs which we have learned to regard as "body." The objective body is the body seen through the eyes of natural science, described in terms of third-person processes, the body as "it" rather than "I". But the body is not an object, although we have learned to regard it as such. Far from being an object, the body is our very means of *having objects* (a world) at all. We do not *have* bodies, we *are* bodies, and it is only through our bodies that a world may appear. The body understood in this way, as the ground of our existence, is the lived body. The lived body is the embodied subjectivity of the person in his/her concrete life situation. The lived body is both mind and body together harmoniously living the world. Mind, body and world are one system. This notion breaks up the dichotomy between mind and body which dualism has imposed upon us. We need to think about mind and body and world in a new way. For Merleau-Ponty, consciousness can *live* in its objects and can be completely immersed in them, without ceasing to be consciousness. Likewise, the body lives meaning, a meaning which is not the work of a universal constituting consciousness but of a general, rudimentary kind. To blur the distinction between mind and body in this way is not to say that mind is body and body is mind, but rather to acknowledge the ambiguity of our lives, the seepage between the organic biological levels and thematic consciousness which is characteristic for man. There is nothing in our bodily existence as human beings which does not possess some kind of mind, and there are no purely psychological moments in our lives which are not conditioned by our embodiment. Just as mind and body are not completely distinct, neither is the subject isolated from the world (classical subject/object distinction). The lived body is the nave at the center of the world. As Merleau-Ponty writes: "Our own body is in the world as the heart is in the organism; it keeps the visible spectacle constantly alive, it breathes life into it and sustains it inwardly, and with it forms a system."[25] This is something quite other

---

[25] *Phenomenology of Perception* (1945/1962) hereafter referred to as *PP*, p. 203.

than the objective body. Merleau-Ponty compares the human body not to a physical object, but to a work of art. The meaning of the poem or painting is not completely arbitrary, capable of being anything, neither is it to be found outside of the work, floating above in some kind of Platonic heaven of ideas. The meaning is *there* in the work, inseparable from the brushstrokes, the colors and the rhythm. The expression is indistinguishable from the thing expressed. In a similar way the body is "the nexus of living meanings"[26]which can only be properly understood directly and intuitively, like the work of art.

Most of the time, the mind, just like the body, is completely immersed in the world, finding there both its anchoring and its continual upheaval. Living the world in this way, as embodied, self-conscious subjectivity, is to ceaselessly confirm, reaffirm, and transform the significance of the world. Significance, or *sens* (which in French means both "meaning" and "direction") is always both mind and body together. The lived body is the only place where meaning can emerge. This position is one which breaks radically from our usual ways of thinking, and for that reason it will need to be presented at some length in chapter 6. For now, I merely wish to introduce the notion of the thinking, interpreting, understanding body, although what this actually means must be further explicated later on. To have a world in this way, to be a body in this way, is specifically human, and no machine or animal can boast of this form of life.

This is not to say that the objectified body is not useful in certain contexts. After all, it is thanks to the biomedical model that we have made such tremendous progress in medicine and health care. This is not to be doubted. But biomedicine has *not* helped us to understand specifically psychosomatic problems. In fact, much of our traditional thinking about health, ill health and disease actually hinders a genuine understanding of psychosomatic pathology. The objective body can never illuminate the concrete subject in his/her life situation, an omission which is serious if one wishes to try to explain psychosomatic conditions. Psy-

---

[26] Ibid., p. 151.

chosomatic theory should not be about the objective body, but the <u>lived body</u>. Unfortunately, traditional psychosomatic theories have not in fact made this distinction, and consequently have not been able to move forward.[27] Biomedical knowledge about the workings of an objective body gives us valuable information about the body as a mechanical system, and although the body can be seen from this perspective, the *psycho*somatic is lost. To bring out the importance of the distinction between the lived body and the objective body, I would like to briefly present some issues from the philosophy of science.

Explanation in psychosomatic theory

A well-known controversy within the history of the philosophy of science is the so-called "explanation/understanding (*Erklären/Verstehen*) debate". Traditionally, explanation is said to belong to the domain of the natural sciences, while understanding is the trademark of the human sciences. Today, the debate is no longer an either/or battle between the two approaches. We admit that it is possible to take different perspectives when studying various phenomena, and we no longer say that the one approach is better than the other, although one of the two approaches may be more *appropriate* than the other for studying a specific phenomenon. Because psychosomatics is concerned with both psyche (meaning) and soma (matter), it is important to reflect upon which approach we are using when we study this phenomenon. For example, what kind of body are we talking about in our theories (the lived body or the objective body)? What criteria are we using when we present theoretical "explanations" within this field? Because the lived body and the objective body are not synonymous,[28] the question arises, what is the

---

27 See chapters 2-5 for the critique of traditional theories.

28 The relationship between the lived body and the objective body is to be understood as follows: the lived body is primordial, while the objective body is a derived, constructed perspective *upon* this lived body. The objective body is an interpretation of the lived body, based upon a specific scientific ideal and perspective. This is comparable to the relationship between the *Lebenswelt* and the natural scientific interpretation of the world. (see Husserl 1954/1970).

proper approach to be used when trying to construct a psychosomatic theory?

The distinction between explanation and understanding was first introduced by the German historian and philosopher Droysen in 1858. This distinction was further worked out by Dilthey (1883), also an historian and philosopher. Dilthey wanted to delineate distinct regions of inquiry and, more specifically, to argue for the methodological autonomy of the human sciences, the *Geisteswissenschaften*. The *Erklären/Verstehen* debate at that time centered around the question as to whether the newer "human sciences" should follow the methodology and scientific ideals of the natural sciences, or whether the specific nature of the region, that is, human beings and their activities, justified developing new, human scientific methods of inquiry and different categories of understanding. The proponents of the autonomy of the human sciences argued that the nomological, causal theories which worked so well in natural science may not be relevant or even applicable to the study of man. The guiding scientific ideal for the natural sciences such as physics and chemistry is the search for universal laws. A natural scientific explanation answers the question "why" something has occurred (in nature) by formulating general (and often causal) laws.[29] These laws say not only why something *must* have occurred, given those specific circumstances, but more often than not why, under the same circumstances, this something will necessarily occur again. This is quite handy for natural science,

---

[29] The most common form of scientific explanation is the so-called "deductive model" which is expressed as a formal argument, where the explanandum (that which is to be explained) is a logically necessary consequence of the explanatory premises (the explanans), consisting of at least one universal law and a number of initial conditions. The explanandum must not logically imply the premises, nor should the premises be equivalent to the explanandum. Finally, at least one of the premises must be more general than that which is being explained. An example of the deductive scientific explanation is Hempel's "deductive nomological explanation." The deductive model is the one most often used in natural scientific explanations, and the one which has been studied the most thoroughly. Other forms of explanations are probabilistic explanations, functional or teleological explanations, and genetic explanations. See Nagel, E. (1961) for further discussion of the different models of explanation used in science.

whose primary knowledge interest is to be able to predict and control the territory under investigation. Although some consider prediction and explanation to be basically identical forms of thought, merely differing in time perspective (the so-called "structural identity of explanation and prediction"), the alleged symmetry of explanation and prediction is an issue of debate.[30]

Is the natural scientific explanatory ideal described above one which the human sciences can appropriate? Although some would claim that it is not inappropriate (for example, behaviorists), many theorists from within the human scientific tradition would reject it as irrelevant to the study of human beings as psychological, social, cultural beings. According to Dilthey, we need not reconstruct our subject matter (human existence) using the abstractions and constructions of natural science. We experience life immediately "from within". We do not "explain" in the human sciences: rather, we "understand".[31] Interpretation is an important tool for the human sciences. Dilthey is sometimes called the father of hermeneutics,[32] although hermeneutical exegesis of holy texts is a practice which goes back thousands of years. That which is relevant to

---

[30] See Hempel (1965).

[31] A rather famous passage from Dilthey (1894/1977) captures the flavor of the human science project and gives some idea of the controversy at the time: "The human sciences are distinguished from the natural sciences in that the latter take as their object features which appear to consciousness as coming from outside, and as given in particulars; for the former (human sciences), in contrast, the object appears as coming from within, as a reality and as a vivid original whole. It follows therefore that for the natural sciences an ordering of nature is achieved only through a succession of conclusions by means of linking of hypotheses. For the human sciences, on the contrary, it follows that the connectedness of psychic life is given as an original and general foundation. Nature we explain, the life of the soul we understand."

[32] The word "hermeneutics" comes from the Greek verb "*hermèneuein*" which means to interpret. In Greek mythology, Hermes was the winged-footed God who brought down messages from the Gods on Olympus to human beings. His role was to translate or convey that which was beyond the comprehension of mortal human beings into a message which humans could understand. To "interpret" is to transform into comprehensibility, although just how this is done is a matter of debate within the hermeneutical tradition. See Bleicher (1980) and Ricoeur (1981a) for a discussion of these issues and controversies.

the discussion at hand is the epistemological standpoint that there does not exist any one method which will guarantee truth, nor any objective point of view from which one can observe. We are always already within the hermeneutical circle of understanding, which is characterized by a linguistic, cultural pre-understanding, sometimes also called our "situatedness." Instead of fighting against this situatedness (striving to rid the observation of the observer, as natural science requires), hermeneuticians wish to use this horizon of meaning in order to deepen our understanding of how we constitute the world and experience meaning. Hermeneutics deals specifically with meaning, intentionality, interpretation and understanding. Phenomenological philosophy, starting with the work of Edmund Husserl (1859-1938), devotes itself entirely to this project, and investigates how the world shows itself in and through consciousness. I will have more to say about the phenomenological project in part II. Suffice to say here that both the human scientific approach and phenomenology are concerned with a different project and another perspective than those of natural science, although they are by no means "unscientific" for that reason. It has been a rather common notion that what is "scientific" are those theories and statements which are couched in the language and concepts of the natural sciences, conceived through the rigorous application of their methods. The most influential wave of natural scientific thinking and ideals in modern times came with the advent of the positivism[33] of the Vienna circle during the 1920s.

---

33 The term "positivism" was first used by August Comte (1798-1857) to denote his own new "positive" philosophy. However, many of his ideas could already be found in the work of Francis Bacon (1561-1626), especially the conviction that one could only attain true knowledge of the world by means of a specific, rigorous, systematic type of observation. This certain knowledge, acquired in this way, should be distinguished from all forms of "metaphysical speculation," which had no place in science. Modern positivism, (also called "neopositivism", "logical positivism" or "logical empiricism") began with a small group of philosophers and scientists gathered around Moritz Schlick in Vienna. This group was inspired by Wittgenstein's dissertation *Tractatus logico-philosophicus* of 1922, where it was stated that language can only accurately (truly) reflect states of affairs, or facts, (like "the cat is on the mat"). Only states of affairs can be verified empirically, consequently only statements concerning states of affairs can be true or false. One may of course speak of other things, but

The explanation/understanding controversy is not really an either/or matter, since explanation and understanding intertwine in real life, transforming and influencing each other. Our "scientific" knowledge (e.g. the fact that we know that the earth revolves around the sun, or that our bodies have an immunological defense system) influences the way in which we understand the world and, in turn, our understanding of the world influences the way in which we formulate the metaphors which constitute our knowledge.[34] The core of the dispute, if there is one, between positivists and hermeneuticians concerns the issue of primordiality, that is, which comes *first*, a world of meaning, or a world of facts? The positivist maintains that events described in natural scientific terms are primordial, that is, they are prior to and causally responsible for the things going on around us which we then "understand" in various ways. A hermeneutical (phenomenological) position is that understanding always precedes explanation, or put in another way, as soon as I "explain" something, I have presupposed a prior understanding, built upon a lived experience of the world. Proponents of the human scientific approach, since Dilthey, have wished to legitimate the possibility of investigating the realm of the subjective in a rigorous, scientific way, without having to have recourse to the constructs of natural science. Since understanding is prior to explanation, the human sciences have an important task, namely, to clarify and explicate the primordial, subjective realm of understanding. To prioritize this task does not in any way deny the impor-

---

such statements do not yield true knowledge. The Vienna circle came to the conclusion that because philosophy and science are supposed to be dealing with true knowledge, these disciplines should hereafter confine themselves to verifiable statements. In one fell swoop, the bulk of philosophical, metaphysical questions were banned from philosophy and science. Even in some circles today, that which is "scientific" is that which can be verified through ritualized observation. In light of positivistic ideals, the human sciences have a hard time gaining scientific acceptance for their methods and results.

34 An interesting anecdote in this context is the observation that the Chinese science of acupuncture, with its notions about blocked energy meridians and energy flow patterns, came from a culture (early China) which had tremendous problems with sewage canals in the cities. One can wonder what traditional Chinese medicine would look like if there had been adequate plumbing.

tance or signification of explanation or the natural sciences: on the contrary, it attempts to do them justice by accounting for the ground (prescientific understanding) upon which they are built.

If we relate this discussion to the field of psychosomatics, it is obvious that we may speak of the body in two ways. The body can be seen as an objective body (no one's/everyone's body), described in terms of neurological, chemical, physical components, or we may refer to the lived body, which is the embodied subjectivity of someone in particular. We have, on the level of the objectified body, legitimate descriptions of physiological processes, processes which can be a part of reasonable explanatory statements. Mrs. G. has a cold because she has a virus in her body, which her immunological defenses were not able to get rid of in time. We can locate the virus and likewise find out which part of her immune system is deficient. We do not need to refer to any specific person in order to explain why someone catches a cold, at this level of signification. But we also have the level of the lived body of personal experience, *the body of Mrs. G,* the psychosomatic body which is the body of interest for psychosomatic theory . Let us say, for example, that Mrs. G. had recently gotten divorced, and her work was not going well. After a particularly bad meeting at work, she went home and came down with a cold. It is first here that we begin to approach the *psychosomatic* level of understanding. The common kernel in all psychosomatic theory is the inclusion of psychosocial factors in the explanation of certain kinds of pathology. A variety of factors contributed to the development of the cold, factors which cannot be measured and observed in the same way that the virus and the immunological deficiency can be located. What shall we call this level of understanding? Are we dealing with explanations at the psychosomatic level, and if so, what kind of explanation is it?[35] Traditional biomedicine has expert knowledge of the objectified

---

[35] To take an exaggerated example, a traditional "covering law" type of explanation (natural science) would attempt to formulate a general law such as "any person P who gets a divorce, has a bad day at work, and comes into contact with a virus, will catch a cold." This is obviously not substantiated empirically. The next step is to specify the "law" further by going into greater and greater detail, such as "anyone who is a

body, but little knowledge of the lived body. Paying specific attention to the lived body has only recently made its way into the medical community, and then often introduced by clinicians rather than theoretical researchers.[36]

What is the relevance of the explanation/understanding debate for understanding psychosomatics? As Merleau-Ponty has pointed out, our experience of our body is essentially ambiguous. The body is both a quasi-object (something I can observe as if it were a thing) yet at the same time it is *me*, it is the very medium through which there can *be* objects at all. The body is, then, a special kind of "thing" which I cannot really observe, although something about the body (its corporeality) makes me think that I can observe it like any other thing in the world. The science of medicine, focusing upon one side of this ambiguity[37] has

---

middle-aged woman, who has difficulties with separation, who gets a divorce, who has a job which exceeds her capacities..." which finally boils down to "anyone who is Mrs. G." It is clear that such a narrow "law" is worthless in the traditional scientific sense. Some theorists would object to this characterization, and claim that they are not attempting to formulate general laws, that it is enough to understand why Mrs. G. caught her cold. However, if one looks closely at psychosomatic theory, one finds there an attempt to formulate laws and strive towards nomothetic generalizations. The implicit goal of medical theory is not simply to understand, but to predict and control. The goal of psychosomatic theory is thus to be able to formulate law-like relationships between various factors in the development and maintenance of psychosomatic pathology. This agenda is especially salient in psychosomatic medicine (see chapter 3). The question we must ask is, is this a reasonable goal, given the nature of the psychosomatic, which has to do with the lived body? We must remember that a discourse on psychosomatic pathology may reflect two different levels of existence, the objectified body and the lived body. Which level is being addressed in the psychosomatic theories, and is the level relevant to the nature of the subject matter under study? This is an important point which needs to be clarified and addressed.

36 See Hellström (1994); Rudebeck (1991).

37 It has been pointed out that the mechanization of the body (getting rid of its "soul") was a prerequisite for the development of modern medicine. Without the anatomical dissection of corpses and experimentation on the living, modern medicine could never have made such progress. Pragmatic interests have thus gone hand in hand with dualistic tendencies, reinforcing each other. An example of this can be seen when the Catholic Church finally allowed anatomical dissection, after much debate, proclaiming in a decree that while the soul is essential to the person, the body is not. In this way, any ethical objections to the new medical methods were effectively removed.

during the course of the last few centuries sedimented a notion of the body that we all subscribe to, namely that it is first and foremost a collection of physiological processes, bones, tissues, fluids and cells. The body can be prodded and examined, both inside and out. But this objectified body regarded in this way is not *my* body, it is not the body which is the vehicle for my existence, the lived body. The objectified body is a construction, a very useful one, but a construction nevertheless. Studying the mechanized, objectified body can explain processes and events in terms of material causes, but it cannot tell us anything about the way in which this person lives his/her world. We may *explain* the eczema of Mr. B. as being caused by an allergic reaction, but we can also *understand* it as a reaction to the life-long "smother love" of his overprotective mother. These two kinds of descriptions do not contradict one another, but they correspond to two different types of "why" questions, on two different levels of signification. In the first case, we are dealing with causes understood in natural scientific terms, in the second, we are concerned with motivation and reasons. Causes conform to the rules set down for scientific explanation, and reasons are understood, interpreted and argued for in line with hermeneutical canons.[38] Psychosomatic theory claims to address both these levels (psycho-social meaning components as well as somatic functioning) but as we shall see in the following chapters, the lived body is hardly discernible, much less addressed, in the literature. In terms of clinical practice, it is often the objectified body which occupies the doctor's attention, while the patient tries desperately to introduce his/her lived body into the consulting room.[39]

---

[38] It is true that certain philosophers consider reasons and motives to be causal as well (Davidson, 1968), but this is a rather complicated internal debate within the philosophy of action which would take us far afield. See Stoutland (1982) on the issue of motivation as causation.

[39] See Toombs (1992) for an excellent account of the different worlds which the doctor and patient inhabit as they try to communicate with each other about the patient's illness/disease. The meaning of the disease/illness is not the same for the doctor and for the patient. Disease for the doctor is a collection of signs and symptoms, which must be ordered through tests and diagnosis. For the patient, the disease is a total disruption of the world. The doctor's objectification of the patient's body into a

On a final note, it is important to remember that "why" questions are never posed in a vacuum. If we ask the question, "Why is that bird black?" we can expect a variety of answers depending upon which frame of reference we situate ourselves in when we ask it. "Because it is a raven, and all ravens are black" is the typical deductive-nomological answer. We may accept this as an answer to our question, or we may be dissatisfied and wonder, does this really tell us *why* the bird is black? The natural scientist can further respond by explaining that the raven is black because it happens to live where it does; were it to live in the polar regions, its feathers would turn white. If we are still not satisfied, and push further, we get answers like "Because it can effectively hide from its predators if it's black" or "Because God made it that way", or "There is in fact no *reason* for its being black!"[40] The question of why Mr. B. has eczema can likewise be understood on different levels of signification and from within different frameworks. What is important to realize is that the level of explanation which biomedicine has so successfully worked out relates to the objectified body, and does not address the lived body. On the level of the lived body, it is perfectly acceptable to ask "why" questions, although the answers given will not be expressed in terms of natural scientific causal explanation.

On causes and reasons

The literature on causation is vast, and a detailed discussion of the distinctions, controversies and fine points of this issue would bring us too far from the subject matter of this dissertation.[41] However, I would like

---

"medical body" is highly disturbing to the patient. The doctor, likewise, is irritated when the patient is not satisfied with the "scientific" explanation s/he has been given concerning the disease/illness.

40 Black bird example in Nagel, E. (1961).

41 In the history of philosophy, David Hume's (1888/1961) *A Treatise of Human Nature* and *An Inquiry Concerning Human Understanding* are classical texts. Hume is famous for his characterization of causation as mere regular succession, and, most importantly, as regular succession which is linked together by psychological association in the mind. According to Hume, although we ascribe causation to states of affairs in

to take some time to present the intentionalist/teleological explanation of human action[42], as it is directly relevant to the discussion of psychosomatics. Intentionalist explanation has to do with how to understand intentions, reasons and motives, concepts which pertain exclusively to human beings, not to things. If "causes", defined in a strict Humean sense (expressed in deductive-nomological terms), describe relationships between things in nature, then we need some other terms and models in order to express the kind of causation operating in human beings and their actions. It is possible that one may subscribe to the view that the causality effectuating events in nature is the very same as that which makes human beings do what they do. A caricature of this position would be that I write this dissertation right now because I have a lot of chemical substances floating about in my body which cause things to happen in my brain, and muscles and organs etc. Presented in this way, it seems patently absurd. However, oddly enough, some of the theorists whom I will examine later on seem to subscribe to this position, or at least it is a conclusion which can be drawn from their way of expressing themselves. But back to intentional explanations.

Von Wright begins his *Explanation and Understanding* by wondering how a subsumption theory of explanation (like the deductive-nomological model) could successfully account for intentional human actions. The positivistic project would be to discover and formulate general laws of sufficient complexity (or banality) so that all surplus in the form of intentions or meaning will disappear. Hempel thought that the general laws of history needed in order to fully comprehend historical developments were too complex, and our knowledge of them too incomplete, for the human sciences to ever be able to imitate the precise, causal ex-

---

the world, causation is really just "ties of thoughts" rather than "ties between things." Hume came up with three necessary and sufficient conditions for something to count as a cause, but for our purposes we need only understand that in Humean causation the cause and effect must be logically independent of one another. In intentional causality, which I will present shortly, cause and effect are not logically independent. Someone's intention to do X (the cause of the action) and its effect, actually doing X, are logically dependent.

42 See von Wright (1971; 1974).

planations of the natural sciences. Popper, on the other hand, proposed that the reason why general laws are not formulated in historical explanations is that they are too trivial to deserve mention. In either case, neither of them found it to be in principle inappropriate to try to emulate the natural sciences in an attempt to find general, law-like explanations for the human sciences. Von Wright rejects the validity of these kinds of explanations for human actions. He proposes instead the practical syllogism[43] as a model of explanation for the human and social sciences. Briefly, von Wright's practical syllogism explains the behavior of a person (why did Peter do X?) in two premises: 1) a premise which expresses what Peter's intention was when he performed the action we wish to have explained; and 2) a premise which states what Peter knew, thought or believed to be necessary in order to perform the action. If we know these two premises and take them to be true, we know why Peter performed action X. Because human agents have motives, intentions and goals, we need to develop a human scientific concept of causation which takes these specifically human factors into account. Von Wright admits that there is a level of description where human actions can be described in terms of natural scientific causation, which he refers to as the "outer aspect" of a behavior, consisting of two parts, which he calls the "immediate" and the "remote" outer aspects of an action. The immediate outer aspect would be, for example, the muscular activity which is needed when I raise my arm in order to open the window, and the remote outer aspect is some event for which this muscular activity is causally responsible, that is, the actual turning of the handle which opens the window. The "inner aspect" is the intentionality behind the outer manifestation of the action. For example, I wanted to open the window because it was stuffy in the room, and I knew that if I moved my arm in such and such

---

43   The practical syllogism comes originally from Aristotle. It comprises a major premise of someone wanting X, and a minor premise consisting of a belief about what would lead to the attainment of X, and a conclusion consisting of the actual using of this means to this end. Just what kind of "proof" this syllogism can offer is not clear. But this should not stand in the way of trying to use this kind of reasoning in order to explain human action, according to von Wright.

a way, I could open the window and let in some air. This is why I opened the window (according to the practical syllogism). The same action can be described in terms of the outer aspects, expressed in mechanized thing-language: I opened the window because of chemical transmitter substances activating nerve synapses, resulting in muscle contractions, and so on. By now I hope the distinction between these two levels of signification is clear.

Just as explanation and understanding do not stand in mutually exclusive opposition, neither does causality in the natural scientific sense necessarily stand in opposition to an analysis of meaning and motivation. As long as we are clear about what level of the human being we are referring to, we may use either one of these models. When discussing psychosomatics, it is important to keep in mind whether the body being discussed is the objectified body (a collection of physiological processes, obeying natural, physical laws) or the lived body (*this* particular body/person). We may use "causality" in a loose fashion to describe occurrences on both these levels; however, to be rigorous we should speak of motives, intentions and reasons when referring to the lived body. This does not exclude the possibility that we may even here use reasons in a counterfactual way: for example, if *this* had not happened, then *that* would not have occurred. In terms of psychosomatic theory, we may say that if Mrs. C's husband had not died, she would not have developed cancer. We relate bereavement to the development of cancer, and we may be correct in doing so, but how should we understand the relationship between bereavement and cancer, which levels are addressed, and what kind of generality can we actually ascribe to this relationship? Can we construct theories on psychosomatic pathology which will reveal law-like relationships? Can we ever enumerate all the factors involved? Is this even a viable project? What kind of theory can be built around psychosocial factors, which are so intimately tied up with the way in which individuals experience and interpret their lives? These questions should be kept in mind in the coming chapters, when we examine what influential theorists have to say about psychosomatics.

The object of the study and the outline of the dissertation

The aim of this study is to critically examine traditional theories on psychosomatic theory, paying special attention to certain philosophical issues such as the mind-body problem and efficacious mechanisms of interaction between meaning (psycho-social factors) and that which is traditionally considered the somatic body (objective, material processes). Afterwards, an alternative approach to psychosomatic theory is worked out, drawing inspiration from the phenomenology of Merleau-Ponty. Specifically, the first part of the dissertation (chapters 2-5) is made up of analyses of the following four schools of thought (or orientations) on psychosomatic pathology: 1) psychodynamic theory, 2) psychosomatic medicine, 3) stress theory as well as neuroimmunology and neuroendocrinology, and 4) the work of the psychobiologist Herbert Weiner. I have chosen to examine these four particular orientations because they have all in one way or another played a role in forming our (lay and professional) understanding of psychosomatics.[44] Those authors within these orientations who have written theoretical texts relevant to my philosophical interests have been included in the analyses. To my knowledge, a collected and systematic philosophical analysis of psychosomatic theories has not been performed before. I have tried to present a systematic overview of the theories, paying special attention to the aforementioned philosophical problems. The questions I have posed with regard to the texts concern: 1) the *ontological* issues; such as, what *is* psychosomatic pathology according to these particular theories, and how does it differ from "purely" somatic disturbances (if such exist)? Because psychosomatic conditions are already conceptualized by their very nature as a relation between psyche and soma, the question arises, how do theore-

---

[44] Due to considerations of space and focus, I have not included in my analyses any of the body-oriented psychotherapies which exist today, such as Lowen's (1975) bioenergetics, Rosen therapy (Brenner & Rosen 1991), *psykomotorisk* physiotherapy (Bunkan 1983),or Downing's (1980) body-oriented psychotherapy. The texts coming from these authors are most often clinical rather than theoretical, which is the reason why they have been excluded. However, many of these therapies are based upon the work of the psychoanalyst Wilhelm Reich (1933), who will be discussed in chapter 2.

ticians understand the interaction between the mind and the body in psychosomatic pathology?; 2) the *etiological* issues: How do the theories understand the nature of the mechanisms which ultimately lead to psychosomatic disease and ill health? The problem of symptom specificity belongs here, that is, why develop one disease/symptom and not another?; 3) the *cure*: What are the treatment principles, given a particular theory of psychosomatics? Which factors are involved in the cure? What are the actual mechanisms by which a psychosomatic patient is cured? It will be through trying to answer these questions that the four theories of psychosomatic pathology will be examined.

The phenomenological alternative worked out in part II of the dissertation is an attempt to break up dualistic ways of thinking and theorizing. The starting point is not how can mind influence body, but rather, how is the mind/body unity lived, and what categories of understanding open up when the person/world field (lived body) becomes the focus of investigation? The aim is not to solve mind-body dualism, but to give up futile questions and unproductive ways of theorizing in favor of a philosophical perspective which gives an adequate starting point for studying the phenomenon in question. A rather tricky initial question is, what do I mean by "psychosomatic pathology" or "psychosomatic conditions"? What psychosomatic pathology *is* must be defined before building one's theory, and yet once it has been defined, a theory has in some sense already been given, or rather a theory may very well be presupposed in the definition. For example, psychodynamic theoreticians call "psychosomatic" those bodily lesions and experiences which are thought to have a psychological cause in repressed unconscious conflict (psychogenesis). The concept of psychogenesis is a theoretical hypothesis, not a neutral description. Another traditional answer would be to simply list specific diseases and symptoms as psychosomatic. As we shall see in chapter 5, this is a questionable strategy, since most diseases are heterogeneous in nature, meaning that the pathogenesis of one instance of a disease need not be etiologically identical with that of another instance of the same disease For example, one form of ulcer may very well be stress-related, while another is bacterial. Since I want to try to present a new perspective or alternative way of theorizing about psychosomatics, the relationship between definition and theory is especially problematic for me. To give a comprehensible definition of psychosomatic pathology at this stage (before having outlined the phenomenological theory) is difficult, but nevertheless necessary in order to delineate the area of study undertaken in this dissertation. My definition of psychosomatic pathology is two-fold. First of all, any and all symptoms and diseases coming from any and all parts of the body can be *used* psychosomatically, that is, in such a way that they replace a symbolic, verbal utterance. This means that according to the first wide definition, psychosomatic pathology is a particular way of living and using the body as a means of expression. It is "pathological" because the body is used in these cases in situations which would be better handled by thoughts, feelings and actions. I will describe the inadequacy of the "psychosomatic solution" in detail in part II. Secondly, a narrow definition of psychosomatic pathology concerns specific psychosomatic *etiology*.[45] In this case, *meaning* (psychosocial factors) is a necessary condition for the initiation and maintenance of the body pathology/experience.[46] Thus, according to the smaller definition the bacterial ulcer is not a psychosomatic condition, although according to the wider definition it *could become* one, if the person in question takes up and uses this bacterial ulcer in a particular way. Most importantly, my definition seeks to delineate those conditions in which the being-in-the-world of the patient is transformed. According to my definition, psychosomatic pathology is the result of a breakdown in meaning constitution. The body steps in when thoughts, feelings and actions have become impossible. Meaning is lived and expressed as body. Translated into clinical practice, an operational definition of psychosomatic pathology would be that psychosomatic patients are trying to communicate something with

---

[45] I will discuss the notion of psychosomatic etiology in my theory in chapter 10.

[46] I use the term "body pathology/experience" in order to remain open to the possibility that psychosomatic conditions need not entail objectively verifiable lesions. It is enough that the person in question *experiences* his/her body as not functioning.

their bodies. Those patients who do not have something to *communicate* do not have a psychosomatic condition. My definition of psychosomatic pathology will sometimes overlap with the definitions given by traditional theories, but at other times my delineation of the field will not correspond to "psychosomatic" as conceptualized by others.[47] The nature of my definition and the dynamics of the somatization process will become clear in part II of the dissertation.

In all the psychosomatic theories examined in this dissertation the experience of meaning is held to be somehow essentially involved in the formation of psychosomatic symptoms and diseases. However, none of these theories have dealt adequately with this interesting observation. Their authors have either started their investigations with the objective body and therefore have been forced to admit to various "mysteries" concerning mind-body interaction, or they have reduced meaning to physiology, and thereby forfeited a truly *psycho*somatic theory. The phenomenological theory to be presented in part II begins not with the objective body, but with the *lived body.* It is the being-in-the-world of the lived body (embodied subject) which will provide us with insights into psychosomatic conditions, insights which cannot be revealed until the mind and the body have been reunited and the subject-world relationship comes into focus. The shortcomings of the biomedical model are today apparent even to medical doctors, who have begun to show an interest in interdisciplinary research and cooperation. This dissertation can be seen as one attempt to open a dialogue with theoretically interested

---

[47] The phenomenological theory developed in part II of the dissertation can be seen as an alternative to traditional theories in that it takes up the perspective of the lived body rather than the objective body. It is *alternative* because it is designed to address issues and develop ideas which are not possible to investigate from within traditional theorizing. However, the phenomenological theory does not deny the importance of the work done in, for example, stress research or psychoanalytic theory. My theory can also be seen as a *complement* to the work of traditional theories, if traditional researchers should be interested in incorporating the perspective of the lived body into their own theories and working out the implications of my theory for their own perspective.

clinicians. Although I will be dealing with abstract philosophical issues, my hope is that even non-philosophers can find it worthwhile to read this dissertation. The method of investigation is philosophical examination and phenomenological reflection.[48]

---

[48] See chapter 6 for an introduction to phenomenology.

CHAPTER 2

Psychodynamic theory of psychosomatics

"Why the formation of symptoms in conversion hysteria should be such a particularly obscure thing I do not know. But the fact provides us with a good reason for quitting such an unproductive field of inquiry."[1]

"...the leap from a mental process to a somatic innervation- hysterical conversion- which can never be fully comprehensible to us."[2]

Introduction

The two quotes above can serve as an indication of Freud's resignation in the face of the mysterious nature of psychosomatic pathology. The peculiar mind-body interaction involved in these conditions constituted a theoretical problem which he never solved during his lifetime. His early writings on conversion hysteria[3] as well as the texts concerning the actual neuroses[4] were the beginnings of a psychoanalytic theory of psychosomatic pathology, but at this stage it was a theory which raised more questions than answers. Freud intended to address some of the conceptual difficulties raised by the phenomenon of psychosomatics (conversion hysteria) in his *Preliminaries to a Metapsychology*. This book was to

---

[1] Freud (1926) Inhibitions, Symptoms and Anxiety, *Standard edition of the complete works of Sigmund Freud*, Vol. XX, London: The Hogarth Press, p. 112.

[2] Freud (1909) Notes Upon a Case of Obsessional Neurosis, *SE*, Vol. X, London: The Hogarth Press, p. 157.

[3] See Freud (1893-1895) Studies on Hysteria, *SE*, Vol. II, for the presentation of "conversion hysteria".

[4] See Freud on actual neuroses: (1898), *SE*, Vol. III, pp. 263-285; (1914), *SE*, Vol. XIV, pp. 73-102; (1916-1917), *SE*, Vol. XVI, pp. 378-91. See also footnote 21.

contain twelve papers addressing various theoretical problems which had arisen during the first decades of psychoanalytic practice. *Preliminaries* was intended to provide a solid theoretical foundation for the science of psychoanalysis. Five of the twelve papers were actually written, published in 1915 as the "Papers on Metapsychology", but the seven remaining papers which were to follow never appeared. It is assumed that Freud never wrote them, or that he destroyed them, as he left no trace of them in any manuscript or letter form.[5] The difficult subject of conversion hysteria was to be the topic of one of these lost (or never written) papers. It would be up to other psychoanalysts to develop psychoanalytic thinking in the area of psychosomatic pathology.

Because Freud's ideas have had such an impact on our modern conceptions of the functioning of mental life, and have, in particular, influenced many clinicians in their thinking about psychosomatics, I will examine psychodynamic theory in this dissertation. Whether or not Freud is loved or hated, revered or reviled, his influence is incontestable. A short introduction to the Freudian system will be presented, focusing upon the hypothetical constructions and terms which we need to be familiar with in order to understand the psychodynamic theory of psychosomatics. A number of psychoanalysts and psychodynamic theoreticians have written on the subject of psychosomatics after Freud. I will however limit myself to mentioning briefly two psychoanalytic theoreticians of major importance in the field of psychosomatics, namely Franz Alexander and Joyce McDougall.[6] I will then move on to a critical examination of the psychodynamic theory of psychosomatics, in terms of ontology, etiology and cure.

---

[5] See "Editor's Introduction" to Papers on metapsychology (1915), *SE,* Vol. XIV, pp. 105-107 on the missing metapsychological papers.

[6] I debated whether or not Wilhelm Reich should merit a section of his own as well. I decided against this, since his later work is considered to deviate considerably from classical psychoanalytic theory, while his early work falls in line with classical psychoanalytic theory. I will however discuss his ideas when relevant during the course of my analysis. Other authors from within the psychoanalytic tradition will be examined in the analysis.

The Freudian (psychodynamic) metapsychology

Was Freud primarily interested in building a theory of mental life which would both emulate and be founded upon the natural sciences, (biology, brain anatomy, physiology), or was he a pioneer, creating a truly inter-disciplinary science of mind, encompassing man as a biological being as well as the creature who inhabits a world of meaning? The scientific status (natural scientific or hermeneutic) of Freud's metapsychology is still debated today, both within the psychoanalytic movement and with-out.[7] The fact that there is such a debate, and that it is unresolved, testi-fies to the ambiguity of Freud's position. Freud stands with one foot firmly rooted in 19th-century neuroscience,[8] and the other clearly plan-ted in the hermeneutical tradition,[9] with his interest in symbol, inter-pretation, intentionality and meaning. Even today it is still debated whether psychodynamic theory is scientific, and in such a case, what is meant by "scientific".[10] Perhaps the tension underlying the Freudian metapsychology lies precisely in its attempt to study man as the distinc-tive *psycho*biological being he is. Man is conceptualized in Freud's texts both as the product of "forces" or "energies" in need of "abreaction"[11] and as the *wishing* creature, motivated by desires. Ricoeur[12] has pointed out that there is something paradoxical about this dual characterization of man, as one can neither *interpret* forces nor *quantify* desire (qua de-sire). One may resolve the paradox by simply taking sides for one or the other aspect (explanation in terms of energy or understanding in terms

---

7 See Amacher (1965); David-Ménard (1983/1989); Kitcher (1992); Ricoeur (1970; 1981b); Sulloway (1979).

8 See Kitcher (1992).

9 See Ricoeur (1970).

10 See Grunbaum (1984); Habermaas (1972); Lesche & Stjernholm-Madsen (1976).

11 Abreaction entails the idea that psychical energy must be discharged in order to maintain psychical equilibrium. Normal abreaction occurs, for example, after trauma and/or inner conflict, if one can react with emotions and actions, or if one manages to resolve inner psychical conflict through reflection or modification of values. When these options are not available, the psychical energy surrounding repressed uncon-scious ideas or memories becomes pathogenic, causing neuroses, or in the case of conversion hysteria, leading to the formation of somatic symptoms.

12 Ricoeur (1970).

of meaning), but Freud wanted to have both. It is beyond the scope of this dissertation to take a stand on the issue of the scientific status of Freud's metapsychology. It will suffice here to draw attention to the ambiguity of his concepts and show the consequences of these ambiguities for the psychodynamic understanding of psychosomatics.

The Freudian metapsychology is a theoretical construction which aims at specifying how the various Freudian hypotheses (terms such as "reaction-formation", "condensation", "displacement" "primary process") relate to the clinical material which they are meant to explain. The metapsychology rests upon three pillars: the **dynamic,** which describes mental life in terms of conflict, the **topographical,** which structures the psyche into different systems with different functions,[13] and the **economical,** which rests upon a neurophysiological drive discharge model.[14] How does this system work? To give an example, we do not need a Freudian hypothesis in order to understand a person who becomes angry over his wife's infidelity. This is a reaction we can all understand without having to appeal to any theory. However, if we find a person who is chronically jealous and suspicious of his wife, without reasonable cause, we have to begin to wonder what is going on with this person. We cannot immediately understand the situation with our commonsense point of reference, so we turn to a theory (introduce theoretical, non-empirical terms) in order to make sense of the behavior. A Freudian hypothesis in this case could be that the jealous man is actually fighting off his own unconscious homosexual impulses, which he has projected upon his

---

[13] The first "topographical" distinction concerned the division between the unconscious, the preconscious and the conscious, while the second (dated from 1920 onward) described the three agencies of the id, the ego and the superego. The topographical demarcations essentially have to do with barriers between different systems, specifically barriers of *force,* which keep psychical material from crossing from one system into an other.

[14] Sometimes one sees the "genetic" point of view included in the definition of the Freudian metapsychology, although Freud never placed it explicitly there himself. The genetic aspect of psychical life does not refer to heredity, but to the way in which the past exerts an influence on the presence. That which we have experienced in our lives is never erased, merely covered over. See Holder (1990) on the genetic perspective.

wife: It is *she* who wishes to sleep with other men (not he), and he must control his wife in order to control his own impulses. The Freudian explanation of this psychological maneuver is that it is a *projection*, a defense mechanism whereby one defends oneself against conflictual thoughts and feelings by attributing them to another person. These impulses are not available to the person directly, they are *unconscious*. Because they are both conflictual and unconscious, they give rise to continual *psychical tension* and therefore need to be controlled. According to the economical pillar of the metapsychology, psychical energy which is not properly taken care of through thoughts and actions will continue to harass the person until they have either solved the conflict (i.e. are able to think and act regarding these ideas and feelings) or developed some kind of symptom, in this case the pathological jealousy. The clinical hypothesis of unconscious, projected homosexual impulses thus finds its theoretical justification in the dynamic, topographic and economical constructions.[15]

The Freudian metapsychology is a vast topic in itself, but I hope that it will suffice here to indicate that Freud's intention was to be able to chart mental life in terms of these three coordinates (dynamic, topographic and economical). For our purposes, we need only concern ourselves with the basic tenets, i.e. that there is a psychical energy associated with/attached to ideas and feelings, and that these ideas and feelings are capable of "going underground" (becoming repressed and thereby unconscious) so that we no longer have access to them. Unconscious conflictual material as well as the "energy" surrounding it continues to influence us in obscure ways which we cannot immediately understand. One of the ways we may be affected by these unconscious conflictual ideas and feelings is to develop a somatic symptom. This famous "leap to the somatic" is Freud's own conceptualization of the process which he found in his somatizing patients. He called this conversion somatization "conversion hysteria."

---

15 For further reading on the role of the metapsychology and its relation to clinical hypotheses, see Rubenstein (1967).

Conversion hysteria

It has been said that Freud actually had two theories of conversion, one which he formulated together with Josef Breuer early on in his career, and a later one which was less neurological and more sophisticated than the first. The second theory of conversion was considered to be especially interesting, according to some, because it opened up for the possibility of the symbolic, speaking body. However, Freud himself was unable to develop this line of thought because of his dualistic framework.[16] The first theory of conversion placed emphasis upon the transformation (conversion) of psychic energy into somatic innervation. The term "conversion" appeared first in 1894,[17] and was then characterized as the process by which a sum of excitation is transformed into something somatic. In 1910,[18] Freud explained the same process in terms of "'strangulated' affects...put to an abnormal use." In the "Papers on Metapsychology" from 1915, Freud wrote: "In conversion hysteria the instinctual cathexis of the repressed idea is changed into the innervation of the symptom. How far and in what circumstances the unconscious idea is drained empty by this discharge into innervation, so that it can relinquish its pressure upon the system *Cs.-* these and similar questions had better be reserved for a special investigation of hysteria."[19] We are informed by an editor's footnote that this last quote probably refers to the missing metapsychological paper on conversion hysteria. Even if Freud did not manage to explicate the mechanisms involved in conversion (specifically, the process *from* mind *to* body), he nevertheless did have some ideas about how this strange conversion process could be understood.

His first attempt to understand the conversion mechanism was to attribute it to what he called "somatic compliance", which is the constitutional or acquired disposition of the body to provide an outlet for the energy either through congenital weakness or acquired injury. The pathogenic energy seeks an outlet at the body's weak point, as an electri-

---

16 See David-Ménard (1983/1989).
17 Freud (1894) The Neuro-Psychosis of Defense, *SE*, Vol. III, p. 194.
18 Freud (1910) Five Lectures on psychoanalysis, *SE*, Vol. XI, p. 18.
19 Freud (1915) The Unconscious, *SE*, Vol. XIV, p. 184.

cal current will break through a badly insulated conducting line. However, Freud found cases where symptoms occurred without this organic predisposition, and in these cases he noticed that the part of the body afflicted had in some way become associated with the trauma or conflict involved. For example, a patient who had smelled burning porridge at the very instant she experienced an intense conflict continued to hallucinate the burning porridge, until she managed to become conscious of her conflictual feelings. As with any symptom formation, conversion is only a partial solution. One has managed to get rid of the disturbing idea/ affect, but at the price of maintaining it as a physical remembrance (symptom). The disturbing elements have been isolated from the rest of the psyche (the conscious system), but they are nevertheless retained in a converted, physical form, which continues to disturb the person via the body.

The second theory of conversion can be said to concern Freud's interest in the symptom as a form of communication. He began to pay attention to the way in which the patient's aches and pains seemed to take part in the analytic sessions, making themselves known at certain points in the course of the hour. The psychosomatic symptom could be seen as trying to communicate something which is not (yet) experienced on a verbal, symbolic level. As mentioned earlier, for whatever reasons, Freud did not further develop this second theory of conversion hysteria. He stuck to the *economical* approach, that is, conversion hysteria is understood as the conversion (diversion[20]) of psychic energy from repressed ideas and affects into somatic tracks. But we must remember that this process is by no means a purely neurophysiological occurrence for Freud. The conversion symptoms do have a *symbolic meaning*, although the meaning is unconscious and distorted, and as such unavailable to the person in question. As a final comment on Freud's work, later psycho-

---

[20] It is unclear whether or not we have a different form of energy involved in the symptom formation. If the energy is the same, "conversion" is a misleading term, as it suggests a transformation from one kind of energy into another. If all that has happened is that this energy has changed its route, it would be more proper to speak of "diversion" rather than conversion.

analysts writing on psychosomatics will concentrate upon a distinction made between the conversion symptoms (those dealing with repressed material) and the so-called "vegetative neuroses" (Alexander), where the symptom is seen as mere physiological activity which does not express a neurotic conflict. The body activity involved in the vegetative neuroses is not considered to be an *expression* of anything, it is simply the result of the organism's physiological adjustment to chronic emotional stress. In such cases, the symptom does not express emotion, it *accompanies* it. While the conversion symptom is an expression of a conflict, the vegetative neuroses have no meaning.[21] Where conversion symptoms are distorted expressions of wishful, conflictual thoughts and fantasies, the pathological physiology of the organism found in vegetative neuroses cannot be interpreted.

To sum up Freud's work on conversion hysteria, we find an emphasis upon the economical aspect of the metapsychology, where conflictual, repressed ideas/affects together with their "cathexis" (psychical energy) find an outlet through somatic innervation. The "choice" of the symptom is related either to 1) somatic compliance, 2) association to the repressed material, or 3) some kind of symbolic body expression, a primitive form of communication. Freud was himself unable to explicate the process from mental processes to body innervation, and he left the problem for others to tackle. One of the first and certainly most prominent psychoanalysts to take up the challenge is Franz Alexander, who founded the Chicago Institute for Psychoanalysis in 1932. Alexander is considered to be one of the foremost theoreticians of psychosomatics. His work will be briefly presented below.

---

21 This form of psychosomatic functioning can be compared to Freud's "actual neuroses," which were thought to be those conditions marked by strong affect, consciously experienced, yet not related to clearly defined mental representations. The actual neuroses were, according to Freud: 1) neurasthenia, 2) anxiety neuroses, and later on, 3) hypochondria. Freud attributed these neuroses to blocked libidinal energy, resulting from an unsatisfactory sexual life. The psycho-neuroses, by contrast, had their origin in repressed, neurotic conflicts.

Alexander's psychosomatic theory

As mentioned above, Alexander[22] is most well-known for his distinction between the *vegetative neuroses* which, according to him, concern the organs of the body innervated by the autonomic nervous system, and the symptoms of classical conversion hysteria, which express themselves primarily in pathology of the neuromuscular and sensory-perceptive systems. Besides introducing the notion of the vegetative neurosis, his basic contribution to the field of psychosomatics is the idea that *chronically repressed emotion* is essential to the development of psychosomatic diseases. He had his own version of organ specificity,[23] whereby he maintained that the physiological responses which accompany chronically repressed emotions will vary according to the nature of the emotion repressed. For example, chronic, unconscious rage stimulates an abnormal secretion of adrenaline, which may in turn lead to hypertension. The excess secretion of stomach acids which accompanies the passive state of waiting to receive food (love) may result in a "gastric neurosis". According to Alexander, these types of physiological functioning do not *express* emotions, they are the body's natural corollary of the emotions which are repressed. Therefore it is the chronic nature of the emotional tension which is harmful. The non-neurotic person is able to get rid of emotional tension by expressing it, or mentally working it through.

Alexander concentrated on investigating seven typical psychosomatic diseases (asthma, ulcerative colitis, ulcers, rheumatoid arthritis, thyrotoxicosis, certain types of eczema and hypertension), later to be known as "Alexander's holy seven." He concluded that specific unconscious conflicts and defenses against them played a role in the formation of the diseases, although he did not follow Dunbar's [24] specific personality profile. He believed in a multifactoral model of disease, where psychological,

---

22 Alexander (1939;1948;1950).
23 The notion of "specificity" has to do with the search for common characteristics in patients with specific psychosomatic diseases (such as specific personality types), as well as the correlation of specific emotional problems to specific somatic symptoms (organ "choices").
24 Dunbar (1943).

physical and societal factors all contributed to the development of disease (the "triple threat" hypothesis). Alexander's distinction between vegetative neuroses as well as his version of organ specificity have been criticized,[25] but his multifactorial model of disease (where disease will develop only in the presence of a "weakness" or vulnerability in the organ system, in combination with specific conflicts and defenses as well as particular external events or circumstances) holds up well to modern thinking about psychosomatic etiology.

McDougall's psychosomatic theory

Joyce McDougall[26] is probably one of the foremost contemporary psychoanalytic theoreticians of psychosomatics. She belongs to the French school of psychoanalysts and supports the "psychic deficit" theory, which maintains that disturbances in the early mother-child relationship lead to a deficiency in the psychic structure of the individual. According to McDougall's theory, because the child is denied ways in which to differentiate from the mother and form his/her own psychic reality independently of her, a line of psychological development ensues where instinctual aims and archaic ideas and fantasies live a primitive life of their own, beyond symbolization, completely cut off from the person's conscious/preconscious life. Mental pain and conflict are "ejected"[27] violently from the psychical apparatus, with no possibility of mental representation or psychical defense, resulting in the need for some kind of outlet, usually through various addictive behaviors (acting out) such as alcoholism, eating disorders, sexaholism, workaholism, and in some cases, chronic somatization.

---

25 See Engel & Schmale (1967); Fenichel (1946); Schur (1955).
26 McDougall (1982/1986;1989).
27 Freud (1918) used the term "foreclosure" to denote the mechanism whereby the psyche ejects mental content from the psychical apparatus. Foreclosure was thought to be a psychotic mechanism of defense, to be distinguished from the neurotic notion of repression.

McDougall takes up the modern theme of psychosomatics as a form of communication. The body as ill/diseased is seen as a preverbal type of symbolization. It is, however, the symbolization of a regressed psyche, where the level of expression is one of the infant, still tied to the mother-body. McDougall comments that Freud did not leave much room for the idea that anything could go seriously wrong between the infant and its mother, as he idealized the mother-infant relationship. McDougall focuses her attention on this relationship, and develops a theory of psychosomatic pathology which underlines the importance of the early relationship to the mother. Because psychosomatic pathology has such an early debut, she likens the psychosomatic development to the psychotic one. They reveal similar structures, as both psychosomatics and psychosis are attempts to keep archaic terror at bay. The anxieties of the neurotic person have to do with the right to a love life and adult sexual pleasures, while the psychosomatic/psychotic anxieties revolve around the right to exist, the right to possess one's own body, to develop a self independent of mother. There are, however important differences between psychosis and psychosomatics: in psychosis, thought processes and contact with the external world are delusional, in psychosomatics, the body functions are delusional. The symptoms make no biological sense, it is the body which is crazy, while the psychosomatic person is able to function well in their relation to the external world.

I will conclude with a remark concerning the way in which I refer to "the psychodynamics" of psychosomatic pathology in this chapter, as if we were dealing with one homogeneous theory. On a fine level of analysis, there are some differences in orientation amongst psychoanalysts coming from different schools and different periods of time.[28] However,

---

[28] I will not go into the different schools or orientations of psychoanalysis, such as ego-psychology, object relations, Self Psychology (Kohut) or Klienian psychoanalysis. There are differences of emphasis within the different orientations, but for the purposes of this chapter I have decided that a detailed account of the various schools would take me too far afield from the topic at hand. I have chosen instead to discuss the work of specific authors on psychosomatic theory, without specifying the school to which they belong. See Haugsgjerd (1986) and Pines (1990) for an overview of psychoanalytic orientations.

despite these variations, I think it is fair to say that psychodynamic theory exhibits a nucleus of theoretical standpoints. It will suffice for our purposes to stick to the metapsychology as described in the beginning of the chapter, and the basic conversion premise in order to delineate the psychosomatic theory addressed in this chapter. We will be looking for answers to basic questions which must be addressed to a theory of psychosomatics, answers which will reflect the psychodynamic standpoint in general on these issues.

The ontological questions

The above brief presentation of conversion hysteria, Alexander's vegetative neuroses and McDougall's psychosomatosis can provide us with an initial, general kind of answer to the question, what is psychosomatic pathology in psychoanalytic theory? Roughly, psychosomatic conditions are those bodily diseases and symptoms (with or without lesions) which arise as a result of psychical conflict (or chronic emotion, in the case of the vegetative neuroses), and which serve some function (economical or communicative) in the equilibrium of the patient. These conflicts/emotions are not thematically available to the patient (unconscious or foreclosed), and the body will continue to "use" symptoms and disease until some resolution of the underlying psychological problems is achieved. The criterion for distinguishing "psychosomatic" pathology from other forms of physical ailments is the specifically psychodynamic psychogenesis said to be involved in their formation. In principle, any part or system of the body may be used in this pathological way. That which is distinctive about the psychodynamic conceptualization of psychosomatic pathology is its emphasis upon the importance of underlying unconscious conflicts for the development of psychosomatic conditions, and the economical interpretation of the initiation and maintenance of the pathology. As we shall see later on, these specifically psychodynamic characteristics will be questioned by other theoretical traditions.

In order to have a theory about psychosomatics, one must be able to explicate the nature of the mind and how it relates to the body, as well as give an account of how the mind/body relationship in particular instances leads to the development of disease/symptoms. Freud himself didn't get very far with these ontological questions. He was rather pessimistic about ever being able to comprehend the "mysterious leap"[29] from mental processes to somatic innervation. It should be said in his defense that his primary interest was not theorizing about the philosophical mind-body problem, but attempting to build a science of mental life. Freud's position on the mind-body issue is debated.[30] He has been called a parallelist, a vitalist and a dualist, as well as a universal monist. It is generally agreed, at any rate, that he was very much the product of his 19th-century neurological education. He was schooled in the Helmholtz tradition, studying as a young medical student from 1876 to 1882 under one of its founders, Ernst Brücke. It was accepted practice at that time to assume that mental processes were paralleled by physical ones. Thus the neurologists of Freud's day could be called parallelists because they assumed that all mental processes were paralleled by concomitant physical processes. As a classical philosophical position, parallelism sees mind and body as two separate tracts which do not interact; or, in a weaker version, sees body as able to act on mind, but not vice versa. Strictly, this is a form of dualism. However, at the same time, Freud and his contemporaries expressed monistic characterizations of mind and body which made it possible for them to shift from speaking about mind/consciousness to physiological descriptions of processes going on in the brain and nervous system, as if they referred to one and the same event. In classical terms, this position could be compared to the so-called "double aspect" position (neutral monism), which holds that mind and matter are different arrangements of a single substance. The neurologists at the turn of the century were biased, as were all scientists of

---

[29] The term was first used by Freud in the "Rat Man" paper from 1909, *SE*, vol. X.

[30] Felix Deutsch (1959) devotes an entire book to "the riddle of the mind-body correlations" as he calls it, a book written in celebration of the centenary of Freud's birth, consisting of a number of psychoanalysts discussing in workshop form what Freud could have meant by the "mysterious leap", and how they themselves attempt to understand the issue.

that time, towards materialism.[31] Their practical business was to ground the understanding of mental functioning in the neurophysiology of the day. Freud was no exception, as the introduction to his *Project* from 1885 clearly states.[32] These pioneers of psychology were convinced that whatever they did not yet understand would one day become clear as the science of neurology advanced. This hopeful attitude of "waiting for neurology" was one which Freud shared, although he simultaneously held that the *psychological* could by no means be reduced to physiological, neurological processes.[33] He was not very clear about the relationship between the psychological realm and the neurophyiological "substratum," as he sometimes called it. His well known conceptualization of the instinctual drive (*Trieb*) as being "a concept on the frontier between the somatic and the mental"[34] is an example of the ambiguity of his thinking on the mind-body issue. Sometimes the instinct was conceptualized as being a *psychical* representative of a somatic force, and yet at other times he stated that an instinct can never become an object of consciousness. This second characterization is the one found most often in the later papers, where the instinct is clearly discussed as something

---

31 It is true that the introspectionists Wundt, Fechner and Titchner of the 1800s became somewhat popular outside of German academic society, but since they rejected materialism they were not in line with the mainstream thinking of the time.

32 "The intention is to furnish a psychology that shall be a natural science: that is, to represent psychical processes as quantitatively determinate states of specifiable material particles, thus making those processes perspicuous and free from contradiction." "Project for a Scientific Psychology" (1885) *SE*, vol I., p. 295. Some may argue that this position is the "early Freud", and was abandoned by him in his later writings. Kitcher (1992) has argued that Freud never abandoned the natural scientific intentions expressed so clearly in *Project*.

33 Freud (1938/1940): "We know two kinds of things about what we call our psyche (or mental life); firstly, its bodily organ and scene of action, the brain (or nervous system) and, on the other hand, our acts of consciousness, which are immediate data and cannot be further explained by any sort of description. Everything that lies between is unknown to us, and the data do not include any direct relation between these two terminal points of our knowledge. If it existed, it would at the most afford an exact localization of the processes of consciousness and would give us no help towards understanding them" (p. 144).

34 Freud (1915), *SE,* Vol. XIV, pp. 121-122.

non-psychical.[35] If Freud himself was unclear about the ontological problems involved in his concepts and theories, let us see if his followers fared a bit better.

Alexander goes right to the heart of the matter in his introduction to the first issue of the journal *Psychosomatic Medicine,* wishing to make "a clear statement" on the confusing philosophical mind-body issue: "Emphasis is put on the thesis that there is no logical distinction between 'mind and body', mental and physical. It is assumed that the complex neurophysiology of mood, instinct and intellect differs from other physiology in degree of complexity, but not in quality...It takes for granted that psychic and somatic phenomena take place in the same biological system and are probably two aspects of the same process, that psychological phenomena should be studied in their psychological causality with intrinsically psychological methods, and physiological phenomena in their physical causality with the methods of physics and chemistry."[36] This is an identity-theory[37] position, where mind and brain refer to the same (physical) thing, although we have access to this mind/ brain thing through introspection, which gives rise to the subjective realm of experience, demanding its own special forms of investigation and understanding. It is worth noting that while psychical and somatic phenomena are seen as being (probably) two aspects of the same process, this process is conceptualized in terms of neurophysiology, taking place in a "biological system". Although Alexander does not want to give up psychological methods which will be able to illuminate "psychological causality", he is clearly ambivalent on this point. Sometimes he seems to express the hope that one day we will have the necessary neurological knowledge so that we can dispense with psychological explications. He wrote some years after the introductory statement, "Psychosomatic research deals with such processes in which certain links in the causal chain of events lend themselves, *at the present state of our knowl-*

---

[35] See Editor's Introduction to *SE,* Vol. XIV, pp. 111 ff. on the "frontier concept" of the instinct and the ambiguity of its ontological status.

[36] Introductory Statement, *Psychosom. Med.* 1939, 1:1.

[37] See chapter 1 on Feigl's identity theory.

edge, more readily to a study by psychological methods than by physiological methods, since the detailed investigation of emotions as brain processes is not far enough advanced."(my italics).[38] However, in the very next sentence he expresses his conviction that even if the physiological bases of psychological phenomena become well-specified, we will not be able to dispense with psychological study. This ambivalence is typical for psychodynamic theory. There is a distinctively psychological level to human reality which cannot be understood in biochemical or neurophysiological terms, while at the same time that which is *referred* to (the processes which underlie the "double aspect") are ultimately physical processes, which will one day be properly understood as such. Alexander thus shows his materialistic bias when answering the *ontological* question of what the psychological realm *is,* while the *epistemological* question, how can we know it?, is answered in psychological terms, since psychical processes are experienced subjectively.[39]

Roy Grinker[40] describes mind-body relations as a form of parallelism whereby the relationship between the psychical and the physical is understood as one of concomitant vectors. The mental and the physical can neither be separated, nor understood in terms of cause and effect. The result of this concomitance is a strange variety of mixed descriptions. There is for example "excessive *psychological* excitation which passes beyond the capacity of the ego for *symbolic discharge*..."(my italics)[41] and "The *amount of such regression* is probably one quantitative factor in neurosis." (my italics)[42] and finally "they (autonomic nerve system functions) are also effective in directing the external discharge of tensions which are basically internal and instinctual, the energy which we term 'emo-

---

38 Alexander (1948), p. 4.
39 For example, Alexander (1948), "When we speak of emotions we refer always to definite physical processes in the brain, which, however, can be studied psychologically because these brain processes are perceived subjectively as emotions and can be communicated to others by the use of language" (p. 29).
40 Grinker (1948).
41 Ibid., p. 76.
42 Ibid., p. 79.

tion."[43]The notion of <u>excitation</u> is here characterized as *psychological*, although the term has its common usage on a physicalistic level of description; <u>discharge</u>, a physiological term, is capable of symbolism; <u>regression</u>, which usually refers to the return to a previous phase of function, is here quantified; and <u>emotion</u>, which normally refers to qualitative intentional content, is defined in terms of discharged energy. Morton Reiser[44] approaches the mind-body problem from a slightly different angle. He wants to develop an isomorphic[45] model in the hope that one day it will be possible to integrate parallel psychological and physiological theories. This means that those physiological states of the brain which allow for pathological discharge "may be the same ones which are detected psychologically as altered ego (consciousness) states."[46] This is another identity-theory conceptualization of the mind-body relationship.

Otto Fennichel[47] does not like the expression "psychosomatic", because it suggests a dualism which does not really exist. Every disease is in a sense "psychosomatic" because no somatic condition is free from psychical influences. This use of the term "psychosomatic" refers to a method of approach, rather than to a diagnostic criterion for specific psychosomatic diseases. Modern psychosomaticians make this distinction between the psychosomatic "approach" and specifically diagnosed psychosomatic diseases and symptoms. But if psychosomatics is this wide, encompassing everything that happens in the body, do we have a useful term? Fenichel himself abandons the wider use of the term and goes on in the same article to describe the field of psychosomatics as "bound on one side by the purely organic diseases and on the other by conversion."[48] Here he seems to be using the term "psychosomatic" di-

---

43 Ibid., p. 54.

44 Reiser (1966)

45 Isomorphism states that two systems or structures are isomorphic if every element in the one system can be linked to a corresponding element in the second. The correlation in our context would be between physiological processes in the brain and psychological, experiential content.

46 Reiser (1966), p. 579.

47 Fenichel (1946).

48 Ibid.,p. 307.

agnostically, for if there is "pure organic disease", there must be something *else* going on in "psychosomatic" conditions. We are by now familiar with the conversion symptoms (the distorted expression of repressed conflictual ideas/affects/memories), but what lies in between "purely" organic disease and conversion? According to Fenichel, we find four different classes of organ-neurotic symptoms,[49] the most interesting of which is that of "affect equivalents".[50] Affect equivalents are the physical expressions of a given affect without the consciousness of the affect. This phenomenon is also described as the way in which the physical attitudes which have become associated with an emotion in childhood get used later on in life as a distorted expression of the emotion, an "equivalent". One is not aware of the significance of the physical expression, yet it is nevertheless used as a substitute. What is interesting about affect equivalents is that we seem to have a form of body-knowledge, or body expression, which cannot be further developed within this framework. It will not be until we have a phenomenological understanding of the mind-body unity that we can make sense of, and use these kinds of ideas. All Fenichel can do with affect equivalents is to state that they have a "diminished discharge value as compared with fully experienced affects",[51] a characterization clearly tied to the economical, neuro-physiological underpinnings of the Freudian metapsychology.

If the ontological mind-body issue is scantily addressed in the early psychoanalytic writings, it is virtually absent in later authors. Why this is so is hard to say. Perhaps the early writers were still grappling with the relationship between the psychological and the neurophysiological. Today, psychoanalysts are no longer particularly interested in grounding psychodynamic theory in neurology, and most of them take a hermeneutical position, that is, that psychoanalysis (and psychodynamic the-

---

[49] (1) affect equivalents; (2) results of changes in the chemistry of the unsatisfied and dammed-up person; (3) physical results of unconscious attitudes or of unconsciously determined behavior patterns; (4) all kinds of combinations of these three possibilities. In ibid., p. 309.

[50] A term taken from Deutsch, "The Choice of Organ in Organ Neuroses", *Int. J. Psa.,* Vol. 20, 1939.

[51] Fenichel (1946), pp. 309-310.

ory) is concerned first and foremost with meaning, not with brain processes.[52] If we examine McDougall's writings, what are her answers to the ontological questions?

For McDougall, the psychosomatic condition is a primitive form of *communication*, where symptoms are used in the same way as the cries of the infant, intending to affect another human being. The psychosomatic communication is a regression to the level of non-purposive, uncontrolled organ functioning. The reason for this deficient functioning is that the psychosomatic patient uses the primitive defense maneuver foreclosure, whereby psychic content is completely ejected from the psyche. And where there is no thought or affect, there will only be a void, and the physical symptom. It is difficult to find answers to the ontological questions in McDougall's theory of psychosomatics. Psychosomatics is conceptualized as a form of communication as well as a specific form of mental functioning. That this particular form of defective psychological development and functioning leads to, or results in, somatization is postulated as a fact rather than investigated as a phenomenon. Sometimes, the relationship between the defective mental functioning and the psychosomatic symptom formation is unclear, as in her own definition of psychosomatosis, for example: "When patients face inner conflict and outer stress with no other mental mechanisms than psychic ejection of every affect-charged idea or perception...and when *in addition* they produce severe or continual maladies, the form of psychic equilibrium maintained in this way deserves the name *psychosomatosis.* This kind of mental functioning does not primarily depend upon repression or denial."(first italics mine).[53] Psychosomatosis can thus be understood as the way in which patients use their bodies in order to maintain their "psychic equilibrium", an interesting idea, although it is not developed any further by McDougall. McDougall exhibits a dualistic framework in her thinking, as seen in the following: "What links may be found between the specific hyperactivity or underactivity of certain chemical me-

---

52 See Schafer (1976).
53 McDougall (1982/1986), p. 165.

diators in the synaptic transmission of a given patient's *neuroanatomical* system and the specific *psychological* system developed by that same patient for dealing with thoughts, affects, fantasies, and desires? A scientific synapsis may be required to link our different findings!"[54] (italics in original) It seems that we are still in the business of "linking" from one realm to another, although psychodynamic theory has not gotten much further than Freud's work on conversion hysteria.

The main problem with the implicit ontology found in psychodynamic theory is that it is ambivalent in its conceptualization of the psychosomatic field. Mind is conceived of as a psychological phenomenon, non-reducible to neurophysiology, although much of the explication of the mental is conceptualized in quasi-mechanistic terms or metaphors. The life of the mind is not to be confused with brain processes, the mind or mental life is something other than neurophysiology, although we have been offered no way of understanding how the mental realm and the somatic relate to one another.[55] If one cannot make sense out of the basic tenets of one's theory (conversion from mind to body), it should be a matter of importance to either revise the theory, or give it up in favor of more useful concepts and hypotheses. Psychodynamic theoreticians have unfortunately done neither. They are stuck with a mysterious mind-body transaction which seems to elude our powers of comprehension. As David-Ménard expresses it: "How can a thought be diverted into bodily innervation while at the same time it remains a thought--given that the

---

[54] Ibid., p. 161.

[55] Rubenstein (1965) attempts to argue for the necessity of formulating psychoanalytic theory in such a way that it can be verified *both* psychologically and neurophysiologically. In order to do this, all terms must be 1) reducible to terms describing observable and/or directly inferable psychological relationships as well as 2) translatable into neurophysiological terms. However, his ontological position is that "the referents of psychoanalytical theoretical terms are not psychological but neurophysiological events" (p. 52). If this is so, then there is really no mind-body problem, it is simply a matter of translating from the psychological descriptive language into the "real" underlying neurophysiological events. He agrees with this characterization, but immediately counters that "just because they may be translatable does not mean that as soon as it is feasible we should go ahead and translate them" (p.53). This ambivalence is typical of psychodynamic theory.

hysterical symptom takes the place of an utterance? There is no solution to this problem within the framework of a dualist epistemology."[56]

The etiological questions

As mentioned earlier, for Freud the somatization process is a particular kind of *defense maneuver*. Conversion hysteria is conceptualized first and foremost in economical terms, as the result of pathogenic energy being converted into somatic innervation, leading to physical symptom formation. It has been suggested by some[57] that Freud's second theory of conversion was on the way to explicating the interactive, communicative aspect of the symptoms, approaching the idea of the "speaking body". Nevertheless, the conversion hysteria mechanism is, for Freud, basically a peculiar form of repression. It is precipitated, like all defense, in the face of unbearable psychical conflict and its accompanying "tension". Because of the psycho-mechanical nature of the conversion idea, with its emphasis on energy and abreaction, the symptom will be maintained as long as the conflict remains repressed, together with its psychical energy, seething, as it were, in the depths of the unconscious. That which cannot be reacted to, thought about, contained and/or acted upon will continue to harass the person physically. How does this defense maneuver come about? Freud states that "the splitting of consciousness in these cases of acquired hysteria is accordingly a deliberate and intentional one. At least it is often *introduced* by an act of volition; for the actual outcome is something different from what the subject intended"[58](italics in original). But why the conversion to somatic symptoms? Why not some other form of neurotic symptom formation? Freud has no answer to this, beyond the previously mentioned theories of somatic compliance and symptom by association. Somatic compliance proved to be empirically unsound, and although both the notion of symptom by association and his (second) conversion theory of psychosomatics as a primitive commu-

---

[56]   David-Ménard (1983/1989), p. 13.
[57]   Ibid.; Mattis (1994).
[58]   Freud (1893-1895), Studies on hysteria, *SE*, Vol, II., p. 123.

nication raise some interesting questions such as "How does the body formulate, express and communicate meaning?" and "What form of self-understanding is operating when a physical expression replaces a verbal utterance?" these questions cannot be discussed within Freud's theoretical framework.[59]

Max Schur[60] sees somatization as a response to either internal, instinctual danger (threatening impulses not acceptable to the ego), or a reaction to reactivated traumas brought about by external life situations. Somatization is a form of *regression* whereby the ego loses two important capacities: the ability to think in accordance with secondary process, and the ability to use neutralized energy.[61] According to Schur, there is a direct interdependence between the ego's ability to use secondary processes and neutralized energy, and the "desomatization" of responses, that is, the ability to react in a non-psychosomatic fashion. The person who somatizes is thus incapable of thinking and reacting in a mature way.

---

[59] In his later work Wilhelm Reich did attempt to formulate a theory of the expressiveness of the entire organism. For Reich, psychopathology of the human being shows itself at the psychogical level in terms of character armor (rigid, chronic forms of ego-defense) as well as muscular armor, the point of which is to hold back the flow of what he called "the cosmic orgone energy". He concluded that his "vegetotherapy" had left the realm of depth psychology and transcended physiology entering the realm of "protoplasmatic functions" (Reich 1933, p. 359). These excursions into cosmic energy and protoplasms were a bit too radical for most of his colleagues to accept. His therapeutic technique of having physical contact with patients was also a decisive step away from classical psychoanalysis. He was expelled from the International Psychoanalytic Association in 1934, after heated debate concerning, among other things his mental health status.

[60] Schur (1955).

[61] The notion of secondary process and neutralized energy (or "bound energy" in Freud's terminology) belong together in the metapsychological theory. Primary process thinking is the primitive, timeless, illogical thought pattern found in the unconscious, in dreams, in very young children and psychotics. The secondary process is what we usually mean by "thinking", that is, thought which has been schooled by the reality principle, where thinking follows logical patterns, obeys the principle of non-contradiction etc. The economical aspects of primary and secondary process are as follows: in primary process, the energy is free-flowing, it tends towards discharge by the speediest route; the secondary process, however, concerns bound (or "neutralized") energy which is checked and controlled.

There is an initial stress situation, in the face of which the person in question cannot mobilize the necessary (psychological and physiological) responses. Schur could not identify any specific psychosomatic personality, but he did find some common attributes in his psychosomatic patients.[62] In the field of psychosomatics, we are diagnostically dealing with what Schur calls "constellations", that is, certain types of libidinal and ego development, certain types of organs and organ systems and certain environmental influences. These factors relate to one another proportionately, that is, the more the organ response is genetically determined, the less neurosis is involved.

For Schur, the psychosomatic patient is someone who has regressed to an infantile stage of development, reacting with diffuse discharge phenomena and lack of thought (cf. McDougall). This form of "physiological regression," as Schur calls it, can in fact occur quite suddenly: "The long and painful path of maturation may be reversed in an instant, the ego loses the capacity of secondary process thinking. It uses unneutralized energy and desomatization fails."[63] However, the loss of these important ego functions does not always result in physiological regression. Schur states that physiological regression also depends upon innate and environmental factors. Although we seem to have a multifactorial model, Schur places special emphasis upon the role of the ego failure, specifically failure to perform secondary process thinking and energy neutralization. For Schur, the conceptualization of ego function and thought is tied up with the *economical* aspect of the metapsychology, with discharge and energy terms in the foreground. We have once again the mixed descriptions of physiological processes in some kind of relationship to descriptions of intentional, symbolic significance (meaning). We find the thinking human being who reacts to his environment and inner life, as well as the mechanical, anonymous system of neutralized/unneutralized

---

[62] Briefly: 1) presentation of a variety of neurotic symptoms; 2) narcissistic and pregenital libido development (conflicts around exhibitionism); 3) widespread impairment of ego functions; 4) tenuous, ambivalent object relations; 5) unusual amount of early traumatizations.

[63] Schur (1955), p. 126.

energy. Because of this implicit dualism, Schur is one more psychoanalyst who must admit, "It is hard to explain and harder still to comprehend how unconscious thought or conflict can influence somatic functions."[64] Schur is perhaps also "waiting for neurology", as he writes that "our knowledge of the intrapersonal pathway from the emotional to the somatic sphere is very scanty."[65] As long as we insist upon building bridges and finding pathways *from* mind *to* body, we will have trouble with our etiological questions.

Fenichel is an author who does not hesitate to use the word "causality" in a variety of contexts. He explains that "'unconscious affects' apparently cause quantitatively and qualitatively different hormonal secretions and in this way influence the vegetative nervous system and the physical functions."[66] Attitudes rooted in unconscious instinctual conflicts (e.g. the wish to perform fellatio) *cause* certain behavior (like compulsively clearing one's throat), which in turn *causes* somatic changes in tissue (pharyngitis). The first "cause" is that of psychical determinism, while the second is the more traditional one. But unconscious attitudes may also "influence the hormonal function".[67] For example, to wish to belong to the opposite sex may influence the production of hormones, although this mechanism is not explained. To "cause" and to "influence" are not specified further, and for that reason are not able to illuminate more precisely the nature of interaction between mind and body. They seem to be used as bridges across the mind-body gap. Fenichel is, as are his fellow psychoanalysts, committed to the economical discharge model,[68] with its accompanying dualistic problem namely, to bring together the level of neurophysiology and the level of psychological signification.

---

[64] Schur (1950), p. 243.

[65] Ibid., p. 265.

[66] Fenichel (1946), p. 312.

[67] Ibid., p. 315.

[68] "...unconscious warded-off impulses which cannot find an adequate outlet but seek again and again to find discharge and to produce derivatives have less obvious and more lasting effects. Continued or repeated attempts at substitute outlets may eventually produce physical alterations." Ibid., p. 312.

George Engel and Arthur Schmale are a bit more careful on the issue of causality. They point out that it is one thing to ascertain temporal correlations between occurrences of particular psychological processes, and the development of a specific somatic disorder, and another thing to establish causality. A temporal correlation in itself does not constitute a causal relationship. In order to show causation one must demonstrate that the "*physiological or biochemical* processes associated with the psychic state in question either have a pathogenic influence or facilitate such a somatic reaction that disease may occur"(my italics).[69] So although it would seem that there is an attempt to explicate a causal relationship between the psychical and the physical, we see that it is the *physiological aspects* associated with specific psychological events which are capable of causal efficacy, not the content, meaning or signification as psychical. The level of description is the objectified body, not the lived body. In spite of this physicalistic position, the authors' own contribution to the field of psychosomatic theory is the introduction of two *psychological* attitudes (described as such), called the "giving up - given up" complex. These attitudes (or their physiology?) are thought to act as a nonspecific onset condition of the predisease state. The first attitude has helplessness as its major affect, while the second is characterized by hopelessness. Patients who develop this complex are more or less prone to reacting in one of these two ways in the face of real, symbolic or threatened loss. The giving up - given up complex is an ego state, characterized by a particular disposition of affects, attitude, self-perception and so on. The giving up - given up complex is not a sufficient causal factor in the development of psychosomatic illness, as it is not always followed by somatic disease. Neither is it a necessary condition for the development of psychosomatic pathology. It is seen as a possible contributing cause of the emergence of psychosomatic pathology only if other predisposing factors are also present. Thus, specific biological predisposition and/or factors in the environment interact with the "giving up - given up" complex to result in a psychobiological state conducive to falling ill. The introduction of this

---

[69] Engel & Schmale (1967), p. 353.

new complex has not clarified the mechanisms involved in the development of psychosomatics, but has given us one more factor, together with other factors, which is said to contribute to the emergence of psychosomatic disease. We have, then, another multifactorial theory.

Alexander introduced the idea that motivation can be regarded as a form of causation. Since psychoanalysis is a motivational theory (why people do the things they do), it is natural that he wanted to give motivation a central role in the understanding of psychosomatic pathology. In order to do this, he had to do battle with physicians who refuse to allow motivation (psychological explanations) the same status as somatic, physicalistic causation. What does motivation as causation contribute to the theory of psychosomatics? Psychological descriptions can tell us (explain for us) the reasons for (causes of?) people's attitudes, thoughts, feelings and behavior, all of which seem to play a vital role in the development of psychosomatic diseases. That which is "causal" here is the psychical determination from the unconscious. It is psychoanalysis which will give medicine the tools necessary to understand unconscious conflicts and tensions and their role in the development of somatic pathology. How does the psychical (ideas, feelings, wishes) affect the physical? This is, of course, the crux of the matter. Like many other psychosomatic theoreticians, Alexander prefers to speak of emotions in this context, because it is easy to show how chronic intense emotion influences body processes (heightened adrenaline, blood pressure and so on). "Emotion" is convenient because it is clearly a "frontier" concept, which seems to partake equally of physiology and psychology. Emotions have both intentional meaning content and bodily aspects.[70] But what if one leaves emotions aside, and speaks about wishes? For example, how can a person's wish to change sex "cause" or influence their hormones? How does a repressed incest fantasy "cause" somatic symptoms? This is harder to understand. In fact, it is first and foremost "unconscious emotional attitudes" which can be regarded as causative, according to Alexander.

---

[70] This is at least the case in strong emotions, such as rage, fear, desire, depression, joy and remorse. It is in fact rather hard to imagine a strong emotion without a corresponding body component.

The mechanism involved is by now familiar: these repressed emotional tendencies, denied conscious elaboration and motor outlet, lead to chronic somatic dysfunction. That which is causative in the mind-body chain is once again the somatic, physiological correlate of the psychological (cf. Engel & Schmale above).

McDougall has characterized the psychosomatic mechanism as one of primitive defense, the psychic repudiation of unthinkable content. No repression takes place, there is no link between psyche and soma, there is just the void, and the somatic symptom. Furthermore, the attack on one's own body is simultaneously an attack on the mother's body, since the psychosomatic individual lacks representations of differentiation from the mother-body. McDougall explains this attachment to the mother-body in terms of the "cork-child", whose function is to repair and fill up the mother. In terms of psychological development, the mother has not been able to help the child contain, reflect and work through anxiety-provoking thoughts, feelings and fantasies. The child has the option to either take a psychotic line of development, or follow the psychosomatic development.[71] The psychosomatic person "chooses" to squash and annihilate emotion and fantasy, since they are dangerously tinted with archaic, primitive longings and fears. In order to do this, a radical split is introduced between mind and body (a process nowhere explicated further). This split enables the person to make use of the body as a repository for this dangerous material, now in the form of purely somatic activity. It should be noted that this process is different from the one described by Freud in the case of conversion hysteria. For McDougall, in this chronic form of psychosomatization, there has never been any symbolic verbal representation of these dangerous ideas and affects. Had they reached that level, it would have been possible to deal with them, either by consciously working through them or by repressing them

---

[71] McDougall wonders herself why children brought up in such a difficult situation do not become psychotic. Her tentative suggestion is that according to her clinical experience, it would seem that the psychosomatic patients remembered their fathers as being active and interested in them during latency and adolescence. This may have some kind of "normalizing" function.

to the unconscious, as the normal neurotic does. The problem for the psychosomatic person is no longer threatening ideas and fantasies, but life-threatening somatic conditions, which become exacerbated when life situations stir up the archaic psychical material. We have in McDougall's psychosomatic theory the same basic psychodynamic mechanism again: that psychical content (in this case, primitive, archaic fears and fantasies) gets transformed into something somatic which causes, or in some way leads to physical pathology. In her terminology, the threatening psychical content is ejected from the psyche into the body, where it there creates havoc with somatic processes.

Some further theoretical additions to the psychodynamic theory of psychosomatics come from two French psychoanalysts, Pierre Marty and Michel de M'Uzan,[72] who discovered a special style of thinking in a certain group of patients, some of whom had psychosomatic diseases. They called this very concrete style of thinking "la pensée opératoire" (operational thinking). These patients focused entirely upon outside reality and external events, and seemed to be incapable of elaborating fantasy, symbolic thinking or their inner life. John Nemiah & P.E. Sifneos,[73] working in Boston, discovered a group of patients with a similar type of problem, people who seemed incapable of describing what they were feeling. Nemiah and Sifneos coined the Greek term "alexithymia" (no words for feelings) to refer to this particular disturbance in thinking and feeling. The relationship between alexithymia and psychosomatic disease is not clear, and many controversies about it are still going on.[74] Whatever the relationship may be between disturbed thinking and feeling and somatization, these authors have not provided any clarifying answers as to why and how psychosomatic pathology occurs.

Psychoanalytic authors have over the years added new theoretical constructs and terminology to the psychodynamic theory of psychosomatics (physiological regression, giving up - given up complex, motivational causality, vegetative neuroses, the "cork child", pensée opératoire,

---

[72] Marty & de M'Uzan (1963).
[73] Nemiah & Sifneos (1970).
[74] See Lolas & von Rad (1989), pp. 218-221.

alexithymia), but they have not radically investigated nor called into question the basic premise of conversion. We have seen in this section that the mechanisms involved in the formation of psychosomatic symptoms are intelligible only when that which is repressed is an emotion, since emotions are convenient "frontier concepts", involving both physiological processes and psychological signification. However, as soon as we leave emotions for repressed wishes, fantasies and so on, we lose efficacious mechanisms. In general, we are dealing with two levels of discourse in psychodynamic theory: the language of energy and the language of meaning. In the attempt to explicate the etiology of the psychosomatic pathology, there is more often than not a mixture of these two levels involved. Patients become psychosomatically ill because they are said to be reacting to their wishes, expectations and desires in a particular way, and at the same time their condition is conceptualized in terms of their being mechanically acted upon by tensions, energies and forces. The psychical life is often described in quasi-neurological terms. The mixed descriptions found in psychoanalytic theory are in fact characteristic of the Freudian framework. [75]

The cure

Psychoanalysis has been called "the talking cure", a term actually coined by one of Breuer's patients[76]. It became clear to Freud that his patients became cured from (or at least less interested in) their somatic symptoms when they became conscious of unconscious conflicts. Not only did they succeed in becoming conscious of these disturbing ideas and wishes, they also managed to work through[77] them in the course of the psychoanaly-

---

[75] See Ricoeur (1970) for a thorough investigation of psychoanalysis as the combination of these two discourses.

[76] See Freud (1910), Five Lectures on Psycho-Analysis, *SE*, Vol. XI, p. 13.

[77] "Working through" is an important curative factor in classical psychoanalysis. It is not curative in itself to simply become conscious of previously repressed material. The patient must psychically integrate the ideas and feelings with the rest of the conscious ego system. This process takes considerable time and effort. One gradually accepts, mourns and reconciles oneself with the previously unacceptable ideas, wishes

sis. The psychoanalytic treatment setting is such that the patient can relax and associate freely, thanks to the neutrality and regularity of the treatment situation. The frequency of the sessions and the fact that the patient lies down on the couch, out of the sight of the analyst, facilitates both regression and transference. Regression and transference make it possible for unconscious material to present itself, albeit in disguised form. The analyst does not direct or advise the patient, but uses the special situation in order to point out (interpret) the unconscious material presented, as well as the patient's resistance to becoming conscious of it. Because of the neutrality of the analyst, as well as his/her importance to the patient, the wishes, fears and anxieties which the patient has experienced in the past in relation to significant others are projected onto the analyst. In the treatment setting, the patient can finally come to grips with these past difficulties and thereby free herself/himself from the neurotic solutions to these problems. The mechanisms involved in the psychoanalytic cure can be easily placed within the metapsychological system: patients succeed in overcoming their inner conflicts (the dynamic aspect), they become conscious of unconscious material (the topographical aspect), and the pathogenic energy which once "fed" the symptoms can once again be discharged into acceptable thought and motor patterns (the economical aspect).

The question regarding the nature of the cure involved in the treatment of psychosomatic patients is less thematically addressed in the post-Freudian literature than the previous two categories (ontology, etiology). It is taken for granted that the patients should undergo some form of psychotherapeutic treatment, and that the psychotherapeutic treatment will cure them of their somatizations, in line with the classical Freudian tenets outlined above. It is emphasized that the cause of the emotional tension (psychical conflicts) must be dealt with before one can expect re-

---

and feelings of which one has now become aware. Without "working through", one may achieve a certain intellectual understanding, but there is no cure. The risk is that without working through, there remains considerable resistance to the material, and accordingly continuation of the neurotic defenses against it.

lief from psychosomatic symptoms. Leon Saul[78] writes that the curative effects of the psychoanalytic treatment depend upon making conscious those "emotional energies" such as love, hate and fear which act as stimuli to the nervous system, gradually resulting in symptoms.[79] Reich was the psychoanalyst who took this cathartic idea to the limits, conceptualizing the cure in terms of the mobilization of the patient's "plasmatic currents." The goal of Reich's orgone therapy is the destruction of character armor and muscular defense, in order to allow for the reestablishement of plasma mobility, which is the uninhibited expressiveness of the organism. For Reich, this ideally entailed the appearance of what he called "the orgasm reflex," an attitude of giving at all levels (interpersonal, muscular, emotional). Another basic tenet in the psychoanalytic conceptualization of the cure is that consciousness is said to have a "buffer effect" against somatizations. It is in and through conscious activity that one can effectively deal with emotional problems. Schur is very specific about the salutogenic role of conscious processes. Procedures of thought and verbalization actually counteract ego regression, which is, for Schur, the most important factor in the development of psychosomatic pathology. Verbalized thoughts belong to secondary process, and, as such, lead energy away from dreams, fantasies, and other forms of more loosely flowing primary process thinking. Secondary process thinking allows the patient to distinguish between "my father", "my husband", "my boss" as well to be able to differentiate between "there and then" and "here and now". As soon as the patient has established (or re-established) secondary thought processes, s/he will no longer have any need to think, feel and act with her/his body.

McDougall describes one of her psychosomatic patients in therapy as having "crossed the frontier" from pure body sensations (something is sinking in my stomach) to articulated thoughts and feelings. What was

---

[78] Saul (1948).

[79] This explanation leans heavily on the economical pillar of the metapsychology. It is the physiological aspects of mental life, specifically the body components involved in emotion (their physiology), which are responsible for the psychosomatic pathology, and it is likewise relief from them which accounts for symptom abatement.

once only body sensation becomes verbalized, elaborated symbolizations, with specific affects and ideas relating to specific people and situations. This same theme is found in the previous authors mentioned, namely that it is the curative factor *par excellence* to be able to verbally formulate thoughts and feelings. Just why this should be so is explained in economical terms for McDougall as well. It is because words are the most effective way to contain and channel the "energy" associated with drives and fantasies. When the latter cannot be taken care of in this way, they will either become neurotic symptoms or psychosomatic pathology.

The psychoanalysts are in agreement about treatment principles and hypothesized mechanisms of cure. The psychotherapeutical enterprise: 1) relieves emotional tensions by making unconscious material conscious; 2) facilitates verbalization of conflictual material, which counteracts the failure of ego defenses and the regression to primary process functioning; 3) makes possible the "working through" process, whereby previously conflictual material is integrated into the rest of the personality. The more conflictual material one has integrated into the conscious system, the less vulnerable one is to the risk of future somatizations. The theoreticians examined ultimately embrace the economical explanation of the cure, which concerns energies and their proper/improper channels of discharge.

Summary of the psychodynamic theory of psychosomatic pathology

I stated in the beginning of the chapter that the analysis of the theoreticians examined in this section should give us the psychodynamic answers to the basic questions concerning a theory of psychosomatic pathology. Those authors who deal with the ontological mind/body issues fall in line with a form of identity-theory where psychical processes are said to exist, in their own right, demanding their own methods and forms of understanding, yet at the same time it is assumed that the psychical is another side of neurophysiological processes. The nature of the relationship between the psychical and the neurophysiological was a problem which Freud could never solve, nor any of his disciples. The early writers decided to "wait for neurology", while the later theoreticians no longer address the issue. I have found that those factors which are said to be efficacious in the formation of symptoms are ultimately those *physiological* processes associated with the psychical level of signification (meaning). That which is thus efficacious is either psychical energy (cathexis surrounding repressed ideas, wishes, fantasies) or repressed emotions. Emotions are conceivable causes of psychosomatic symptomology because they are good examples of "frontier" concepts which involve both physiological and psychological components. It is harder to see how unconscious wishes and fantasies can effect physiological processes in the body, since efficacious mechanisms from mind to body seem to be lacking. The only way to make sense of this interaction is to appeal to *economical* aspect of the metapsychology, where ideas and fantasies are attached to/surrounded by psychical energy. It is in fact the economical explanation which is invoked by all the theoreticians in order to explain both the mechanisms behind somatization and the cure. Although we find multifactorial theories from Alexander onward, the basic notion of conversion, that is, the transformation of psychical content (conflicts, traumas) into somatic innervations, is never abandoned as the cornerstone to understanding psychosomatic pathology.

That which is specific to a psychodynamic theory of psychosomatic pathology is the hypothesis of unconscious conflicts and their accompanying energy (cathexis).Without the **unconscious**, there is no psychodynamic theory of psychosomatics. Without the **economical** pillar of the metapsychology, there is no way to understand either the formation of symptoms nor the phenomenon of cure. The critique of psychodynamic theory rests upon whether or not these two specifically Freudian notions are illuminating, or whether they can be abandoned in favor of more useful theoretical constructions. Do we need the unconscious to understand psychosomatics? Are we satisfied with the economical explanation of causation? Have we won a genuine understanding of the psychosomatic condition with these theoretical constructs? My answer to these questions is that we do not need the unconscious, at least not the unconscious as it has been *formulated by Freud*; neither does the economical explanation of causation further our understanding of psychosomatic functioning. There are some interesting ideas to be found within psychodynamic theory, such as the "speaking body" of Freud's second conversion theory, "affect equivalents" and the curative role of verbalization (the talking cure). However, the further development of these ideas within psychodynamic literature has been hindered by the dualistic conversion premise and adherence to the economical pillar of the metapsychology. I will in the second part of the dissertation develop a phenomenological alternative which will attempt to remedy some of these problems and reformulate the ground for a truly psychosomatic theory. But first, let us examine the next theoretical orientation in psychosomatic theory, psychosomatic medicine.

CHAPTER 3

Psychosomatic medicine and psychosomatic theory

"It is more important to know what sort of person has a disease than to know what sort of disease a person has."

--Hippocrates

"The cure of many diseases is unknown to the physicians of Hellas, because they disregard the whole which ought to be studied also, for the part can never be well unless the whole is well."

--Plato

Introduction

Psychosomatic medicine as the branch of Western medicine specifically concerned with mind-body relations has a rather short history, usually dated from the publication in 1935 of Flanders Dunbar's *Emotions and Bodily Changes, A Survey of Literature on Psychosomatic Interrelationships*, and the first appearance in 1939 of the *Journal of Psychosomatic Medicine*. Dunbar's book was an attempt to collect and synthesize all available literature up to that time (2251 articles) on the relationship between somatic functioning and the emotions. The intention of the *Journal* was to delineate this new psychosomatic field of study, and set up guidelines for further medical research. The "Introductory Statement" in the first issue of the *Journal*, often quoted and referred to, can be seen as a kind of credo, which to this day is more or less regarded as the official position of psychosomatic medicine. The Statement defines the role of psychosomatic medicine as follows: "Its object is to study in their interrelation the psychological and physiological aspects of all normal and abnormal bodily functions and thus to integrate somatic therapy and psychotherapy."[1] Despite the relatively short history of psychosomatic medicine as a discipline, the field of psychosomatic inquiry itself is ancient, as is witnessed by the two quotations above. Zbigniew Lipowsky[2] has pointed out that our modern understanding of "psychosomatic" incorporates two very old conceptions within Western thought, namely, the holistic[3] conception of man and the idea of the psychogenesis[4] of illness, formerly understood in terms of "the passions". Although psychosomatic medicine has decided to dismiss the notion of psychogensis (as it is understood by the psychoanalysts), the holistic understanding of health and disease is alive and well in psychosomatic medicine.

Psychosomatic medicine has a complicated relationship to psychoanalysis. Many of the first proponents of psychosomatic medicine were also psychoanalysts.[5] The field of psychosomatic medicine was dominated by psychoanalytic theory from the 1930's until the mid 1950's. This orientation led to an emphasis upon the influences of psychological factors on somatic functioning. The psychoanalyst Franz Alexander, mentioned in the previous chapter, exerted a strong influence on the development of psychosomatic theory within psychosomatic medicine. Issues of specificity were in the foreground, and much research was concerned with trying to validate correlations between specific unconscious conflicts and specific diseases. This line of research proved to be unfruitful, and Alexander's specificity hypothesis has been heavily chal-

---

1   Introductory Statement, *J Psychosom Med* 1: 3.

2   Lipowsky (1984).

3   The term "holistic" comes from the Greek "holos" which means whole. The term holistic generally refers to the position that mind (soul) and body are one. Man is an inseparably unity. For the ancient Greeks, the psyche/soma unity was a life form. Today, a holistic approach means that mind and body are considered to be two distinct, yet integral aspects of the human being.

4   Psychogenesis means that psychological factors are thought to play a causative role in the formation of disease. The word "psychogenic" was first used in 1894, by a German psychiatrist by the name of Sommer, when referring to hysteria. By the 1920's the term "psychogenic" could be applied to a variety of somatic problems imagined to have a psychological origin.

5   See Wittkower (1974).

lenged by both psychoanalysts and non-analysts. Today the hypothesis of linear psychological specificity in the development of psychosomatic conditions (in terms of specific unconscious conflicts as well as Dunbar's personality-illness specificity) is regarded as an historical phase in the development of psychosomatic medicine. During the 1970's the shift was made from the psychodynamic interest in unconscious conflicts, motivation and defenses to a psycho-physiological approach, focusing on the so-called "mediating mechanisms"[6] between symbolic "stimuli" and their physiological response. This orientation picked up on a thread existing alongside of the psychoanalytic approach, namely the tradition of stress theory, beginning with the work of Walter Cannon and Hans Selye.[7]

The psycho-physiological approach is a modern version of the theme of the impact of the passions on the body.[8] In modern thinking, emotions alone are not considered to be sufficient causes of disease, but they are one of the variables (an extremely important one) which may "intervene" between man and his environment in a detrimental way. It is probable that the rising influence of natural scientific ideals within medicine and psychology was at least partly responsible for the abandonment of psychoanalytic thinking in favor of physiological laboratory studies and experiments. A variety of animal and human experiments were performed in order to test quantitative hypotheses concerning correlations between specific testable variables and the development of disease. If the early phase of psychosomatic medicine can be said to overlap with psychodynamic theory, the later development has an interface with research on the physiology of stress. The discipline of psychosomatic medicine can therefore be said to spring from two different streams of thought, with one influence coming from psychoanalytic thinking and

---

6 Also referred to as "intervening variables". Sometimes the term "mechanisms" seems to be reserved for physiological factors, while "variables" refers to more subjective factors. But this is not always the case. Mediating mechanisms and intervening variables will be examined in the etiology section of this chapter.

7 The work of Cannon and Selye will be dealt with specifically in the next chapter.

8 The idea that the "passions" have a negative impact on health is referred to in the medical textbooks of the seventeenth and eighteenth centuries. See Bynum & Porter (1993); Margetts (1954).

the other from experimental psychology and stress research. That which is specific to modern psychosomatic medicine is the insistence upon a complex interplay of many factors, psychological, physiological, social and cultural, which together contribute, in varying degrees, to the development of disease and ill health. Because psychosomatic medicine overlaps into both psychoanalytic theory and stress theory, it has been somewhat difficult to choose which authors should be discussed in this chapter. I have simply decided to analyze relevant texts from those authors whose names are strongly associated with psychosomatic medicine, even if the person in question also happens to be a psychoanalyst or a physiologist/stress theoretician.[9] I will in this chapter address the common theoretical kernel which unites the various authors being discussed here under the heading "psychosomatic medicine." Where there are relevant or interesting differences in their theories, I will bring these differences up.

How does this marriage work, then, this historical union between the psychoanalytic interest in subjective, mental life and the quantitatively oriented physiology of stress? For although the idea of psychogenesis as a linear, causal factor in the development of disease has been abandoned, psychosomatic medicine does not wish to throw out all psychoanalytic ideas on mental functioning. Theoreticians within modern psychosomatic medicine are quite open to the idea that there is a connection between the affective life of the individual and vulnerability to disease, although it is no longer accepted that intra-psychical conflicts are necessarily responsible for the development of ill health. Taylor et al.[10] write that the theoretical limitations of the psychoanalytic conflict paradigm became apparent during the 1950's, when psychoanalytic therapy did not prove to be as effective as hoped for in the treatment of psychosomatically ill patients. Psychogensis is considered to be a reductionistic

---

[9] I will however not deal with the work of Alexander in this chapter, as his ideas have already been examined in the previous chapter. For some classical references from the history of psychosomatic medicine, see: Alexander (1948); Mirsky (1958); Ruesch (1948); Weiner et al (1957); Wolff (1953).

[10] Taylor et al. (1991).

concept, and it has given way to a multifactorial theory of psychosomatics. Lipowsky[11]summarizes the development of psychosomatic medicine as a distilling down over the years into a blend of psychophysiology and the holistic approach to health and disease.[12] What, then, has been retained from psychodynamic theory? The main legacy from psychoanalytic thinking is the (medical) legitimization of subjectivity as a vital factor in the development of pathological conditions.[13] That which differentiates psychosomatic medicine from the discipline of physiology is the importance that is placed upon the meaning of experience for the subject. However, psychosomatic medicine is not interested in the meaning found in unconscious conflicts and fantasies, but focuses upon the way in which the individual *cognitively* perceives and understands his situation. The way someone responds to a situation depends upon his or her individual personality traits, habits and coping skills. The way information is taken in, responded to and dealt with is vital to the understanding of the relationship between the subjective experience of the person and the outer environment with its "stressors", life events and hardships. It is within the relationship between man (with his emotions, cognitions, coping) and his environment (situations and events occurring on the physical, individual, social and cultural levels) that one should look for the factors which lead to disease and illness.

Authors within the field of psychosomatic medicine view the subjective dimension somewhat differently from authors within the field of psychoanalysis do, on several points. Psychosomatic medicine places em-

---

[11] Lipowsky (1984).

[12] Cheren (1989) has been kinder to psychoanalysis and includes "psychodynamic psychiatry" as one of the three main endeavors of modern psychosomatic medicine, together with psychophysiological research and biobehavioral approaches.

[13] This is not to say that medicine had completely ignored subjectivity until psychoanalysis came onto the scene. In fact, the biomedical model with its emphasis upon "objective" laboratory findings is a relatively recent phenomenon in the long history of medicine. Jewson (1975) has pointed out that it was after Virchow's success with microbiology that medicine paid less and less attention to the patient's psychological, social and economic situation. One could say that it was only with the coming of psychoanalysis that medicine *recalled* its interest in the life of the patient.

phasis on the importance of cognitive processes and coping (one could say "adapting" as well) instead of unconscious conflicts and defenses. An important shift has also occurred from an *intra-psychical* perspective (the problem is *in* the person's psychical make-up) to an *inter-relational* systems approach, where several systems are seen as operating together (physiological, psychological, social, cultural, environmental) to produce disease. Just how this mulitfactorial theory is to be understood will be discussed in this chapter. As mentioned above, psychosomatic medicine has abandoned the psychoanalytic interest in psychological specificity in favor of the so-called psychosomatic approach, which claims that events and situations in a person's life, in collaboration with his or her intrapsychical make-up, overt behavior, genetic make-up and sociocultural environment, co-determine, to a varying degree, the predisposition to and the cause of every human ailment.

For psychosomatic medicine, the field of psychosomatic pathology is the study of the complex interaction and interdependence between bio-, psycho-, social factors found in the onset and outcome of all human disease.[14] The theoretical aim of psychosomatic medicine is to define and verify correlations between various factors ("intervening variables") and the development of disease. Where psychoanalysts reserved "psychosomatic" pathology for those conditions with a clear psychogensis, psychosomatic medicine advocates a multifactorial theory of psychosomatics, including various etiological factors. Whether or not any and all health problems which afflict man are actually the result of psychosomatic processes is not specifically spelled out, over and above the general psychosomatic approach, i.e. that diseases and symptoms can all be considered "psychosomatic" in a wide sense of the term. But what does this really mean? Are we to understand that every back pain *is* psychosomatic, or do we find criteria for distinguishing psychosomatic back pain from "purely" somatic pain? This is a matter of diagnostics, not approach. Often, the specific diseases and symptoms referred to as "psychosomatic"

---

[14] Lipowsky (1984) points out that health and disease are more or less arbitrarily defined states of the organism, co-determined by psychological, social and biological factors.

in the literature are the classical ones, thus implying that in fact some diseases/symptoms are *more* psychosomatic than others. This switching back and forth from the general psychosomatic approach to specific psychosomatic diagnoses makes it hard to determine the exact nature of psychosomatic diseases and symptoms. In the first case (the approach) the claim is that psychosomatic processes constitute a totality (any and all diseases and symptoms), while in the second case (diagnostics) they are a partial class in the totality.

The method of investigation for the psychoanalysts was the qualitative, descriptive study of individual clinical cases (the case histories), whereas proponents of psychosomatic medicine wish to present quantified, testable hypotheses concerning variables which are thought to intervene between the subject and his environment in a detrimental way.[15] One very important clinical outcome of psychosomatic medicine has been the development of liaison-consultation psychiatry, which deals with helping both patients and somatically oriented doctors understand the psychosomatic approach to disease and ill health. I will return to the clinical applications of psychosomatic medicine later on.

While psychosomatic medicine rejects the idea of linear psychogenesis in the development of disease, the efficacious role of the emotions has fared much better. As shown in the previous chapter, it is not surprising that emotions are important to the understanding of psychosomatic pathology, as they can be conceptualized as "frontier concepts" between the psychical, having to do with the subjective realm of meaning, and the physical, having to do with physiological processes in the body. Psychosomatic medicine is extremely interested in emotion as an important intervening variable between cognition (taking in "information") and physiological arousal. The importance of emotions has to do with their physiological aspects, which may affect the body in several important systems, for example, the autonomic nervous system, the immune system

---

[15] Lipowsky (1976) states this agenda clearly: "The task of psychosomatic research is to break down the enormous complexity of this interaction and formulate hypotheses about causal links and correlations among clearly defined and quantifiable variables" (p. 9).

and the endocrine functions. What is detrimental about emotions is their potential to arouse the system. Indeed, *arousal* is one of the major factors found in the sequence from health to disease. Before going into the specific analysis of ontology, etiology and mechanisms of cure, I will briefly state the issues which I find to be of central importance for the psychosomatic theory of psychosomatic medicine. These issues are as follows: Does psychosomatic medicine have any mechanisms to account for the relationship between, for example, life events, psychological make-up and physiological response? Where psychodynamic theory had problems accounting for the "leap" from mind to body, psychosomatic medicine must be able to explain how "intervening variables" actually intervene. Are we dealing with causality, concomitance, or mere statistical correlations? Finally, how are we to understand "multifactorial" etiology? We find terms such as "interactions" and "influences", but what do these terms actually mean?

The ontological questions

The mind-body problem is implicit in the very field of psychosomatic medicine itself, as it is specifically concerned with the *relationship* between psychological/social/cultural factors and physiological processes in the body. Although psychosomatic medicine sees its role as investigating the mind-body relationship, little emphasis has been placed upon a philosophical discussion of the issue. Lipowsky[16]writes that although psychosomatic medicine is concerned with investigating theories about bio-psycho-social relationships, and "while all this activity may be regarded as highly relevant to the debate about the mind-body problem, the latter cannot be viewed as the subject matter of psychosomatic medicine, which is an empirical not a philosophic discipline." This empirical approach nevertheless needs some kind of operational working definition of mind and body, and several of the authors who bring up the subject explicitly refer to David Graham's "linguistic parallelism"[17]as a reason-

---

[16] Lipowsky (1984), p. 168.
[17] Graham (1967).

able standpoint on the mind-body issue. Linguistic parallelism states that the dualism which exists between mind and body is a *linguistic* dualism, based upon two different discourses of description, the one psychological, the other physical/physiological. According to linguistic parallelism, different languages may be used to describe *the same event*. The mental and the physical are often thought of as referring to different types of events, but this is a mistake, according to linguistic parallelism. There is only one event, described in different ways. However, this position is not the same as Feigl's identity theory, where the position is that we have two avenues of knowledge to the same (mind/brain) thing. Graham distinguishes his own linguistic parallelism from Feigl's identity theory in the following way, "...Feigl's position, which he at one time called a 'two language theory'. He later suggested that 'two avenues of knowledge' would be a better designation. The position of the present essay is that even when there is only one avenue to knowledge, the choice of two languages remains."[18]So even when we choose to speak only about subjective experience (known via introspection), we can *still* choose to speak about it in one of these two languages. Linguistic parallelism does not say that mind and body are two aspects of the same thing, it says the parallelism consists in the fact that we have two potentially different ways of describing the *same thing* or aspect.[19] The parallelism involved is linguistic rather than ontological.[20] However, we do not find a strict parallelism here, since the physical descriptions are always available, no matter

---

[18] Ibid., p. 57.

[19] "Aspects' refers to *different* observational data, obtained--to take a basic example--by looking at something from two different vantage points...Patients can be thought of as having different aspects, but any aspect is suitable for description in the somatic language, and many in the psychological." Ibid. p. 57.

[20] Graham is not primarily interested in ontological questions, but he does state at one point that linguistic parallelism "most closely resembles psychophysical parallelism and might be considered a special case of that. However, the parallelism lies in the ways of describing events, and not in the operation of two mysterious things called 'mind' and 'body.' It might therefore be called a theory of linguistic parallelism." Ibid. p. 57.

what the "event", while the reverse is not true. This has consequences which I will take up shortly.

Psychosomatic medicine is pragmatic, not philosophical in its interests. Its aim is to be able to isolate variables which influence and/or cause the pathological body processes leading to disease/illness, and explain the actual mechanisms responsible for the psychosomatic conditions. Where psychoanalysts were tuned into the possibility that psychosomatic suffering need not be accompanied by structural, organic changes, psychosomatic medicine focuses on diseases with clearly defined somatic pathology. This is most probably due to the fact that physiology is one of the two "roots" of psychosomatic medicine. Despite decades of work in the field of psychosomatic medicine, the yield has been meager.[21] The bridge between psychoanalysis (dealing with the subjective, lived world of the patient) and the physiology of the body has not been built. The reason why psychosomatic medicine has not been able to illuminate the relationship between the psychological and the physiological is that the dualistic starting point makes this task difficult, if not impossible. The "dualism" in language, accepted by psychosomatic medicine in its doctrine of "linguistic parallelism", is also a dualism in method, a dualism in understanding, and at the highest level a dualism in the very meta-theory of psychosomatic medicine itself.[22] There is tension between the "interrelationship" project of psychosomatic medicine and its holistic approach. Dunbar herself had misgivings about the term "psychosomatic interrelationships" as not doing justice to the fundamental unity of man. The holistic understanding of man conceptualizes the human being as an indivisible unity . The mind-body split found in psychosomatic medicine is not dualistic in the traditional sense, where mind and body refer to two different kinds of "entities" or spheres of being, but dualistic in its

---

[21] "Despite much research effort, psychosomatic research has-from a medical point of view-in large been a disappointment. It has failed to produce knowledge to control any of the major health care problems...a large amount of empirical observations have accumulated, but the problem is that many of the findings cannot easily be related to one another" Jern & Carlsson (1990), p. 4:1.

[22] See Jern & Carlsson (1990).

interactionistic stance. When the lived unity of man (as embodied meaning and lived body) is theoretically broken up, effort will have to be spent trying to "put Humpty-dumpty together again". Time and energy is spent on this project, instead of investigating the nature of the lived unity of man. Given this split, how are mind and body conceived of in psychosomatic medicine?

Psychosomatic medicine has no trouble in identifying what is (the objective) body. It is within the somatic disciplines that Western medicine has made such tremendous progress. With ever finer calibrated methods, the scientist uncovers the secrets of the body. The "body" which is investigated here is the objectified body, the body observed in the third person, divorced from any of the subjective elements which characterize the lived body. When the scientist is caught up in fascination with the intricate, yet comprehensible workings of neurophysiological mechanisms, it seems to be relatively easy for the psychological side of the "interrelations" project to get lost. That which was to be the specialty of psychosomatic medicine, namely to study and explicate the nature of the *relationship* between the psychological and the physiological, often gives way to the one-sided explication of physiological and neurological functioning, reflecting the naturalistic bias of the biomedical model.[23] This tendency is seen most clearly in what I would term "the misrepresentation of meaning as physiology". The following excerpt from Kiely[24] provides a good example of this: "A tripartite hub composed of the reticular formation, limbic system, and hypothalamus, all richly interconnected makes up the central core anatomically. Direct and indirect neocortical connections with the subcortical hub provide mechanisms whereby behavior is organized in respect to long-term *purposes, opportunities* and *dangers*" (my italics). How do these cerebral "mechan-

---

[23] Engel (1977) is one of the authors who has complained of the slow progress made in the psychosomatic project to bridge the gap between the biological and the psychological. He points out that not only is the subject matter "complex", but there are pressures put upon psychosomatic medicine to conform to mechanistic and reductionistic methodologies which are inappropriate for the problems under study.

[24] Kiely (1977), p. 207.

isms" relate to purposes, opportunities and dangers? Does the physicalistic explication of neocortical connections help us to understand something about the relationship between psychological and physiological processes? Brain processes are physiological occurrences in the nervous system, which have been investigated extensively, but as such, they do not help us to understand subjective experiences of constituting the world in terms of dangerous or opportune, nor do they illuminate the nature of the relationship between meaning and physiology. What happens in these types of maneuvers is that the subjective, psychological element disappears; or rather, gets subsumed under physicalistic description. This is legitimate if one has the explicit conviction that the psychological is reducible to or directly translatable into physiological descriptions. And although Graham would have nothing against translating from the one language into the other, the project of psychosomatic medicine is not one of translation. The specifically psychosomatic profile involves asserting that there are good reasons for using psychological language, as it is seen as adequately describing an important aspect of human reality. Psychosomatic medicine considers the psychological/social realm to be meaningful, important, and efficacious in the development of disease. The problem is that physiology and neuroscience are not capable of addressing these aspects of human life.

Proponents of the biomedical model, however, would feel quite at home with the Kiely quotation. For the average medical doctor, physicalistic descriptions are considered to be superior to, or at least more "scientific" than the language of meaning. This naturalistic bias creeps into the psychosomatic literature, in more or less open forms. For example Kimball,[25] praises the physiological side of psychosomatic medicine and states "The hope of these workers is to arrive at a basic physiology and biochemistry of the emotions and defenses whereby illnesses characterized by organ responses mediated by these hormones may be understood." It is clear that the plan is to ultimately derive psychological signification from the "solid" natural sciences. Biomedical dogma thus

---

25 Kimball (1970), p. 308.

threatens the very *raison d'être* of the psychosomatic discipline. It is possible that linguistic parallelism permits the equation of physiology with psychology, but if this is so, it is important to understand what this "equation" means. Together with the biomedical model, the "parallelism" between mind and body tends to slip into reductionism. Linguistic parallelism is ambiguous. On the one hand, emphasis is placed upon the importance of psychological, sociological and physiological multifactorial interdependence. No one description/language is said to be superior, and using one language does not exclude using another language meaningfully about the same data. On the other hand, we find in linguistic parallelism a naturalistic bias which gives primordiality to physicalistic descriptions. *Any observation whatsoever* can be described in physical terms, but not necessarily the other way around.[26] All psychological signification is said to have a physical "parallel" description. This may not seem so controversial at first glance, since man is, after all, always embodied. However, let us reflect upon the following from Graham:[27] "'Anger' can, for instance, be said to be a cause of shouting, if it is remembered that 'anger' must refer, directly or indirectly, to a state of affairs which could in principle have been described in the physical language, as, for instance, a pattern of excitation in the brain." Although this statement is concerned with the question of causation, it does state that anger could, in principle, be defined in physicalistic terms. Is there really nothing left unaccounted for in "anger" when it is described in physicalistic language? If the psychological is capable, in principle, of being understood in this way, as neurons firing in the brain, one hardly has any need of psychosomatic medicine. The discipline of neurology will do fine. But if there is a dimension of human existence known as "the subjective", meaning, mind, signification etc. (a dimension which is implied in the bio-psycho-social model espoused by psychosomatic medicine) which is not adequately described nor understood in the lan-

---

26 "All observations of people can be put in physical language terms, so that for any psychological statement whatever there must be a parallel physical statement. The reverse is not true;..." Graham (1967), p. 56. See also footnote 19.

27 Ibid. (1967), p. 62.

guage of physiology, then we should expect more of our theoreticians than this form of reductionism.[28]

Linguistic parallelism rests upon the possibility of two types of language (psychological and physiological) which can both be applied to human beings. However, behind this duality of parallel languages we find an implicit ontological position which seems to be a form of double aspect/neutral monism, which states that there is only one substance in the universe. This one substance, or event (applicable when speaking of human beings), can be known, described and understood in various ways, and we have developed two different languages in order to understand this one event. The psychological and the physical are both legitimate descriptions, although we should understand that we are actually talking about one and the same thing/event in two different ways. And because of the materialistic bias found in psychosomatic medicine, the things we are talking about are ultimately physical things.[29] We can always find physical descriptions for anything we wish to describe (an emotion, a wish, an action, a fantasy), and the fact that we sometimes use psychological language to describe certain things has to do with the fact that: 1) we do not yet know the corresponding physicalistic description; 2) it is sometimes more economical/informative to use psychological descriptions, although one could use a physical description as well. To conclude, the project of psychosomatic medicine (to understand man in his psychological, biological, and social nature), is both interactionistic (see the "Introductory Statement"), parallelistic (psychophysical parallelism) and in some sense "dualistic", since it allows for the legitimacy

---

[28] Backus & Dudley (1977) show some sensitivity to this issue, as they call attention to the fact that psychosocial factors are not quantifiable. However, in the same article it is indicated that perhaps this problem (and they do see it as a problem) is merely a reflection of our current inability to measure, and that one day this quantification will be achieved. We have, then, a methodological problem, not a principle one. This is probably what Graham means when he states that the psychological could *in principle* (one day) be understood physicalistically.

[29] A position which deviates from strict neutral monism, which claims that there is neither mind nor matter, but something else which is the basic reality behind all things.

of dual (linguistic) conceptualizations.[30] But if it is interactionistic, what is interacting with what? If we only have one "event", it is not correct to speak of interaction. Why is there always a physicalistic description, but not a psychological one? This could be a reflection of a positivistic ideal where the psychological is ultimately understood physicalistically.[31] Psychosomatic medicine has appropriated a philosophical position which sediments a duality in the understanding of man, as well as strengthens the biomedical preference for giving explanatory priority to the material over the subjective dimension of existence.

The etiological questions

In the introduction to this chapter I asked whether psychosomatic medicine has any specific mechanisms to account for the relationship between life events, intra-psychic make-up and physiology. I will here try to answer the question and examine the nature of explanation given. The explanatory terms found most often in psychosomatic medicine are "intervening variables" and "mediating mechanisms". The terms "intervene" and "mediate" convey the very important idea in this tradition that disease and ill health arise due to the *interaction* between man and his environment, which is clearly a theoretical step forward from both the psychoanalytic solipsism of intra-psychical determinism, and the naturalistic reductionism of the biomedical model. Intervening variables are said to

---

[30] "Mind-body dualism is correct; but the *duality is in the languages used*" (italics in original). Graham (1967), p. 66.

[31] Consider the following parallelism offered by Graham (1967): "John Smith was frightened when he saw the cat. When light rays from the cat reached John Smith's retina, various biochemical processes were set up that resulted in the passage of impulses over the optic nerve to the occipital cortex, with activation of sympathetic hypothalamic nuclei, and increased activity in sympathetic nerves to the heart, leading to tachycardia" (p. 58). In fairness to Graham, in the context of his article this was meant to illustrate how clumsy and uneconomical the second description would be. But my point is that the second description is not a description of "fright" at all. Biochemical processes refer to the objectified body. Fright is a psychological phenomenon belonging to the realm of meaning and experience (the lived body), which cannot be captured in these physicalistic terms.

influence individuals in varying degrees, depending upon the person, the situation, and the disease in question. How they "influence" will also be examined in the following section. But to begin with, what are these factors, variables and mechanisms?

Intervening mechanisms can be found in any system (bio-psycho-social). They can be anything from an increased hormone level .in the blood to a fantasy to a social network. These various factors are said to often work together, in terms of feed-back loops between the different systems. For example, information (something which is cognitively/perceptually attended to by the subject in his/her environment) may give rise to physiological arousal, resulting in changes in the autonomic nervous system and endocrine functions. These physiological changes may lead to conscious sensations (dry mouth, weak knees etc.) which in turn may activate memories, thoughts and fantasies. These thoughts and fantasies may stimulate feelings/fears which further increase the intensity of the physiological response, thus producing a spiral of negative activity in both the mind and the body. However, these very same physical sensations, in another person, may not provoke this accelerating spiral, but may instead lead to what is generally called "coping," [32] where the person is able to muster up thoughts, attitudes and perhaps action which succeed in quieting down the system and ultimately reducing the physiological arousal with its concomitant thoughts and feelings. The ability to cope is considered to be an intervening variable, a variable which may differ both from person to person in the same situation, and from situation to situation in the same person. Coping is an extremely important salutogenic factor. But "coping" is a slippery thing, not comparable to immunity from viral infections for example. One cannot say that a person who has "coping abilities" will always cope. One reason which is given for the temporary or habitual inability to cope is that physiological (and possibly emotional) arousal is maintained at such a high level for such a long time that the individual is overwhelmed, and thereby rendered incapable of thinking. The theme of *arousal* is often invoked as a

---

[32] The notion of coping will be dealt with specifically in the next chapter.

hindrance to the ability to think. Where psychoanalysts had chronic arousal (as repressed emotion and/cathected ideas) being discharged into the body via somatic symptoms, psychosomatic medicine conceptualizes the detrimental effect of extensive prolonged arousal in terms of: 1) its detrimental effect on the body's homeostatic balance, and 2) its tendency to block out a key salutogenic factor, namely a person's ability to think and to cope. Psychoanalysts also found thinking to be salutogenic, but not for the same reasons.[33] The emphasis upon thinking in psychosomatic medicine may be due to the influence from the computational "information processing" model. Man is conceptualized as an organism who "receives, stores, processes, creates, and transmits information, and assigns meaning to it, which in turn elicits emotional responses."[34] Coping, or lack of coping, is cited by many authors as an important mechanism which mediates between the subject and the "stressful" situation. Because thinking is an essential part of coping, it is understandable that psychosomatic medicine emphasizes the importance of cognition for maintaining health.

That which is said to be efficacious in the thinking/coping process is that it is imagined to counteract the detrimental effects of prolonged physiological arousal. This detrimental form of physiological arousal[35] can be experienced by the person as overwhelming emotion or, if one is unable to represent emotion consciously, merely as unbearable "tension." Bastiaans writes that psychosomatic symptoms arise "only at those moments when the patient's inner tension and his related emotional insta-

---

[33] As seen in chapter 2, psychoanalysts maintain that (secondary) thought processes: 1) counteract regressive tendencies towards primary process; 2) bind cathectic energy in verbalization and conscious motor activity; 3) facilitate the "working through" of trauma and consolidate the functioning of the reality principle.

[34] Lipowsky (1984) p. 168.

[35] Not all physiological arousal is detrimental to health or unpleasant. Sexual activity, as well as many of life's tasks, require a certain amount of arousal in order for things to get done. It is also well-known that certain individuals enjoy what others would consider to be excessive excitement and stimulation. Witness scenes from any stock market in the world on this point.

bility have reached a certain level of intensity and chronicity." [36] This inner tension, or arousal, has also been called "stress". It is said that the physiological and emotional disruption associated with stressful stimuli is directly responsible for the vulnerability to disease and ill health. The chain of events can be said to go from meaning (the perception of the "stimuli" or life situation) to physiology (reactions in the autonomic and hormonal systems) to (possible) further loops (thoughts and fantasies which augment physiological reaction), leading finally to the breakdown of the body in various forms of disease/ill health. This chain differs somewhat from the psychodynamic scenario, with its repressed unconscious conflicts, defenses and energy cathexes. That which is reminiscent of psychodynamic theory here is the idea that prolonged tension is bad, as well as the idea that there is a *psychological* moment which initiates the chain. It is important for both psychosomatic medicine and psychodynamic theory to show how the subject constitutes the subjective meaning of his/her lived situation, although that which is said to be of etiological significance differs within the two orientations.

But it is not only psychological factors which can "intervene" in a detrimental way. Overt behavior as well as social factors are thought of as playing role in the development of disease and ill health. According to Weiss,[37] it is rather rare that psychosomatic symptoms arise directly as the result of an emotion. An example of a direct interaction between emotion and symptom would be cases where the onset of a psychological state is simultaneous (or near simultaneous) with the onset of symptoms. For example, an asthmatic patient receives some exciting news, for example that s/he has been elected to some high office, and immediately upon hearing this begins to experience a tightening in the chest, starts wheezing and shortly thereafter has an asthma attack. Weiss states that the most common sequence of events, at least in asthma, is that emotion leads to mediating behavior which then induces symptoms. An example of this would be anger which leads to fighting, which leads to asthma. It

---

[36] Bastiaans (1977), p. 90.
[37] Weiss (1977).

is not the emotion *per se* which is an etiological factor, but the emotion in this particular person tends to lead to a *behavior* which is directly detrimental to the person's health. An interesting sociological investigation has been presented by Moss[38] where he studied a group of Zulus who had moved from their rural tribal existence to an urban city environment. He found that those subjects who developed hypertension were those who had problems with what he called "information incongruity". Information incongruity occurred when the person was unable to understand their urban experiences in terms of the information repertoire which they had with them from rural life. If information incongruity is not resolved, according to Moss, it may *lead to* physiological changes which alter the susceptibility to disease. How is this to be understood? Moss presents the mechanism operating between social variables (information incongruity) and physiology in the following way: "If social behavior is itself to produce changes in health, it must be through the central nervous system, since all that enters the body in social interaction is information."[39] Here we can see both the cognitive information- processing influence and what I have called "the misrepresentation of meaning as physiology". That which is fruitful about the interesting concept of information incongruity cannot be found at the level of the workings of the nervous system, for it is not there that we reach an understanding of what is significant about how these individuals perceive, constitute and respond to their lived experiences. In part II of this dissertation, I will show how it is possible to understand a concept like "information congruity" in terms of the lived body, however, this concept will not be discussed in terms of neural functioning.

To sum up this far, intervening variables or mechanisms, which are said to influence the interaction between the subject and his environment, range from physiological changes in the body, to thoughts, feelings and fantasies on the cognitive level, to emotions (with their physiological arousal as well as cognitive content), personality traits and abili-

---

[38] Moss (1977).
[39] Ibid., p. 92.

ties (including coping skills), social factors such as networks and group identity. These variables do not appear alone, but work together in feedback loops, between systems, leading to either augmented prolonged physiological arousal (causing somatic changes in the body's homeostasis, as well as possibly hindering the individual's capacity to think and cope), or to a reduction of arousal, due primarily to coping behavior (thought and possibly action). The cognitive information processing model exerts an influence on the explanatory theory of psychosomatic medicine in its conceptualization of stimuli "input" in terms of information and "responses" which are elicited from the individual. Let us now examine *how* these intervening factors actually intervene.

As late as 1991 Taylor[40] et al. had to concede that "Psychosomatic medicine is founded on the premise that emotions and personality can influence bodily functions and contribute to the etiology and pathogenesis of disease. The mechanisms by which these interactions occur, however, are not well understood." The terms I have found used to characterize the nature of the intervention in the literature are as follows: factors "influence" from one system to another (e.g. from the psychological to the physiological, or the other way around); they "activate" a response (also from one system to another); they "interact reciprocally"; they may "induce" or "result in" concrete changes in another system; finally, factors from one system can "cause" changes in another system. Etiology is almost always *multifactorial*, which is to say that no one factor alone is responsible for producing the disease. The weight of each class of factors (psychological, physiological, social) varies from disease to disease and from individual to individual. All of this makes it virtually impossible to construct a nomothetic theory of *the* etiology of, for example asthma or heart disease. It will be a matter of this particular person in this particular life situation who, for various reasons, develops this particular disease at this particular time. Just how the intervening factors intervene will be highly idiosyncratic. Instead of linear psychogenesis, we find a variant of systems theory in which parts of a whole interact with each other in

---

40 Taylor et. al. (1991), p. 153.

complex open-ended relationships. Despite the enormous complexity of this systems approach, Jern & Carlsson write that "a causality model appropriate for psychosomatic research should meet two criteria: 1) it should enable clarification of the precise effects of each causal factor in the system, and 2) it should tell which factors are necessary for disease to develop and which are not." [41] This is a tall order. It's not enough to identify factors which may influence people in various ways, one should be able to explicitly state how these factors influence, activate, interact, and ultimately together cause disease and ill health. Rooymans states that "multicausality remains an empty concept if no attempt is made to accurately describe and order the diverse causes and, if possible, to assess the relative importance of these causes." [42]

We must, then, get beyond correlation to causal explanations. It is not enough to state that certain "stressors" have been correlated with specific psychological and physiological changes, or that correlations exist between certain somatic dysfunctions and specific feelings, or to point out the fact that some social factors have been seen to "influence" the course and outcome of illness. Theoreticians in psychosomatic medicine wish to conform to the ideals of natural (nomothetic) science. [43] Causal connections should be demonstrated, validated and then explained theoretically. But how can this be accomplished, when the entire psychosomatic approach is based upon the importance of subjective idiosyncratic factors? How can causal relations be established when such complex and almost endless combinations of factors interact, such as the contributions of specific personality traits, coping skills, physiological make-up, social status, and finally, the *individual* meaning which every person ascribes to life events and situations. How can all of this be formulated into laws and causal chains? The problem is not that psychosomatic medicine pro-

---

[41] Jern & Carlsson (1990), p. 4:9.

[42] Rooymans (1974), p. 306.

[43] Birley & Connolly (1976) on this issue: "It is no longer good enough to predict 'illness' from 'life-events', or to fail to do so. The aim should be to postulate certain mechanisms and then attempt to confirm or refute their existence by well-designed experiments" (p. 162).

poses a complex mulitfactorial theory of illness and disease, but that it seeks to combine this open-ended, idiosyncratic, meaning-constitution approach with the goal of developing a traditional, nomethetic, general theory of psychosomatics. Psychosomatic medicine will not be able to insist upon the importance of the subjective, while at the same time attempting to formulate general causal explanations about the nature of the interaction between various "systems" in the human organism.

Unfortunately, the literature has been unable to explicate the way in which intervening variables influence each other or the body. The only efficacious link between the subjective and the physiological is to be found in the way in which an intervening variable (be it psychological, social or physiological) initiates and maintains (or in some way hinders the reduction of) <u>prolonged detrimental physiological arousal</u>. Even if this mechanism is comprehensible it is still hard to explicate in terms of interrelations (bridges) between systems. Psychosomatic medicine is left then with emotions, the "frontier concept", just as psychoanalytic theory needed emotions with their physiological manifestations in order to have an efficacious mechanism of interaction between mind and body. Emotional distress (sometimes referred to as "stress") is the only factor or variable which has any comprehensible interface to physiology. "Information" is sometimes attributed to neurological processes, but I have pointed out the misrepresentation involved in this characterization. In terms of the main project, to study and explicate the nature of the interrelations between psychology and physiology, we find no real examples of such interaction but rather examples where physiological characterizations are meant to illustrate interrelations between mind and body. In terms of understanding the etiology of psychosomatic pathology, psychosomatic medicine offers on the one hand an idiographic, open-ended systems approach, emphasizing subjective factors, while on the other hand it falls back upon "hard sciences" which do not contain within their domain any bridges to the psychological subjective aspects of human existence. The split is the result of Western dualistic thinking, with the divergent development of natural science and human science, and the suppression of the lived body in favor of the objective body. That which has been lost is a way to investigate the living, mind/body unity, bound up in its world of meaning. This conceptualization would have been more in line with the holistic approach, and would have allowed psychosomatic medicine to concentrate on psychosomatic processes from a different angle. The interrelations project has not been able to produce comprehensible explanations of the interaction between "systems" nor been able to satisfy natural scientific demands for quantifiable hypotheses concerning causal relationships between variables imagined to produce disease and ill health.

The cure

It will not be surprising to find that theoreticians within psychosomatic medicine recommend a variety of methods and treatments in order to cure psychosomatic pathology. Because psychosomatic medicine espouses a multifactorial theory of etiology, specifically focused upon the complex interplay between systems, treatment will in each case depend upon which variable/variables are causative or contributing to the maintenance of the disease. The psychosomatic approach to disease and ill health stresses the importance of psychosocial elements in the development of disease. This approach is seen clearly in the work of liaison-consultation psychiatry.[44] The psychiatrist who is consulted by his/her somatically oriented colleagues must, according to Krakowski,[45] have a clear understanding of the psychodynamics of illness, understand the doctor-patient relationship, and show sensitivity to the psychosocial adjustment problems of the patient and his/her family. The treatment methods in psychosomatic medicine encompass techniques from psychiatry, psychotherapy, pharmacology, behavioral therapy, various re-

---

[44] The term "liaison" refers to the mediating role which the consulted psychiatrist takes on between the patient and the referring physician. The psychiatrist interprets the meaning of the doctor/medical teams work to the patient, as well as helping to convey the meaning of the patient's illness to the referring doctor/team. The main objective of the liaison psychiatrist is to lift out the psychosocial aspects of the patient's situation and relate them to the patient's biological/somatic difficulties.

[45] Krakowski (1977).

laxation techniques, hypnosis (autogenic training), biofeedback, body awareness training, cognitive therapy, and group therapy. The mechanisms of cure vary, according to which form of psychosomatic problem is presented, as well as according to which camp the specific theoretician belongs to. The psychoanalytic writers within the tradition maintain the classical "discharge" theory of cure, which has been examined in the previous chapter, while other authors argue that insight therapy is a waste of time for psychosomatic patients, who do much better in supportive therapy groups.

Because not all theoreticians in the psychosomatic medicine tradition are psychoanalysts, not all would subscribe to the idea that psychosomatic pathology is the result of a psychoneurosis. Bastiaans[46] writes that while most psychosomatic patients do suffer from neuroses, we should not forget that their psychological problems are often accompanied by certain destructive life-style patterns, maladaptive social behavior and so on, all of which can aggravate their condition. One may even find cases where although the original neurotic problem has been solved, the symptoms remain, having achieved an autonomy of their own. In such cases, without additional forms of treatment simultaneous with (or after) insight psychotherapy, one will not succeed in curing the patient. Because of the multifactorial etiology of disease, it is quite possible that several systems interact in order to maintain the symptoms, which is why it is sometimes recommended that the patient be involved in several different forms of treatment.

The mechanisms of cure which I have found in the literature[47] could be divided into two categories, those following 1) psychodynamic principles of cure and 2) principles of behavioral therapy. We are already familiar with the psychoanalytic cure from chapter 2. Bastianns falls in line with psychoanalytic thinking as he explains that "We can first notice a

---

[46] Bastiaans (1977)

[47] As found in the previous chapter, not much has been written explicitly on this topic, at least not from the theoretical point of view. Most of the texts analyzed concerned themselves explicitly with: 1) questions of etiology; 2) practical clinical issues, and 3) (rarely) the ontological mind-body issue, in that order.

lessening of the intensity of the psychosomatic syndrome as soon as the patient is able to express his inner tensions along normal and verbal pathways in expressive gestures, thus freeing himself of pent-up anger and abnormal stress on his vegetative nervous system and on the related endocrinological pathways." [48] To be able to express oneself is curative, a theme we recognize from the previous chapter. Bastiaans writes again: "If psychosomatic patients are able to express these aforementioned feelings during the first interviews, a rapid diminution or disappearance of the psychosomatic symptom may be expected, provided that the mode of expression is not solely intellectual or rational." [49] This is classical psychodynamic theory. However, one of the problems with psychosomatic patients, is precisely that they cannot express their feelings. A modern variation of psychodynamic theory is presented by Taylor et al.[50], writing in 1991 on alexithymia, who find that these patients have clear deficits in the capacity to cognitively "process" emotion. Their emotional life is diffuse, undifferentiated, and poorly regulated. Alexithymic patients (as well as psychosomatic patients) have a tendency to amplify and misrepresent bodily sensations which accompany emotional arousal. Because they have no way of cognitively processing these sensations, they cannot regulate tension nor control their arousal. Therapy is therefore aimed at raising emotions from the level of primitive sensation to mature, cognitive representations. Working on increased emotional awareness in psychotherapy, through fantasy, dream, play acting etc., will help to reduce the diffuse arousal which becomes abnormally amplified and somatized in psychosomatic patients. The form of psychotherapy may vary, depending upon the degree of neurotization and the introspective capacity of the patient. Alternatives to psychodynamically oriented insight therapy are those techniques which fall under the label "behavior therapy", entailing the second category of "cure" found in psychosomatic medicine.

---

[48]   Bastiaans (1969) p. 307.
[49]   Bastiaans (1977) p. 87.
[50]   Taylor et al. (1991).

Behavioral therapy is concerned with learning, conditioning and cognitive aspects of mental life. Specific therapy forms may focus upon specific behaviors, such as muscle tension, body awareness, or patterns of social interaction. Emphasis is placed upon the patient's behavior, and the basic curative principle involved is the idea that behavior is learned, and can be re-learned (or re-conditioned, if one is a behaviorist) in accordance with cognitive re-orientation. Behavioral therapy can either be a complement to insight therapy, or be the main treatment, if the patient is unable to participate in introspective therapy, or if his/her symptoms are considered to be the result of behavioral problems rather than intrapsychical ones. Many studies emphasize psychosomatic patients' need of support and empathy rather than insight into unconscious conflicts.[51] Some authors even maintain that goading psychosomatic patients into trying to speak about their inner life and fantasies actually *worsens* their condition, since they are often incapable of doing what the therapist is asking of them. The mechanism of cure working in behavioral therapy is that learning skills and alternative patterns of living will enable the patient to choose behavior which is less conducive to disease and ill health. Relaxation techniques, body awareness, assertiveness training, group therapy, all these techniques are intended to broaden the patient's current repertoire and thereby make possible the cure.

Summary of the psychosomatic theory of psychosomatic medicine

We have seen that psychosomatic medicine is the ambitious union of psychoanalytic thinking (or at least, its legacy) and stress-physiology. This marriage was to provide a bridge between the subjective realm of meaning and the physiological functioning of the body. To study mind and body in their interrelation is the credo of psychosomatic medicine. Disease processes, and indeed all health disorders, can be seen as the

---

[51] Nemiah et al. (1976) write: "In sum, it would appear that unless the patient with a psychosomatic illness has a clear-cut readily demonstrable capacity to develop insight, he would be better managed by supportive techniques" (p. 438).

product of complex interactions between factors found in various inter-dependent systems. These systems, (bio-physiological, psychological, social and cultural) interact with each other via feedback loops, mutually "intervening" upon each other. Mechanisms of intervention between man and his world are found on all levels, from the cellular up to the sociocultural. The etiology of disease is said to be multifactorial, that is to say, rarely is one mechanism or variable entirely responsible for the outbreak of disease. Very complex patterns of interaction emerge, as one attempts to map out the various factors which can interact in the development of disease. We find that subjective factors are important, specifically the traits and personality of the patient, his or her coping ability at the time of the onset of disease, and the cognitive and behavior patterns which may (or may not) accompany psychoneurotic impairment. The way in which intervening mechanisms intervene remains unclear. Terms such as "influence", "activate", "induce", "result in" and "cause" are found in the literature, although the only comprehensible explication of interaction can be seen in the cases when specific factors somehow initiate and maintain (or hinder the reduction of) prolonged physiological arousal. The detrimental effect of sustained arousal is a recurrent etiological theme. Emotions are seen as a "link" between subjective meaning and the physiology of the body, similar to the way in which the psychoanalysts found emotions to be a convenient explanatory factor in psychosomatic pathology. Several authors have deplored that psychosomatic medicine has not come very far in its basic aim, which is to explicate the relations between mind and body in disease and ill health. Theoreticians in psychosomatic medicine want to demonstrate causal relationships through verified quantitative hypotheses. There are several inherent conflicts in the discipline of psychosomatic medicine which need to be brought out. The first conflict is between the holistic approach to man and the dualistic "interrelations" project. The second conflict concerns what could be called a clash between conflicting scientific interests, looking for nomothetic laws and at the same time embracing an open-ended idiographic approach.

What does the holistic approach espoused by psychosomatic medicine actually entail? Does it give us something substantial which enhances our understanding of man as an indivisible unity? I cannot find anything in the literature from psychosomatic medicine which would increase our understanding of the lived unity of man. The "holistic approach" as it is illustrated and discussed by the authors seems to be basically just another way of expressing multifactorial etiology. However, as mentioned in the introduction to this chapter, psychosomatic medicine has made the holistic approach one of its most basic tenets. The holistic approach claims that man is an indivisible unity. Mind and body are abstractions from this unity. Not only is man a unity, man is also constantly in interaction with his/her environment. Despite these insights, psychosomatic medicine has from the very start embraced the mind-body dualism prevalent in our culture. It has decided to study the body with objectifying methods, and the psychological/social aspects with other methods and in line with other ideals. The dual-track strategy is justified by "linguistic parallelism". The problem, then, is to unite these two paths again in a single science. Grinker states the problem rather well: "The roots of modern psychosomatic medicine are physiological, derived from the investigations of Pavlov, Cannon and their students, and psychological, derived from psychoanalytic theory. Pursuance of both lines of investigation independently and concurrently, each with its own methods, and *finding some means by which both fields may be viewed and studied simultaneously as properties of a single integrated whole* constitutes the subject matter of much needed psychosomatic investigation" [52] (my italics). The problem is that we need a language and a theory which *begin* with the lived unity of man, rather than with the objectified body and the bodiless mind. Besides the dualism between mind and body, psychosomatic medicine has split off the natural unity of being-in-the-world through its appropriation of the "information-processing model" with input and output, stimulus and response. The final criticism on this point concerns a tendency to reduce the psychological realm into its phy-

---

[52] Grinker (1973) p. 28.

sical "parallel" system. This is an obvious danger when linguistic parallelism aligns itself with the biomedical model. As I have tried to show, although a certain lip service is paid to the importance of the subjective realm, often enough human beings are characterized in terms of physiology and brain processes. I have called this tendency the "misrepresentation of meaning as physiology". It could also be conceptualized as a form of naturalistic reductionism.

The second tension found in psychosomatic medicine concerns its scientific ideals. On the one hand, it wishes to embrace an open-ended systems approach, where highly individual and idiosyncratic patterns are traced out, involving complex combinations of variables.[53] On the other hand, as a medical discipline, psychosomatic medicine demands quantified experimental verification of its theoretical statements, and wants to see at least some causal mechanisms. These two poles are in conflict with each other, and 50 years of psychosomatic medicine has not succeeded in reducing this tension. Neither has five decades of psychosomatic medicine bridged the gap between the mind and the body. My next chapter will take a closer look at stress theory, and the clinical sciences of neuroimmunology and neuroendocrinogy.

---

[53] Jern & Carlsson (1990): "The emphasis on processes and interactions considerably increases the complexity of the research process and to some extent invalidates conventional methods for establishing causal relationships. We have therefore chosen to use models derived from general systems theory, since such models are designed to permit integration of complex interactions" (p. 4:7).

CHAPTER 4

From stress theory to neuroimmunology and neuroendocrinology

Men are disturbed not by things, but by the views which they take of things.

--Epictetus

I. STRESS THEORY

Introduction

In most of the histories of stress theory, Walter Cannon[1] is usually referred to as the founding father of the field, while Hans Selye[2] is considered to be the one who popularized the notion of stress, although Darwin had already some 60 years earlier formulated the idea that the organism must deal with challenges in the environment in order to survive. As we shall soon see, the concept of "stress" has developed over time since the first publications on stress during the 1930s. Newton[3]has pointed out that despite his status as the godfather of stress, Cannon hardly addressed the issue of stress at all in his work. Cannon's primary interest was to develop a physiological theory of emotions and the instincts. When Cannon did explicitly mention "stress",[4] he was most often referring to the noxious stimuli themselves, such as cold, lack of oxy-

---

[1] Cannon (1914; 1929;1932; 1935).
[2] Seyle (1937; 1946; 1950; 1956; 1974).
[3] Newton (1995).
[4] For example, in his paper from 1935 entitled, "The Stresses and Strains of Homeostasis".

gen and loss of blood. These factors would later be referred to as "stressors" by Selye, who wanted to reserve the term "stress" for the physiological state of arousal in the organism arising as a result of the encounter with a noxious agent. Selye called this state of general, nonspecific arousal "The General Adaption Syndrome" (GAS). I will shortly examine Selye's work on the GAS, but first, a brief history of the term "stress".

The term "stress" had a common usage several centuries before its scientific use, which emerged during the 17th century. As early as the 1400's one could find the term stress used to describe hardships, dire straits or adversity. This common usage persisted throughout the 16th century. In these references, the recipients of stress tended to be inanimate objects (often a ship), and the stressor was generally something environmental, outside of one's control, such as the weather.[5] From the 17th century and onwards one can find references to human beings as recipients of stress. The scientific definition of stress, coming from physics and engineering, saw it as the force or pressure applied to a physical object. By the 19th century, the scientific notion of stress formally referred to the internal force generated within a solid object caused by the action of an external force.[6] This force tended to bend or distort the object in question, thereby giving the concept of stress some connotation of elasticity (bending up to the breaking point). Hinkle[7] writes that the 17th-century common-sense idea of stress as hardship and strife was gradually replaced by the scientific concept of force and strain, and it is this latter concept which has been developed by the medical and social sciences. However, Newton has found references in the *Complete Oxford English Dictionary* (Hinkle cites only from the *Shorter Oxford Dictionary)* from the 16th century which come very close to our modern

---

[5] Recounted In Newton (1995), p. 50.

[6] To be completely accurate, "load" was defined as the external force, "stress" was the ratio of the internal force created by the load in proportion to the area over which the force was applied, and "strain" was the actual deformation or distortion of the body in question.

[7] Hinkle (1977).

contemporary usage, for example, "the overpowering pressure of some adverse force or influence."[8] In any case, our modern, everyday concept of stress seems to incorporate both of these ideas, i.e. stress is conceived of as being related to a situation of adversity or strife, which is further conceptualized in terms of some kind of force or pressure which tends to distort or in some way disrupt the system which is affected.

To understand the background of the stress concept, it is worth briefly mentioning another historical development in medicine, namely Claude Bernard's work on the constancy of the "milieu internal". The notion of the internal milieu was a forerunner to Cannon's concept of homeostasis. Bernard, a French physiologist, noticed the body's inherent tendency to return to a "steady state" of equilibrium after disturbances in the internal milieu. He found that living organisms seemed to depend upon maintaining a relatively stable internal environment in order to survive. Cannon studied some of these mechanisms of equilibrium, and wrote in 1935 that "So long as this personal, individual sack of salty water, in which each one of lives and moves and has his being, is protected from change, we are freed from serious peril. Because that protection is afforded by special physiologic agencies, I have suggested that the stable state of the fluid matrix be given the name *homeostasis*."[9] Cannon's research demonstrated that the internal environment of the body was in fact very seldom in a "steady state". The human organism fights a more or less constant battle with disturbances which must be dealt with. Cannon and his colleagues showed that the capacity of the body to recover internal balance depended upon a variety of complex mechanisms. The living body responds continuously to both internal and external signals. It was Selye who would develop the idea that the body's physiological reactions to provocations are an integral aspect of the stress concept.

Cannon is most well-known for the "fight or flight" syndrome. He was primarily interested in the emergency functions of the organism, and his research depicted what happens in the body when the organism is

---

8   Newton (1995), p. 50.
9   Cannon (1935), p. 2.

threatened by extreme stimuli. He subjected animals to various noxious agents and registered what happened in their internal systems. He concentrated basically on the important functions of the catecholamines, epinephrine and norepinephrine.[10] These hormones play a vital role in arousing the organism, thereby enabling it to respond to danger (i.e. to fight or flee). Thus, for Cannon, the stress reaction was conceived of as a form of adaption, something both necessary and expedient. Cannon's main contention was that body's reactions to perturbations were protective and "wise".[11] Cannon was also aware of the fact that prolonged inexpedient stress reactions could ultimately be detrimental to the organism, but this was not his topic of interest. The main thrust of his work was to demonstrate the body's capacity for adaption to environmental hazards.

During 1936, Selye was in the process of investigating the effects of various noxious stimuli on rats in laboratory experiments. During the course of one experiment, he injected extracts of ovary tissue into the rats, and found a triad of physiological responses which were hard to explain, since no known ovarian hormones had any such documented effects. The adrenal glands were enlarged, the thymus shrank, and the rats developed bleeding ulcers. He proceeded to inject extracts from various other tissues into their bodies, and found this same *general* response, regardless of the substance injected. He furthermore exposed them to heat, cold, burns, fractures and radiation, and found time after time the same triad of symptoms. Somewhat later on, Selye[12] divided the rats' behavioral reactions to prolonged contact with these noxious stimuli into three phases. The rats seemed to go from initial alarm, to the stage of resistance (or adaption), to the final stage of collapsing into a state of exhaustion. He called this syndrome the General Adaption Syndrome (GAS). The syndrome was called a "general" adaptive syndrome because it seemed that this reaction was the same independently of which nox-

---

[10] Epinephrine and norepinephrine are the American designations of the more well-known British terms, adrenaline and noradrenaline, respectively.

[11] Canon (1932) *The Wisdom of the Body.*

[12] Selye (1946); Selye & Fortier (1950).

ious stimulus was involved. Although Selye was mainly concerned with physiological responses to physical stimuli, he admitted that even purely psychological events could constitute a "noxious stimuli", and thus provoke GAS. The main theoretical interest of the GAS was Selye's observation that the very same reaction of neuro-humeral mechanisms occurred regardless of the nature of the provocation. GAS was thus a *general* theory, which maintained that the body responded uniformly to any disturbing stimuli. As we recall from the last chapter, psychosomatic medicine was dealing with specificity theories during this time (1930's). Selye's work was seen as giving support to those who wished to argue for a generality hypothesis of disease. Psychoanalytically minded theoreticians wanted to demonstrate correlations between specific types of personality/defenses and the propensity to develop specific diseases. Selye claimed that only one uniform massive reaction to "stressors" could be observed in the body, and it was this general, non-specific arousal which heightened the susceptibility to *any and all* types of disease. He called the diseases which did eventually arise as a result of the GAS "diseases of adaption." Generality theories maintain that because the source of stress is not important, the actual illness or disease which an individual will develop is the result of the different vulnerabilities found in the individual's organic make-up. Specific diseases, then, were not due to any particular type of stress transaction or any specific emotion. It has been pointed out[13] that Selye's GAS syndrome had completely missed the important psycho-social processes which contribute to the response of the organism to the stressors. This very important consideration eventually found a theoretical formulation in the notion of "appraisal", which is the centerpiece of modern stress theory today.

The notion of a GAS syndrome has been criticized by many, and certain studies[14] have shown that various emotions, such as anger and fear, do seem to have their own particular hormonal response patterns. However, the controversy over generality vs. specificity is far from re-

---

[13] See Hinkle (1977); Lazarus (1977); Lazarus & Folkman (1984).
[14] See Mason (1975); Mason et al. (1976).

solved. The main criticism of GAS was that Selye had no way of explaining the "first cause" in the chain of events, that is, what the mechanism is whereby the organism senses danger. Especially if one wants to study human beings, it is obvious that the meaning or signification of the event must somehow find its way into the "stress" equation. Selye did not address himself to this issue. Sapolsky[15] has recounted how irritating it was for experimental physiologists when the psychological camp of stress researchers started to insist that stress responses couldn't be understood apart from psychological and social factors. Just when the concept of stress was getting nicely systematized and measured, these psychologists come onto the scene and muddle everything up. A Yale physiologist John Mason, who was one of the leading figures in the "psychological approach," had a debate with Selye.[16] When Mason referred to the growing literature supporting the importance of the psychological modulation of the stress response, Selye, aware that he was losing the debate, replied peevishly that *all* stress responses couldn't be psychological, since the anesthetized patient still gets a stress response when the surgical incision is made.

We are now ready to begin to look at the modern version of stress theory, whose main and most influential proponent is Richard S. Lazarus.[17] I have chosen to concentrate on the work of Lazarus and his co-workers because I find his notion of appraisal to be an interesting and significant theoretical step forward. His work is influential, psychologically oriented, and belongs to the mainstream tradition. Newton [18] has called attention to the fact that the stress research done by two existing alternatives to the mainstream, namely the psychodynamic group represented by the Tavistock Institute of Human Relations and the Scandinavian researchers of the 1960's (especially Bertil Gardell and the Norwegian group at the Work Research Institute of the University of Oslo), has been more or less ignored by the mainstream tradition. According to

---

15 Sapolsky (1994).
16 Recounted in Ibid., p. 182.
17 Lazarus (1977; 1984; 1993).
18 Newton (1995).

Newton, this is because these alternatives emphasize the organizational, social and political structures involved in stress, while the traditional view places the individual alone and de-contexualized in the center. Be that as it may, I have chosen Lazarus and it is his version of modern stress theory which I will be examining in this chapter.[19] But before I begin, we can first take a look at what has happened to the term "stress" from the time of Cannon and Selye. For Selye and his adepts, stress was a "state" within the organism, recognizable by the presence of certain physiological signs. A stimulus (noxious agent) from without induced or triggered the organism to produce this inner state of stress. Today, the modern notion of stress is interactional: stress is *about* something in the world. The modern lay person conceives of stress as being somehow associated with things like conflicts, intense emotional reactions, having too much to do in little time, or even having too little to do. Furthermore, most people would agree that there seems to be some kind of natural affiliation between stress and anxiety, although the relationship between them is not clear, even in the professional literature. Lazarus[20] states that although the term "stress" did not appear in the *Psychological Abstracts* until 1944, the way in which the term "anxiety" was used before then often approximated what the term stress designates today. Stress was *implied* in the descriptions of psychopathology, and one need not "quibble"[21] about which term is actually used. According to Lazarus, people were reacting to stressful situations (or fantasies) when they became psychologically distressed or psychosomatically ill, even if we did not have the term at that time. The distinction between stress and emotions in general is rather fuzzy in stress literature. Sometimes one even finds the term "stress emotions."

---

19 Because this dissertation is concerned with a philosophical examination of psychosomatic theory, I will not be looking at experimental, pragmatic stress research in this chapter. I will refer to various studies in the course of the chapter, but always in light of what they can tell us about mind-body issues and the theoretical categories of ontology, etiology and cure. A systematic study of the experimental literature lies outside of the scope of this dissertation.

20 Lazarus & Folkman (1984).

21 Ibid., p. 5.

A deconstructionist point of view, somewhat outside of the scope of this dissertation, is the interesting idea put forth by Newton[22] that "the stressed subject" is simply the product of a discourse,[23] constructed in order to maintain power relationships. In this way of thinking, the stressed subject appears as someone whose stress experience is largely due to him/herself, to their personality, their behavior, their "coping style" etc. This a-political subject is thus effectively removed from arenas of power relations, such as those between men and women, employers and employees, superior and subordinate. Another idea absent from the traditional stress literature is Newton's proposal that stress is just a label for the unknown.[24] When we cannot measure or quantify objective causes of illness or death, we turn to the subjective realm. And because the subjective interiority of others is, for the most part, a vast unknown, we need some term which can say something about it. With the "stress label", we can say that the heart attack of Mr. P. was certainly due to stress, even if he didn't *seem* stressed. We can even say that, well, that was his problem, after all, he just couldn't let it out.[25]

The modern, professional, academic understanding of stress is in line with our ordinary language usage, that is, stress is conceptualized as a *relationship* between the person and the environment. The stressed individual has appraised her relationship to the environment (situation) as taxing or exceeding her resources and, as a result of this, as endangering her well-being. There are important cognitive processes going on here, as

---

22 Newton (1995).
23 The word "discourse", used in the Foucauldian sense, refers to bodies of knowledge whose aim is to create "truth effects". A discourse claims to tell us how we know the world. Discourses are in themselves neither true nor false, they are merely claims to truth. Examples of discourses, according to Foucault are psychiatry, psychology, sociology etc.
24 With the exception of Hinkle (1977), who argues that we can dispense with the "stress" concept altogether, and Gatchel (1995), who writes that "Stress is usually viewed as a mediatory, that is, an unobservable inferred construct which is hypothesized to account for a certain observable behavior such as health or illness differences between individuals" (p. 76).
25 Example in Newton (1995), pp. 66-67.

well as physiological components. Gatchel[26] has pointed out that the experimentally observed stress response contains three important aspects; namely, 1) subjective, self-reports (people's conscious experiences); 2) overt motor behaviors which are measured by observing performance of certain tasks; 3) physiological arousal involving first and foremost the sympathetic branch of the autonomic nervous system (having to do with adrenaline and noradrenaline levels). What is interesting is that in the experimental situation, one will not always find agreement between these three aspects. A person may verbally report that he did not feel stressed at all during the experiment, yet he performed quite badly on the tests and registered a high level of adrenaline. The experimental literature does not problematize the relationship between operationalized stress (what is measured and stipulatively called "stress") and the subjectively experienced, everyday phenomenon of stress, as far as I have seen. However, Lazarus is aware of the issue, and admits that in real life, events are never artificially isolated but related to other real events, enmeshed with the person's actual goals, values and conflicts. This entire complex cannot be adequately replicated in an artificial laboratory experiment.

Although the Canon/Selye stress-concept began in the laboratory, modern stress research is interested in the individual's experiences of stress.[27] Stress is no longer simply defined as a state of physiological disequilibrium. The notion that stress is a person-environment interaction is central to modern stress theory. Obviously, the anesthetized patient has a physiological stress-response when the surgeon cuts into his body, but we would hardly wish to call the patient "stressed", especially if we maintain the idea that the *appraisal* of the relationship between the person and his environment is central to the concept of stress. It is time to examine the notion of appraisal and see how this modern formulation of stress theory attempts to explicate the area of the "in-between" (between

---

[26] Gatchel (1995).

[27] Lazarus (1993) writes, "To truly understand coping requires that we zero in on the main threat meanings of a particular stress situation and how they change over time and across situational contexts, regardless of whether the approach to the measurement is an in-depth interview or a standardized inventory" (p. 244).

subject and object), i.e. the area of interaction, which is so important to the understanding of psychosomatic relations.[28] We will see here a further attempt to unite meaning (in this case, understood in terms of appraisal) with physiological processes in the body. I will first just briefly present the theory, before I examine it in terms of the categories of analysis used in the previous chapters (ontology, etiology and the cure).

Lazarus places himself in opposition to the stimulus-response (S - R) understanding of stress found in academic psychology. Even the more modern version, with the formula S -O -R (stimulus-organism-response), presumes that the line of influence is coming from the outside, impinging upon the organism. The fact that the organism also affects the environment, constitutes its meaning, and even chooses one environment or situation over another, is completely ignored in this way of thinking. The most obvious criticism of the S -R model, as pointed out earlier in relation to the critique of Selye's GAS, is that it is not especially illuminating to say that an external stimulus causes a physiological response, since we still don't know what it is about the stimulus that produces the physiological stress response, at least not when we are dealing with specifically human, psychological stressors. A further criticism of the stimulus-response model, related to meaning constitution, is that we now know that not all disruptions of homeostasis are bad. There is in fact "good stress" and "bad stress", and unless we want the term "stress" to simply refer to all changes in homeostasis (which would make it an empty, meaningless concept, since everything in life would be "stress"), it is necessary to investigate the *meaning* of the stimuli in relation to the subject experiencing stress.[29]

---

[28] Lazarus & Folkman (1984) on this point: "Our approach to psychological stress emphasizes cognitive appraisal, which centers on the evaluation of harm, threat and challenge. An appraisal does not refer to the environment or to the person alone, but to the integration of both in a given transaction" (p. 294).

[29] Even Selye (1974) himself admitted later on that the GAS does not occur in all forms of stress, only in certain ones. Thus one could claim that his generality position gradually allowed for a certain degree of specificity, related to what Lazarus and others would call "appraisal".

Lazarus emphasizes that the meaning or signification of a particular transaction between the person and his/her environment depends largely upon how that person appraises that situation. That which is stressful for one person need not be experienced as stressful by another.[30] There are thus no pure "stimuli" in themselves. All stimuli are mediated by the meaning or signification which they have for the person in question.[31] The cognitive appraisal of the situation is an *evaluation* which determines if the situation is potentially stressful or not. The appraisal involves categorizing the encounter in terms of various aspects. <u>Primary appraisal</u> determines if the situation is irrelevant, benign-positive, or stressful (dangerous/threatening). Primary appraisal determines if the situation will be taken up as a threat or a challenge. When we eventually do arrive in a potentially stressful situation, we must begin to imagine what we want to do about it. This further evaluative step Lazarus calls <u>secondary appraisal.</u> Secondary appraisal takes into account which coping options are available, the likelihood that one will succeed in a particular strategy and so on. One should not think of these two forms of appraisal as temporally distinct: indeed, their interplay is complex, and they may shape each other. For example, if I realize that I cannot handle a situation, I am very likely to conceive of it as threatening, compared to a situation where I rather quickly understand that I can easily master the difficulty. A final note on appraisal: Lazarus is quick to point out that

---

[30] This is also Lazarus's criticism of Holmes & Rahe's (1967) life-events approach, where specific life events (often involving a change, such as divorce and unemployment) are seen as being weighted with a certain stress factor. The criticism is that it is not the life change *in itself* which is stressful, but rather the personal significance which is given to the event. Hinkle (1977) has made the empirical observation that major life changes are not always associated with stress and disease.

[31] It is clear that catastrophes, such as earthquakes, war and fire, would most probably be experienced as stressful by most people, but this stress is still to be understood in terms of appraisal, that is, these occurrences are interpreted by most people as constituting a threat to their well-being. The fireman will not experience stress during a fire in the same way as the person whose home is burning down. Regarding the magnitude of the stress situation, Lazarus has preferred to address those stress situations which he refers to as "hassles" rather than cataclysmic events. I will return to this point in the etiology section.

appraisal need not be *conscious* (although it seems to always be cognitive/evaluative). A person may be unaware or unconscious of all the ideas, values and personal agendas which guide his or her understanding of a situation. Appraisals contain not only explicit thoughts, but commitments and beliefs as well. Even these will determine how people take up and understand a situation. Commitments and beliefs are important to the notion of *vulnerability*. The more one is committed to something, the greater the potential for personal harm if the commitment should become threatened.

Because many situations in life are ambiguous in their signification, the way a person will appraise a situation depends upon a variety of factors: their commitments, beliefs, coping strategies and personality dispositions. For example, the type A personality[32] will often ascribe a threat to an ambiguous situation, since there is an underlying tendency towards aggression in this type of personality. Another person would find a different signification in the very same situation. The important point in this approach is that we are dealing with the personal ascribed meaning or signification of an event, based upon a subject's interpretation of the situation. This idea somewhat resembles Merleau-Ponty's phenomenological approach, although the appraisal theory described here is predominantly cognitive, and as such is limited in its ability to do justice to the richness of the interaction between the subject and his world.

A further important aspect of modern stress theory is the concept of coping, briefly mentioned in the previous chapter. This concept can be found in two different traditions, animal research and psychoanalytic ego-psychology. The animal model defines coping as those actions whereby the animal attempts to control adverse environmental conditions. This is a simplistic model, which does not take into account the emotional, cognitive, and meaning aspects of situations as they can be experienced by human beings. Animals are unpleasantly aroused, and

---

[32] A term coined by two cardiologists, Meyer Friedman and Ray Rosenman in the 1960's, meant to refer to a certain personality type, characterized by tendencies of competitiveness, overachieving, hostility and time pressure. This personality type was (and still is today by some) seen as predisposing to cardiovascular disease.

they try to get away from what they consider to be the source of the unpleasantness.[33] Human beings live in a complex world where they are called upon to solve problems and relate to the environment in a variety of ways, even if it means having to endure a certain amount of unpleasantness. Folkman et al. define coping in the following way: "*Coping* refers to the person's cognitive and behavioral efforts to manage (reduce, minimize, master, or tolerate) the internal and external demands of the person-environment transaction that is appraised as taxing or exceeding the person's resources. Coping has two major functions: dealing with the problem that is causing the distress (problem-focused coping) and regulating emotion (emotion-focused coping)" [34] (italics in the original). Various coping mechanisms have been described in the literature: humor, crying, self-control, swearing, boasting, thinking, resigning, hoping, seeking help and so on. Psychoanalytic ego-psychology emphasizes the importance of ego-structures and various ego-related abilities in handling difficulties in life. There is a debate within the theory of coping as to whether coping ability has to do with traits (personality) or styles (referring to whether one uses only one particular coping strategy to deal with a variety of situations, or whether one varies strategy in accordance with the situation). The psychoanalytic approach divides coping styles into more or less healthy forms of coping. Healthy coping means using strategies which are the least regressed, less rigid, and most in touch with reality (e.g. not using denial to an excessive extent). From the late 1970's an emphasis has been placed on coping as a process, which leaves the trait/style debate behind. In terms of process, coping seems to change over time and in accordance with the contexts in which it occurs. For example, denial may be a counter-productive coping strategy when interpreting symptoms and seeking medical care, but denial can be quite

---

[33] In one way, you could say that animals do constitute meaning at some level, as they have experienced the situation as unpleasant, as well as understood the source of unpleasantness, but this is a very low level of meaning, and one which is not specifically human.

[34] Folkman et al. (1986), p. 572.

useful right after coronary hospital care, during the phase when the heart patient must dare to perform his/her activities of daily life.

To sum up, modern stress theory is based upon an interactional model which does not assume a stimulus-response framework, but rather emphasizes the importance of the meaning or signification which the subject ascribes to the particular situation (person-environment encounter). This interpretation has been called "appraisal" by Lazarus, and although appraisal is not necessarily conscious, it nevertheless refers to cognitive evaluations, often in terms of good-bad, beneficial-dangerous etc. Secondary appraisals are those thoughts which arise in connection with the initial evaluation of the situation. The concept of coping is an essential component of modern stress theory. Coping is the way in which the individual manages or handles the demands of potentially stressful situations. Historically, the development of the stress concept has moved from Cannon's interest in homeostasis, to Selye's theory of non-specific general arousal (GAS), to the modern cognitive-appraisal theory of Lazarus. We have still not seen how stress, emotion and coping relate to health and illness. Indeed, Lazarus writes, "That stress, emotion and coping are causal factors in illness is still only a premise, albeit widely assumed..."[35]To this issue I now turn, aided as in the previous section by the categories of analysis.

The ontological questions

As in the previous chapters, the intention of this section is to try to ascertain what ontological presuppositions (implicit and explicit) about the mind/body issue underlie the theories presented. In this case, what view is adopted on the mind/body problem in the stress theory tradition? How do these writers conceive of the relationship between various mental phenomena and the body? Regarding stress theory, we will have to search for the implicit answers to these questions, since the issue has not been explicitly addressed.

---

[35] Lazarus & Folkman (1984), p. 205.

The first question to be asked in this section is, what is a psychosomatic disease/symptom for stress theoreticians? Which diseases are considered to be stress-related? Does stress theory maintain that all diseases could, in principle, be understood as directly or indirectly related to stress? Cannon wrote that many factors could influence the fluid matrix of the internal environment, such as the demands of school, fatigue, the trying periods of old age and puberty, and so on. This insight prompted him to suggest that the "whole gamut of human diseases might be studied from this point of view."[36]Lazarus has likewise stated that since the body functions in a less integrated and harmonious way under stress, it is conceivable that "all or much disease could be stress related."[37]I have not found any clear-cut definition of those specific diseases which are considered to be stress-related. The term "disease" is most often used in the stress literature without qualification as to which disease is referred to. Sometimes the condition under discussion is qualified by "diseases that have psychological determinants", or "stress-related diseases", but this is not always the case. Perhaps it is taken for granted that one is referring to those diseases which can be easily related to the specific physiology of the stress response (catecholamine secretion, heightened blood pressure, sharpened vigilance, energy mobilization etc.). Sapolsky writes that a large portion of the "stress-related diseases" are disorders of excessive stress responses. However, somewhat paradoxical findings have shown that, for example, people who were removed from their middle-class homes and forced into concentration camps during the second world war lost their asthma, ulcers, migraines, ulcerative colitis and other so-called stress-related (psychosomatic) illnesses.[38] It was also found that diabetes diminished in areas under military occupation during this time, and reports of similar phenomena have been reported since World War II. The relationship between stress and vulnerability to various diseases is by no means perfectly clear. While we do not have a clear-cut inventory of stress-related disease, nor any definitive formal relationship between

---

36 Cannon, W. (1935), p. 14.
37 Lazarus (1977), p. 14.
38 Wolff (1953), pp. 119-120.

stress and disease, we do find in stress theory an emphasis upon the importance of psychological variables for the stress experience. To understand stress as the result of psychological processes is a modern idea. But what does "psychological" mean for the stress theorists?

Lazarus uses a variety of concepts (appraisal, coping, beliefs, commitments) which emphasize the way in which the individual understands and relates to his/her environment. Stress is thus a mind-body-world phenomenon. He makes no bones about the fact that in order to understand stress as it is experienced by human beings, we must turn our attention to the way in which individuals evaluate, appraise and understand their situation.[39] The one-sided investigation of the nature of various "stressors" from the early stress research of the 1930's has given way to an interactionistic approach, much in the same way in which psychosomatic medicine has ended up with a multifactorial, open systems approach (see chapter 3). From this interactionist point of view, that which is important is the way in which the subject interprets the meaning of what is happening to him. Human beings are creatures of meaning, although meaning can be understood on low or high levels. Low levels of meaning would be those responses to the world which we share with animals, a kind of phylogenetic tendency to perceive and organize our experience in certain ways. Higher up, we find cognitive structures which are influenced by learning, beliefs, attitudes, emotions, commitments. According to Lazarus, all of these factors, from genetically conditioned behavior and perception to symbolic meanings, are involved in the human stress reaction/experience. Although Lazarus emphasizes cognitive appraisal in his theory, cognitive appraisal or evaluation is just one of the ways in which the world takes on signification. There are other ways to conceptualize "meaning" in his theory, for example in terms of the constellations we call beliefs. For Lazarus, beliefs are personally formed or culturally shared configurations of significance. They tell us

---

39 We are here no longer dealing with the psychological realm as it is understood by the psychoanalysts, with their emphasis upon the unconscious, primary process, defenses, and the like. The move away from psychodynamic theory towards cognition and learning processes has sometimes been called "the cognitive revolution."

what is a "fact", and structure "how things are." They can be general, existential (e.g. God exists) or more specific. Beliefs are relevant to specific appraisals as a general background of meaning. Jensen et al.[40]have found in their study of chronic pain patients that beliefs seem to have an influence on patients' mood, which in turn influences their adjustment and ability to cope with pain. Pain-related beliefs had to do specifically with ideas about general locus of control, specific control over pain (is it up to me or my doctor?), estimations of one's own efficacy, expectancy of outcome, just to give a few examples. What is interesting about beliefs is their pervasiveness as mood, or style. This could be compared to dispositions to act/behave in a certain way within the analytic philosophical tradition. Beliefs seem to guide individuals into typical ways of thinking and behaving. Lazarus himself speaks most often about cognitive evaluative appraisal, but he also addresses the more general level of style, especially in his discussion about coping styles. Finally, Lazarus speaks about commitments (sometimes referred to as "personal agendas") as a further example of one of the ways in which human beings can ascribe meaning to their situation. What is a commitment?

Commitments tell us what is important, what is of value, what is considered worthwhile for the individual in question. Lazarus writes that the most damaging life events are those in which vital commitments are lost. Commitments tell us what is at stake in a specific stressful encounter. Although commitments can be formulated in cognitive terms, they are more than ideas. They refer to a whole complex of choices, preferences, goals and motivations. This commitment network lies underneath cognition, conditioning it and giving it sustenance in each individual encounter. Commitments steer us towards certain situations, and away from others. They shape our sensitivity to the environment, making us attentive to certain "cues" and indifferent to others. As mentioned earlier, we need to take commitments into account in order to understand the concept of vulnerability. The deeper the commitment, the greater the potential harm when this commitment is threatened. However, even

---

[40] Jensen et al. (1991).

here we can see individual variations. For example, one person may take up a situation which calls their commitments into question as a challenge (i.e. a Christian missionary in Africa, a gifted teacher with rebellious students, a politician in a televised debate), while another person could regard these situations as extremely threatening. What makes the difference? The commitments are (let us suppose) the same, equally strong and integrated, the situation is in a certain respect the same, but the attitude to the situation is quite different.[41] As we saw in the case of psychosomatic medicine, we are dealing with extremely idiosyncratic factors, which concern the way the individual ascribes a personal significance to the events in question.

As in the previous chapters, a relevant question for psychosomatic theory is, how does the mind relate to the body, how can disease and ill health be the result of factors which are not somatic/physiological in nature? For stress theory, the question is, how does the experience of stress make one ill/diseased? The specific mechanisms of interaction will be examined in the etiology section, but in this section the question is if stress theory has any general ideas about the way in which mind (psychological, social, and cultural signification) relates to the physiological processes which we associate with stress and stress-related diseases. It is not surprising that even here we find that the notion of emotions plays a central role. Lazarus and Folkman state: "An essential theme of the analysis of stress, coping and health that dominates thinking in behavior medicine is that emotional states of all kinds and intensities accompany appraisals of harm, threat and challenge. The link with illness is the conventional one that massive bodily changes are associated with emotions,

---

[41] An interesting question here is if these two individuals would have the same physiological reaction in this situation, or would they have quite different physiological patterns. Lazarus & Folkman (1984) suggest that in fact the physiological stress response to challenge is different from that in threat. This is a question which belongs to the specificity/generality debate, i.e. does there exist a specific physiology for specific emotions/states/experiences, or do we always find a uniform pattern of arousal, independently of the situation? This question has not found a clear answer at this time.

especially strong, negative ones such as fear and anger."[42] For Lazarus and Folkman, emotion is not to be separated from cognitive processes. It is an error to think that emotions either precede or arrive after thought. Thought and emotion are intertwined with each other and affect each other reciprocally. Emotions are not only tied to thoughts, but are also bound up with a person's goals, commitments and values. Lazarus, paraphrasing Freud, calls emotions "the royal road"[43] to understanding a person's most important agendas. However, emotion is a vast concept, containing within its domain everything from mild sentiments and moods to passions and overwhelming states of disruption.[44] According to Lazarus, the reason that emotions are relevant to stress theory is that they include components from psychology (subjective affect, cognitions, value judgments), behavioral action impulses and physiological changes. Emotions carry with them not only symbolic, cultural connotations, but also specific impulses towards action: for example anger triggers attack, while fear produces the impulse to run away. The connection between emotion and ill health is the idea that repeated chronic emotional arousal is said to inflict wear and tear on the system (either specifically or generally), leading ultimately to disease.[45] By now, this is a familiar theme.

I stated earlier on that it is a difficult task to find answers to the ontological questions in stress theory, since these issues are not problematized as such. *Meaning* (signification, interpretation, constitution) is assumed to be an integral factor in understanding stress, although we do not find any statements about how we are to understand what meaning

---

[42] Lazarus & Folkman (1984), p. 205.

[43] For Freud, dreams were the "royal road" to the unconscious.

[44] Parkinson (1995) has suggested that we reserve the term "emotion" for those intentional states which have a clearly defined object. According to this definition, diffuse feelings such as happiness or boredom would not qualify as emotions. These latter states would be moods, which are by nature objectless, persistent and unfocused.

[45] It seems in this discussion that "emotion" and "stress" are used almost interchangeably. Lazarus (1993) has proposed that we should regard psychological stress as a subset of emotion. "In fact, anger, anxiety, guilt, shame, sadness, envy, jealousy and disgust, which arise out of conflict, are commonly referred to as the stress emotions" (p. 244).

is in this theory, or how meaning relates in principle to body functioning. We do not find any "Introductory Statement" here on the mind-body issue. As in the previous theories, mind-body interaction is supposedly illustrated in the case of the emotions, which are said to build a bridge between meaning/signification and physiology, although this bridge is never actually explicated.[46] If we try to construct an ontological position on the mind-body issue from the concepts at hand, a picture emerges which could be called an ad-hoc ontology, where we begin with etiology (explaining the explanandum) and construct the ontological categories afterwards. The starting point is the fact of the breakdown, the explanandum. The explanatory chain moves backwards from breakdown through coping (lack thereof), personality (including traits, sensibilities, life experiences, commitments, vulnerabilities), appraisal (of a specific situation(s)), to the initial particular person-environment transaction (which can be complex and stretch over a period of time). All of these elements are part of a chain which is hypothesized in order to explain the process leading from health to breakdown. Something in the chain, or a combination of components, is imagined to be responsible for the breakdown explanandum. If the person finds him/herself in a potentially harmful/threatening situation, if s/he appraises it as such, if the person is vulnerable to the threat and if they do not succeed in coping, the result is psychological/somatic breakdown. If Mrs. P. becomes ill after her husband's death, we may appeal to the components mentioned above, although they may just as well be invoked if she does not become ill (it must have been her personality/coping/appraisal which made her ill, or alternatively, kept her well). We need the components to explain breakdown, we do not begin with them as ontological descriptive categories.

If one were to attempt to place Lazarus in line with some classical philosophical position, he could in some sense be called a phenomenologist. That which is phenomenological in his thinking is the interest paid to the way in which individuals constitute the meaning of the person-

---

[46] As in the previous theories examined, emotions are described dualistically, entailing aspects which are mind and aspects which are body. To describe a double aspect-phenomenon is not the same thing as to explicate the relationship of mind to body.

environment transaction. In one text Lazarus actually refers to "our phenomenology,"[47] although he gives no phenomenological references. That which is not phenomcnological is the way in which Lazarus refers to "the objective world" (same text), showing that he has not implemented the phenomenological reduction in order to study the "noematic" object as meant or intended.[48] Nevertheless, there is a phenomenological thread in his approach which stands out in contrast to previously examined theories.

To sum up, the original idea behind stress theory was that hardships and dire straits have a detrimental effect on the organism, an effect which could be seen and measured in terms of physiological changes. One could furthermore ascertain experimentally that performance deteriorated under stress,[49] while verbal reports could confirm that the individuals experienced negative, unpleasant sensations during the "stress" experiment. However, the effect of hardships and difficult environmental situations could not be understood as a mere stimulus-response situation, and for this reason Selye's simplistic GAS model was criticized by the psychologically minded theoreticians. The psychological emphasis placed upon interpretation, meaning and signification was formulated definitively in the cognitive appraisal model of Lazarus. Stress theory has come closer to a theory of the "in-between" (interaction and reciprocal intervention between man and his environment) than both psychodynamic theory and psychosomatic medicine, although stress theory has not had much to say about how this middle ground should be understood. Even though the conceptualization of interaction is the cornerstone of stress theory, Lazarus writes that "although we know much about what happens to the tissues when a person or animal is undergoing a stress emotion, the psychological determinants of emotion, its regula-

---

[47] Lazarus & Folkman (1984), p. 48.
[48] See chapter 6 for an explication of the phenomenological reduction.
[49] Newton (1995) has pointed out that Lazarus and his colleagues were funded in a major research project after the Second World War by the US Air Force, whose main interest was to ascertain the relationship between stress and task performance. It is perhaps not a coincidence that early stress research concentrated on task performance.

tion, and the role of these processes in bodily disease have remained somewhat elusive."[50] Let us now see what stress theory has to say specifically about the etiology of stress-related disease and ill health.

The etiological questions

Within this tradition, as within those dealt with in the preceding chapters, we find a careful optimism concerning etiology, in the face of more or less mysterious processes. The mechanisms which account for the relationship between stress, coping, emotions and disease are not fully understood. Hinkle[51] writes that we now know that the relationship between people and their society can influence the incidence, prevalence, course and mortality of disease, but exactly when, how and to what extent are questions to which "precise answers...will not be forthcoming without a great deal of scientific effort." Lazarus and Folkman[52] maintain that the premise that stress, emotion and coping are tied to illness has been shown to be empirically sound, at least with respect to the relationship between stress and infectious diseases. However, as mentioned earlier, there are empirical studies which show paradoxical patterns. Fletcher and Jones[53] have found stress associated with *lower* blood pressure rather than high blood pressure, while Patkai[54] has demonstrated experimentally that the output of adrenaline and noradrenaline (the socalled "stress hormones") was elicited not only by noxious stimuli, but also by pleasant events. Be that as it may, the underlying assumption in stress theory and stress research is that the connection between stress, coping, emotion and disease is basically sound, although the precise nature of the relationships involved is not yet clear. Let us examine some

---

50 Lazarus (1977), p. 14.
51 Hinkle (1977), p. 47.
52 The mechanisms of psychoimmunology will be dealt with in the next section of this chapter.
53 Fletcher & Jones (1993).
54 Patkai (1971).

ideas about how stress is considered to cause or influence the development of disease.

Cannon, as we recall, was not especially concerned with the question of stress-related disease, although he could imagine that chronic levels of the alarm response might lead to serious disruption of homeostasis, resulting in disturbed physiological functioning. Selye was also quite convinced that disease could result from prolonged GAS, but their hypotheses on this matter were rather undeveloped. It is first with the concept of *psychological* stress that we begin to see some attempts to explicate how the chain from stress to disease might be constructed. Lazarus and Folkman state the complexity of the issue as follows: "...stress alone is not a sufficient cause of disease. To produce stress-linked disease other conditions must also be present such as vulnerable tissue or coping processes that inadequately manage the stress. The primary task of research is to study the contribution of these other variables and processes as mediators of the stress-illness relationship."[55] We thus have a complex network of factors, comparable to the multi-factorial open systems approach of psychosomatic medicine. I have found in my examination of stress theory, as presented by Lazarus and his followers, the following etiological factors: 1) certain potentially stressful situations which arise in the life of the individual. "Situations" are conceived of as man-environment interactions; 2) appraisals of situations, which contain not only conscious and unconscious thoughts, but also have a matrix-like relationship to beliefs, commitments, emotions, motivations, and goals; 3) coping skills and patterns, related to both personality traits and coping style. Coping is furthermore conceptualized as a process, evolving over time, possibly changing even during the course of one and the same stressful situation; 4) physiological reactions in the body, specifically catecholamine secretion, increased blood pressure, sharpened vigilance, energy mobilization with all that it physiologically entails (such as the secretion of glucocorticoids, which block the transport of nutrients into fat cells, the diversion of amino acids to the liver for immediate breakdown into glucose and so

---

[55] Lazarus & Folkman (1984), p. 18.

on). What seems to be the mediating link between all these factors? The notion of appraisal.[56] When a situation is appraised as stressful, and coping mechanisms are not available, the likely result is somatic disturbance, which can, if it is chronic, lead to disease. However, appraisal cannot be understood as distinct from coping. The way the person appraises the situation will in fact depend on his or her coping ability. Coping ability, in turn, has a direct effect upon emotions: the better one can cope, the less disturbing/intense the emotion. And as we have seen many times before, the less chronic emotion, the greater the chances for maintaining health. So although appraisal is the centerpiece of this theory, appraisal cannot be understood apart from the structure: situation---coping---emotion. Let us now examine, in turn, what is a "stressful situation" and what is coping.

As I stated earlier on in a footnote, Lazarus has preferred to address those stressful life situations which he calls "hassles" rather than acute, cataclysmic events. His own research has shown that hassles are more predictive of psychological and somatic symptoms than dramatic life events. Acute life events, in and of themselves, seem to have little impact on health, independently of the daily hassles associated with them. Pancheri et al.[57] came to the same conclusion, and offer the hypothesis that it is perhaps easier to develop a coping strategy during a crisis situation than in constant and repeated daily episodes of stress. What is so debilitating about hassles? If people must continually attend to regular and persistent "low level" stress (like having disturbing neighbors, or being displeased with one's job, or fighting with family members), the attention and effort expended on these hassles are imagined to gradually deplete the person's capacity to cope with subsequent stressors. A seem-

---

56 "Since we cannot move automatically from stress at the social level to stress at the psychological and physiological levels and vice versa, what are the principles that can guide our thinking about the relationships that exist among these levels? ...The links...are established through cognitive appraisal" (p. 289). Further: "Appraisal processes provide a common pathway through which person and environment variables modify psychological response, and hence emotions and their biological concomitants" (p. 224).

57 Pancheri et al. (1979), pp. 193-194, cited in Lazarus & Folkman (1984), p. 239.

ingly banal event may then push the person over the edge and result in a psychological or somatic breakdown. Hassles are pathogenic because they are persistent and taxing. One spends all of one's "energy" dealing with them, leaving nothing in reserve to deal with other problems. The energy metaphor invoked here is not the psychodynamic concept of libido or cathexis (discussed in chapter 2), but seems rather to refer to the individual's (limited) capacity to devote attention, vigilance and thought to events in the environment. It is as if a person has only a certain quantity of these things, and they are wasted, so to speak, on hassles. Furthermore, implicit in the concept of a hassle is the idea that a hassle is a hassle only when it can't be coped with. For example, if a person has a functional coping strategy in order to tolerate his noisy neighbor, this situation will no longer be experienced as a hassle. Let us now take a brief look at the concept of coping, in its general outline. The specific curative mechanisms said to be involved in coping will be discussed in the next section.

Coping is behavior (thoughts and actions, as well as attitudes and beliefs) which: 1) facilitates the solving of problems, as well as 2) helps to regulate the emotional disturbance connected to these problems. If one cannot remove the problem (problem-solving coping), one can at least learn to live with it without too much emotional distress (emotion-regulation coping). Certain problems simply cannot be mastered, for either objective or subjective reasons, and it is therefore just as important that people can learn to somehow tolerate less than desirable situations. Coping is tied to both primary and secondary appraisal. Coping is partly responsible for determining whether a situation will be appraised as threatening, benign or indifferent, and it is an integral aspect of the secondary appraisal question, "What do I do now?" once the stressful situation has arisen. Coping has an impact on how often and to what extent we experience the environment as posing a threat to our well-being (and thus initiating physiological arousal). Coping ability determines to a large extent how good we are at regulating emotional distress, once it does arise. Finally, our particular coping styles may have an impact on our behavior, which can in turn have various effects on our health and well being. For example, drinking heavily may help to regulate emotional distress, but it certainly has a detrimental impact on health.

What is the decisive link between experiences of stress and physiological processes in the body (which may lead to disease)? What are the mechanisms of interaction which can be explicated in a comprehensible way? We have here a situation similar to that of psychosomatic medicine, in that a wide variety of factors are accepted as somehow contributing to the development of disease, factors so diverse as genetic constitution, psychological traits, coping styles, appraisals, emotions and even societal and cultural factors, although the nature of the links between these factors is unspecified.[58] We find in the stress theory literature problems concerning how to explain individual differences in stress-reactions which can be found on all levels.[59] Physiological reactions are not uniformly consistent with the theory of stress-reaction. Stress experiences have been experimentally demonstrated in relation to lower blood pressure (rather than high), and other studies have shown high adrenaline secretion in connection with pleasurable events. It is a documented fact that stress-related (psychosomatic symptoms) diseases such as migraine, ulcers and asthma have in fact been known to disappear during continual stressful situations such as internment in concentration camps and military occupation. Stress breaks down certain functions, but enhances others[60]. What these counter-examples show is that the simple hypothesis that stress leads to disease and ill health has not been empirically demonstrated.[61] Perhaps "stress" is after all just a label we have invented in order to speak of the unknown.

---

[58] Lazarus & Folkman (1984): "...only when we can specify the person and environment antecedent factors determining the nature of the appraisal process, and how these appraisals affect the coping and emotional consequences, can cognitive appraisal go beyond pure description, which is itself a valuable first step" (p. 48).

[59] The studies referred to below have been cited earlier and will not be cited again here.

[60] As early as 1949 Hench et al. demonstrated that the adrenal hormones and the corticosteroids may suppress the development of allergic, rheumatic and collagen diseases.

[61] For further references on the questionability of the stress--illness relationship, see Briner & Reynolds (1993); Cohen & Williamson (1991); Karasek et al. (1987); Kasl (1983); Kessler (1987); Pollock (1988).

If we nevertheless press stress theory for some etiological statement, we find that the theoretical bridge which implicitly supports all the connections between stress and disease (whatever the specific mechanisms may be) is the idea that <u>sustained physiological arousal</u> is detrimental to the organism, the same basic idea expressed in psychosomatic medicine. Sustained physiological activity is the result of various forms of chronic emotion, and the emotions persist as the result of failure to cope with stressful situations (appraised as such). If we look a bit closer at the concept of sustained physiological arousal, as discussed in the stress literature, we discover a legacy from social Darwinism and eugenics,[62] where the basic idea is that our "outmoded biology" is in conflict with the demands of our complex, sophisticated, modern world. The cave man on Wall Street. We are still programmed biologically for gathering sticks and hunting prey. The modern man "turns on" the stress reaction too often and for too long a time. That which was physiologically meant to take care of emergencies has become an unwanted reaction to a variety of non-acute situations. Although outright biologism is considered by many to be outdated and simplistic, it does exert an influence on the stress theory. Cannon's fight-flight syndrome is directly rooted in biological thinking, Selye spoke of "diseases of adaption", and even Lazarus couches his descriptions of stress-related symptoms in terms of adaption/non adaption.[63] So, if we wish to remain healthy, we had better cope with the environment and avoid undue stimulation of the stress-reaction. Although the physiology of the stress-reaction has been nicely mapped out, the link between stress as an experience and the ultimate development of disease (the explanandum) is not clear. What is the nature of the interaction between the meaning (or appraisal) of the situation and the eventual development of disease? Do we really understand what "coping" is? The theoretical problems are similar to those found in psychosomatic medicine, namely which factors interact with each other

---

[62] In Newton (1995), pp. 19-20.

[63] Lazarus (1977): "Above all, we need to see somatic illness as an expression of repeated or persistent forms of adaptive commerce with an environment of some kind" (p. 24).

in what ways (according to what mechanisms?) in order to ultimately produce disease? Do we have a methodological problem here - i.e. we just don't yet know all the factors, and although the picture is very complex, it is not incomprehensible - or are the difficulties in relating stress to disease *principle* ones? My position is that we will never be able to produce the kinds of explanatory links which both stress theory and psychosomatic medicine wish to see between stress experience, physiology, emotion, coping, beliefs, attitudes and the development of disease. This cannot be done because these theories are not dealing with the whole human being in his/her life situation. The natural unity of being-in-the-world has been dissected in order to comply with methodological strategies. How this particular life is lived, psychologically, socially, physiologically, and how to understand the breakdown into disease, demands a different type of inquiry. To understand why this person experiences stress in this situation, or why this person develops just this disease at this time, requires a phenomenological analysis. This theme will be developed in the second part of the dissertation. To wind up the section of this chapter on stress theory, I will now take up the notion of the cure, as it is conceptualized in stress theory.

The cure

The previous sections discussed the importance of coping for mitigating the detrimental effects of stress. The basic idea is that when one can cope with potentially stressful situations, one has a greater chance of maintaining health. There is no consensus today on how coping works, although certain contemporary researchers focus their investigations on the coping process and try to ascertain an understanding of coping strategies and their effect on health and disease.[64] The specific questions in coping research are, why is coping effective? in which situations? by which individuals? what are the antecedent conditions involved in successful coping? Despite a variety of studies on coping, the investigation of coping

---

[64] See especially the Pearlin (1978) study on coping responses in relation to health and disease.

variables has not revealed any generalizable knowledge concerning these questions. Findings have been contradictory, and the evidence suggests that what works for one person in one type of situation might have a damaging effect for another.[65] There are no findings which enable the prediction of successful coping given variables X,Y,Z. Furthermore, there is the rather basic problem of identifying coping behavior. Pearlin[66] admits that it is somewhat difficult to identify what *is* coping, as there is nothing intrinsic in the behavior itself which indicates that it is serving a coping function. Some people watch TV or drink alcohol in order to cope, while others perform these same activities for entirely different reasons. Given these initial remarks, I now turn to specifically examining what stress theory has to say about the cure. What do stress theorists think it is that works in coping, and why?

Within the stress theory tradition, with its cognitive orientation, there are a variety of "stress management" therapies, based on principles of behavior therapy which have been discussed in the previous chapter. Specifically, we find the usual assortment of somatophysiological techniques such as biofeedback, relaxation, meditation, which aim at altering the physiological response patterns, as well as various forms of cognitive therapy ranging from the early "Rational Emotive Therapy" of Albert Ellis to Aaron T. Beck's cognitive behavior therapy. Stress-inoculation, systematic desensitization and other behavioral techniques are also relevant approaches to the management of stress (stressful situations). Even psychoanalysis is considered to be a therapeutical alternative, but then only the ego-psychology orientation with its interests in ego functioning. The orthodox psychoanalytic school with its emphasis upon infantile wishes and defenses does not seem to rank highly in stress management programs. Cognitive and somatophysiological techniques are more important in such programs than psychodynamic psychotherapies. Lazarus & Folkman[67] state that there is no reason to suppose that any one technique is necessarily better than another at bringing about change, al-

---

[65] See Speisman et al. (1964).
[66] Pearlin & Schooler (1978), p. 7.
[67] Lazarus & Folkman (1984).

though they do maintain that for any therapy to be effective, it must in one way or another produce changes in the ways in which people cognitively appraise and cope with stressful situations. Since stress is related to cognition, emotion, and behavior, it is quite natural that a multifactorial treatment is to be recommended. It is not difficult to construct such a program, combining cognitive therapy with relaxation techniques, psychodrama etc. All these techniques must then ultimately be applied in the real-life situation in order for a lasting cure to occur.

A brief look at the content of the cognitive behavioral therapies reveals that the basic "problem" with the stressed person lies in their faulty conceptualization (appraisal) of the situation, and therapy aims at bringing about a cognitive/emotional re-orientation regarding the problem(s) which have brought the person to seek help. Ellis emphasized that people make counter-productive interpretations of events because they entertain irrational ideas and beliefs. His "rational emotive therapy" aimed at bringing about a more rational way of thinking. Beck's cognitive behavioral therapy is somewhat more sophisticated, focusing on a variety of maladaptive thinking patterns (arbitrary inference, overgeneralization, selective abstraction, magnification, all-or-nothing thinking), but the basic idea is the same, i.e. that emotional distress is the result of cognitive processes, be they conscious or unconscious. No effort is made in the cognitive orientation to reconstruct the origin of these maladaptive thoughts and beliefs by asking for example, how they have arisen and what their function is. It is sufficient to become aware of these ideas, gain insight into how they steer one's thinking and behavior, and finally replace them with more adaptive, realistic thinking patterns. The somatophysiological techniques address the emotion-regulation side of coping, that is, they enhance the individuals ability to "cool down" the physical attributes of the stress reaction, such as visceral and motor disturbances. This increased self-control can conceivably also lead to an improved ability to solve problems, since the patient can presumably think clearer and reason better if s/he is not plagued by tachycardia and insomnia. However, Lazarus points out that certain studies have suggested that it may very well be that the efficacy of the somatophysiological therapies lies in the patient's perception of increased mastery and self-control, rather than the physiological effects of the treatment.

The principles of the cure rest not only upon cognitive re-orientation, but also (and importantly) upon emotional factors.[68]This is not surprising, since appraisal, as we recall, is integrally bound up with emotions. There is a relationship between feelings, actions and thoughts which must be taken into account when trying to manage stress. Because the stress hypothesis states that intense emotion (and/or anxiety) disturbs thinking, drains energy, and disrupts bodily functions, the obvious cure is to work backwards so that physiological reactions are calmed down, energy is restored, and the ability to think is reinstated. Since appraisal is the key to stress, we need to develop new ways of evaluation. If one appraises the situation differently, new avenues of coping are imagined to open up.[69]We must learn to think differently, behave differently, and feel differently about what is happening to us. When expressed in this way, there is a an uncomfortably one-sided emphasis on the *individual,* which makes this strategy sound politically naive.[70] In defense of Lazarus, he does not exclude the possibility that situations can be in and of themselves unreasonable. There is, after all, a problem-solving side to coping. But the notion of appraisal and coping is essentially an individual affair and the "stressful situation" is not analyzed in terms of its social and cultural dimensions. How human beings in groups co-constitute situations, construct organizations, socially reproduce prejudices and op-

---

68 "When all is said and done, treatment always centers on the emotional life of the person, and so there must not only be a theory of change, but a theory of emotion as the basis for therapy" (Ibid., p. 357).

69 "Nevertheless, our conceptualization states unequivocally that to produce therapeutic changes in the way people manage their lives, one must in one way or another produce changes in cognitive appraisal and coping" (Ibid., p. 352).

70 Newton (1995) writes, for example: "Managing stress is also, conveniently a private affair, conducted off stage...As such, it supports the tacit constraints on the expression of emotion at work...After all, if employees did openly express their feelings of anger, distress, upset or frustration in the work place, they might be more likely to notice the commonality amongst their feelings, and *even* to express collective grievances in relation to them" (p. 108, italics in original).

pressions etc., are questions which were of interest for the Tavistock Group, but not for Lazarus and his fellows.

A psychoanalyst would find the treatment principles described here shallow and ineffectual. S/he would argue that without addressing people's unconscious motivations, defenses and resistances, one cannot arrive at any real, lasting cure. One can perhaps alter people's cognitions superficially, for a time, but the *reasons* people have for their maladaptive thinking and behavior remain undisclosed and unattended to. Because of this, psychoanalysts claim that new symptoms and disease will arise (symptom substitution) until the basic underlying conflicts are resolved. The controversy between psychodynamically oriented therapists and their cognitive behavioral colleagues has been going on for some time. The controversy cannot be solved here, suffice to say that it is obvious that since psychoanalysts and stress theoreticians have completely different ideas about the psychological life, they will have different ideas about what will cure man of his ills. To sum up this section, let me just say that in terms of the etiological hypotheses, the cognitive-behavioral stress management program is quite rational. However, the precise nature of the cure has not been systematized in any general way. As with psychosomatic medicine, the field is extremely open and idiosyncratic. Relaxation techniques work fine for some people, but create anxiety in others. Certain patterns of coping seem to work well in interpersonal relationships, while they are not equally effective in coping at the work-place. Thoughts are said to shape feelings and actions, but just how they do that is not explicated beyond the idea that not being able to cope (panic and catastrophe thoughts) leads to emotional distress and various maladaptive behavioral patterns. Having "maladaptive" thoughts is also seen as being detrimental to functioning, since one interprets situations in non-adaptive ways. But where do these maladaptive thoughts come from, what sustains them, how are they lived and understood by the person experiencing them? These are typically phenomenological questions, and are therefore not addressed in stress theory.[71]

II. NEUROIMMUNOLOGY AND NEUROENDOCRINOLOGY

Introduction

The relationship between stress theory and neuroimmunology and neuroendocrinology is somewhat ambivalent. On the one hand, some theoreticians from the latter disciplines find the "stress concept" to be more misleading than helpful, and advocate getting rid of the notion entirely. It is considered better to focus on processes and mechanisms which can be measured and investigated (natural) scientifically. On the other hand, there is a great deal of interest paid to the immune system and its relationship to the *experience* of stress. The basic idea is that repeated exposure to stressful situations ultimately leads to decreased immunologic competence. Stress is hypothesized as being an important etiological factor in the development both of infectious diseases and of autoimmunological ones. Neuroimmunology and neuroendocrinology are natural heirs to the laboratory tradition of Cannon and Selye. The physiological workings of the body are in focus. The interactions between the immune system, the endocrine system and the brain are of central interest in this field. Instead of concentrating on the interpretative, meaning-appraisal aspects of stressful situations, neuroimmunology and neuroendocrinology turn inwards in order to map out the intricate workings of the body. The body studied in this manner is the objective body, not the lived body.

I am taking the liberty of clumping neuroimmunoloy and neuroendocrinology together, and treating them somewhat schematically. It is an

---

[71] I have in this part of the chapter been forced to exclude examining the work-related stress tradition, due to considerations of space as well as focus. We have there primarily the Scandinavian research, especially the work of Marianne Frankenhaeuser, Bertil Gardell, Lennart Levi, and Tores Teorell.

accepted fact today that neuroimmunology and neuroendocrinology describe processes which are actually integrated systems in a functioning whole. Hormones have been shown to be involved in the inhibition of immune responses, and antigen responses can, in turn, elicit changes in the neuroendocrine system. Due to considerations of space as well as focus, I will limit myself to trying to ascertain a psychosomatic theory from the literature. Do we find any consideration of the mind/body issue? How are psychological/social factors imagined to interact with the physiology of the body? This analysis will be carried out from within the limitations of my own competence in these fields.

The discipline of immunology has developed since its inception as the study of bacterial immunization. After World War II, immunology focused on the chemical workings of the antigen/antibody pattern (immunochemistry), while today a prominent area of study is the influence of psychological processes on the immune system (psychoneurorimmunology). It is an empirical fact that a population exposed to the same pathogens will not exhibit a uniform pattern of disease. Some people get sick, while others do not. There is something about the "host" which prevents ill health. Quite a few diseases are related to the functioning of the immune system, for example, viral and bacterial infections, the autoimmune diseases and allergies; and even certain forms of cancer are the object of immunological study today. Briefly, how does the immune/endocrine system(s) work?

Basically, the immune system is a collection of circulating cells in the blood stream whose job is to differentiate between "self", that is, those cells which bear the distinctive cellular signature of the organism, and "non-self", cells which are foreign or somehow strange (e.g. cancer) to the body. The invaders must be attacked, while the body's own cells must be protected from attack (horror autotoxicus). When the body does not succeed in getting rid of foreign cells (such as bacteria, virus, parasites, cancer cells) we get sick. When for some reason the immune system attacks its own cells, we develop an autoimmune disease, such as rheumatoid arthritis, thyroiditis, systemic lupus erythematosus, myastenia gravis, to name a few. There are various types of circulating cells involved in immunological defense. These cells (lymphocytes called T- and B-cells, as well as the monocytes) have different functions in the defensive strategy, but the important point in this context is that when these cells do not perform their job, sickness and disease are the result. It has been demonstrated that periods of stress can disrupt immunologic functioning in various ways. Long-term stress appears to dismantle the immune system, although this hypothesis is not accepted by all. If it is so that stress disrupts the immune system, this is somewhat puzzling, since it doesn't make biological sense to suppress immunity when it is needed the most. A variety of hypotheses have been put forth over the years on the question of stress-induced immunological failure,[72] but there is today no consensus about the hypothesis in general or any agreement about why such failure occurs.

The endocrine system is also based on blood-transported chemical messages. Various glands in the body secrete hormones, and these substances travel to various sites in the body. The brain has been shown to be the master gland, especially the hypothalamus, which secretes many of these releasing and inhibiting hormones, which in turn regulate the secretion of hormones further out in peripheral areas of the body. The hormones which are of interest in this context are the so-called "stress hormones", for example epinephrine (adrenaline) and norepinephrine (noradrenaline), mentioned previously in this chapter. These hormones, released by the sympathetic nervous system, act immediately upon the body, giving rise to vigilance, arousal, activation, mobilization etc. Another class of hormones released during stress are the glucocorticoids, which act in a similar way to adrenaline, backing up the immediate adrenal arousal by more long-lasting effects. The pancreas releases a hormone called glucagon, needed for the mobilization of energy. Prolactin is released by the pituitary gland, which among other things suppresses reproduction during stress. Finally, the brain and the pituitary gland release morphine-like substances (endorphins) which serve to blunt the perception of pain. Both immunological processes and hormones are

---

[72] See Sapolsky (1994) pp. 140-146 for the 6 major hypotheses on this issue.

said to be influenced by psychological processes, notably the experience of stress. Let me now highlight the relevant points for a discussion of psychosomatic processes.

Psychosomatics and neuroimmunology/neuroendocrinology

Psychoneuroimmunology (PNI) began in the West with Robert Ader and Nick Cohen's work with conditioned immunosuppression experiments,[73] although the Russians had been performing similar types of experiments already during the 1920's.[74] Briefly, the experiments performed by Ader & Cohen demonstrated that one could pair a neutral stimulus (a distinctly flavored drinking solution) with an immunosuppresive pharmacological drug, and ultimately create the immunosuppresive effect by the neutral stimulus alone. These experiments, performed on sheep, demonstrated that immunological suppression could be conditioned (learned). The sheep which had been subjected to the conditioning showed a weakened immunological response when subsequently injected with a pathogen, even though they were only drinking the neutral substance at the time. This same principle is behind the well-known clinical example of the asthma patient who can have an asthma attack at the sight of a plastic rose. In sheep we would refer to the component of learning or conditioning, while in the human being we would want to include the symbolic level dealing with meaning-constitution, signification and intentionality.[75] The aim of PNI is to attempt to explicate some of the mechanisms which could account for the differences in immunity and resistance to disease in the population. From my review of the literature, there is very little written specifically on the mind/body issue, and it is therefore difficult to construct any ontological position on the

---

73 Ader & Cohen (1975).
74 Metal'nikov & Chorine (1926).
75 It is possible that a behaviorist would object here, and claim that we are dealing with conditioning even in the human being. However, from what I can ascertain from the literature, the theoreticians of psychoneuroimmunology and endocrinology are not behaviorists.

148

status of the psychical, the physiological, and the nature of their interaction.[76] The body and its processes are described in terms of the objectified body studied by natural science,[77] while the characterization of the psychological, if mentioned at all, is reminiscent of the position of psychosomatic medicine. Psychological, social factors are acknowledged as being efficacious in the development of disease, but they are not problematized nor thematized in relation to the physical/physiological. When they are mentioned, they are brought up in quantified equivalents. Reductionism is criticized by several authors as an inadequate method of approach,[78] but there is no specific consideration given to what a multifactorial approach actually entails. A few authors mention systems theory, but then the matter seems to be finished. The bulk of the literature is concerned with etiological questions. I will wind up this chapter with a brief look at the etiology of immunological-endocrinological systems failure and its alleged contribution to the development of disease and ill health.[79]

---

[76] In one of the few explicit references to the mind/body problem, Harte (1992) states: "Attempts to separate 'the mental' from 'the physical' are outdated; instead, we illustrate the interplay between entities of what, in the end, is a biological organism surviving in a biological ecosystem" (p. 43). As was the case with psychosomatic medicine, the result of this new paradigm tends to be the subsuming of the psychological under physiological descriptions. And this is quite natural, given the primacy of the biological perspective.

[77] With the interesting exception of Booth & Ashbridge (1992; 1993), who will be discussed shortly.

[78] See especially Cunningham (1978).

[79] The phenomenon of kindling will not be discussed here, as it has not been linked to any disease processes in humans, with the exception of temporal lobe epilepsy. Kindling refers to the way in which repeated electrical stimulation of the forebrain in rats can eventually lead to convulsive activity in those rats that had initially been unresponsive to stimuli. After the rat has been "kindled", it may have full-strength responses after only one or two stimulations. Even spontaneous convulsions will occur. Certain psychiatric conditions (manic-depressive syndrome, schizophrenia, panic disorder) have been hypothesized to partake of kindling-like mechanisms, but so far this is mere speculation. See Bolwig & Trimble (1989) on kindling.

Solomon[80] hits the nail on the head when he writes that our ability to be convincing about psychosomatic hypotheses rests upon our ability to form a "...clear elucidation of underlying pathogenic mechanisms that lead from experience through the central nervous system to tissue alteration." Unfortunately, nothing like this has been described. What do we find in the literature on the relationship between experience and susceptibility to disease? First and foremost there is the general idea that prolonged stress (experience) will eventually lead to a breakdown of immunological functioning, although this is not always the case. In some cases, stress can actually have an enhancing function for immunological processes. Some authors consider the hypothesis that stress leads to an increased susceptibility to disease to be a speculative idea, yet to be demonstrated,[81] while others dismiss the entire concept of "stress" as a hindrance to truly understanding the processes under study.[82] The explications of the mechanisms leading from experience to tissue alteration are physiological, that is, they begin and end in physiology. For example, "stress" is discussed in its operationalized form, e.g. as the activation of glutocortocoid secretion. One begins, as Selye did, with the on-going physiological process. The "first cause" of the chain is not addressed (in this case, experience). If we begin with on-going physiological processes, it is easy to describe physiological mechanisms, such as how glutocortocoid secretion causes the thymus gland to stop producing new lymphocytes into the blood, thus depleting the body's supply of immunological defense cells. Further descriptions of stress mechanisms are given in purely physiological terms: stress is said to repress the number of circulating "killer cells", which are especially active at stopping tumors from

---

80 Solomon (1981), p. 174.
81 See Palmblad (1981).
82 For example, Ader (1980): "Since different experiential events have different behavioral and physiologic effects that depend upon the stimulation to which the individual is subsequently exposed and the responses the experimenter chooses to measure, the inclusive label 'stress' contributes little to an analysis of the mechanisms that may underline or determine the organism's response. In fact, such labeling, which is descriptive rather than explanatory, may actually impede conceptual and empirical advances..." (p. 312).

growing; glucocorticoids seem to aid the tumor in developing its own set of capillaries (angiogenesis) and so on. These are fine descriptions from within physiology, but they do not provide an answer to Solomon's request for an elucidation of the process *from* experience, through the CNS to tissue alteration. Although the approach here is supposedly multifactorial, the understanding (and contribution) of non-physiological factors is difficult to see. Psychological traits are sometimes connected to genetic constitutions (for example, carcinogen-producing enzymes being associated with particular personality traits), but these studies are not considered to be convincing, and the literature on the relationship between personality and immunological deficiency is not strong.

One exception to the exclusively physiological explication of stress and its relation to disease is found in an interesting concept put forward by Booth & Ashbridge[83] concerning what they call a somatopsychic self-determination model, wherein the "self" is understood to include not only the psychological dimension but also the immunological level (of self, non-self). Instead of seeing the immune system primarily as a protective system, they conceptualize the immunological discrimination of self, non-self as belonging to the same holistic principle of self-determination which can be found on all levels of the organism. In this way, it is no longer possible to isolate the psychological from the immunological. For example, the neonate is both immunologically and psychologically tied to the mother until the maturation process has allowed for the determination of self to emerge, in terms both of one's own antibody defenses and of the psychological experience of identity. The somatopsychic self-determination model interprets these two phenomena as different manifestations of one and the same (self) system. There is a general somatopsychic malleability during the early years, when the self is less defined. The immune system will both determine and be determined by psychological and somatic states, and parallels between experience and physiology should be apparent throughout the life of an individual. The authors argue for the need for a new language in order to address this

---

83 Booth & Ashbridge (1992; 1993).

holistic system, bridging the gap between the language of psychology and the language of neuroimmunology/neuroendocrinology. A true *psycho-neuroimmunology* cannot limit itself to discussing the physiology of the immune system, it must take into account the psychological aspects of the organism. On this view, health is as wide as connectedness and coherence, on all levels, while disease is disconnection and separation, giving us information about the entire somatopsychic existence of the individual at the time of the onset of disease. The work of Booth & Ashbridge is unique in the literature.[84]

To conclude, although the disciplines of psychoneuroimmunology and endocrinology have amassed an impressive bulk of somatic knowledge, they have not made much progress with the *psychosomatic* questions. I will here conclude with some excerpts from the literature on this point:

> "Does the concept of what is necessary and sufficient (for disease) extend beyond genetic predispositions and responses to altered socioenvironmental conditions? We of course assume that it does. Clinical observations, retrospective analyses, and epidemiologic studies strongly suggest that it does. We are, however, lacking systematic biopsychosocial analyses of such disease processes."[85]

> "Many unsolved diseases are abnormalities of immune control, for example various autoimmune and allergic conditions. Tissue transplantation is still bedeviled by rejection problems. Effective immune control of many viral and metazoan parasites, and of course cancer, has not yet been achieved. In these areas we have not advanced much since Pasteur, although our knowledge of immune *mechanisms* has increased enormously since his time" (italics in original).[86]

---

84 The journal *Advances* (1993, vol. 9, no. 2 spring) devoted an issue to the "speculative and controversial" ideas of Booth & Ashbridge, giving rise to a lively debate. The commentators agreed that there is good reason for examining the immune system and its relationship to other systems (the psyche, CNS etc.), but few of them agreed with the authors' propositions.

85 Ader (1980), p. 310.

86 Cunningham (1978), p. 46.

"(Despite these fascinating findings), it remains far from clear just how much chronic stress makes you more vulnerable to diseases that would normally be fought off by the immune system."[87]

"We can come to no conclusion regarding influence of PF (psychosocial factors) on induction of cancer through exogenous carcinogens. We do, however, have a highly speculative, extremely uncertain mechanism by which it could happen."[88]

"The possible physiological mechanism for emotional influence on production of rheumatoid factor, especially if not tied to the concept of psychological distress, which relates to dysfunction of the immunologic system, is unclear."[89]

"To summarize, all these studies have found that life changes and/or emotions evoked by life changes occurring for a rather prolonged period were associated with depression of one, or less frequently, two or more immune reactions. Both the mechanisms and the clinical significance of these observations are unknown."[90]

Summary of stress theory and neuroimmunology/ neuroendocrinology

Stress theory has evolved from the fight/flight syndrome of Cannon through Selye's GAS to modern psychological theories of stress as a person-environment interaction. In this chapter I have examined the work of Lazarus and his co-workers in order to discern a psychosomatic theory, focusing upon the categories of ontology (mind-body interaction), etiology and cure. Selye's notion of GAS was criticized as being psychologically unsophisticated, and Lazarus belongs to those psychologically minded theoreticians who took up the psychological aspects of stress and emphasized the *meaning* of the stressful situation for the subject in question. For Lazarus, the notion of appraisal is integral to understanding the experience of stress. He developed the notions of primary and secondary

---

[87] Sapolsky (1994), p. 147.
[88] Fox (1981), p. 108.
[89] Solomon (1981), p. 176.
[90] Palmblad (1981), p. 244.

appraisal in order to describe the cognitive processes involved in the constitution of a "stressful situation". In Lazarus' texts, stress is sometimes considered to be a subset of emotions ("stress emotions"), and at other times the term is used interchangeably with anxiety. The mind-body issue is not addressed by Lazarus, so we have had to construct an ad-hoc ontology, which starts with the explanandum (the breakdown into disease/ill health) and hypothesizes a chain of events said to be the cause of this breakdown. We do not begin here with ontological descriptions of what is mind, what is body and how do they interact, but rather with a *fait accompli*, a person who has become ill due to stress. The factors said to be of importance for the development of stress-related disease/illness are: the person-environment interaction, appraisal, personality traits, commitments, beliefs, coping, emotion and physiological arousal. The etiological discussion boils down to the same efficacious mechanism operating in the psychosomatic theory of psychosomatic medicine, namely that sustained and prolonged physiological arousal (due to chronic emotion/lack of coping) is detrimental to the functioning of the organism. The cure is to work with appraisal (problem-focused coping) and emotional regulation (emotion-focused coping) in order to reinstate the ability to solve problems and reduce physiological arousal. The main techniques are cognitive therapy and somatophysiological therapy. What coping actually is and why it works remains unclear.

It is difficult to construct a psychosomatic theory from the literature on neuroimmunology and neuroendocrinology. Very few authors take up the notion of mind-body interaction, and most concern themselves exclusively with on-going physiological processes. They do not consider the initiation of the process, the first link in the chain, which has to do with the meaning-constitution (experience) of a stressful situation. Though there is an awareness of the importance of psychological factors for the development of certain diseases, these theoreticians are at a loss to explain how psycho-social factors relate to the workings of the nervous system. In conclusion, neither modern stress theory nor PNI has been able to convincingly demonstrate the path from meaning (the constitution of a stressful situation) through the activity of the nervous system to the ultimate breakdown into disease and illness. In the next chapter we will take a look at one final theoretician from the medical tradition of psychosomatic theory, Herbert Weiner, who attempts to formulate an integrative theory of health, disease and illness.

CHAPTER 5

An integrative model of health, disease and illness: Herbert Weiner's psychobiology

"If the term 'psychosomatic medicine' has any meaning at all, it is a medicine of sick persons not of their diseased organs."[1]

"Most patients seeking medical care do not have diseases but are in ill health."[2]

"(Illnesses) are the manifestations of sick persons not only of disturbances of bodily systems. They may be precipitated by unemployment, marital discord, bereavement, and job dissatisfaction. Curiously, ill-health has not been the major area of investigative interest of psychosomatic medicine."[3]

"Medicine may be the only discipline that lacks a comprehensive Theory. Theories of Art, Aesthetics, Biology, Economics, History, Philosophy, Physics, and Psychology exist. In Medicine the only existing Theory derives from Infectious Disease and is generally acknowledged to be unsatisfactory because it is linear, restrictive, and oversimplified."[4]

Introduction

Herbert Weiner is Professor of Psychiatry and Biobehavioral Sciences at the University of California, Los Angeles. His work could have been discussed in both in chapter 3 (psychosomatic medicine) and chapter 4

---

[1] Weiner (1987), p. 154.
[2] Weiner (1992a), p. 91.
[3] Weiner (1987), p. 153.
[4] Weiner (1977), p. XI.

(stress theory). He has however merited his own chapter for several reasons. To begin with, Weiner stands out from his fellow theoreticians because of his clear understanding of the difference between disease and ill health, a distinction not always made in traditional literature. His "integrative approach" to health, illness[5] and disease is an attempt to integrate experience, behavior, the brain/nervous system and physiology, a project which psychosomatic medicine has called for since its inception. Finally, he discusses explicitly the mind-body problem, the bane of psychosomatic theory. All of these ideas are of central interest to forwarding a real understanding of psychosomatic pathology. In a way, Weiner can be seen as the culmination of these two traditions, as he is clear about the theoretical shortcomings of traditional psychosomatic medicine and stress theory, as well as determined to formulate an integrative theory which will remedy these misconceptions and dead ends. For these reasons I wish to examine Weiner's writings and see if he can give us a new starting point for our theorizing with his integrative approach.

Weiner is primarily interested in adaption. Health is characterized in terms of successful psychobiological adaption to the environment. The integrative model conceptualizes both disease and ill health as the breakdown of adaption, on various levels. Disease is defined as clearly identifiable anatomical lesions (lesions which interfere with the organism's structure or functioning), while ill health is a state of the *person*, characterized by unpleasant feelings of being discomforted, depressed, in pain, or of in general having gone awry in life, without necessarily having structural, organic changes in the body which accompany (or account for) these feelings. According to Weiner, traditional medicine has made the mistake of looking for identifiable syndromes and diseases (organic lesions) as the source of ill health. This is misleading, as ill health always has to do with a person-environment interaction. In ill health there is

---

5 The terms "illness" and "ill health" are not rigorously distinguished in Weiner's writings. When I refer to the two terms, "ill health" will be used as the opposite of health, while the term "illness" refers to the particular state of ill health which the person experiences (e.g. upset stomach, headaches, gastro-intestinal problems etc.) This is in line with Nordenfelt's (1987) work on the philosophy of health.

some demand being placed upon the individual which exceeds his/her capacity for coping. The most common sources of these demands are the family and working life. Disease may result in ill health, as any "stressor" may lead to illness, but the reason for ill health is not the lesion in itself, but the situation which arises as the result of having a disease. It is the total person-environment interaction together with the meaning of that totality for the individual which constitutes ill health. There is, then, no linear, causal relationship between disease and ill health, in contrast with what traditional medicine has taught us. With this insight, we can understand one of the foremost paradoxes of clinical medicine, i.e. that persons may have diseases and yet feel that they are healthy, while others with no lesions are in very bad health.

The above characterization of health, disease and ill health falls in line with modern stress theory. We find the person-environment interaction in focus, as well as an emphasis upon how the individual constitutes the meaning of his/her situation and how s/he copes with it. However, Weiner is also a psychobiologist, and his later characterizations of ill health emphasize its biological/physiological aspects. In 1992 he writes, "A more precise analysis of the manifestations of ill health leads to the conclusion that they represent physiological changes in vital biological functions - respiratory and cardiac rhythms, food intake, digestion, elimination, reproduction, sleep rhythms, pain modulation and mood."[6] Here, we find the idea that ill health is fundamentally related to biological functioning. He expresses this even more clearly later on in the same work: "The tentative conclusion is that ill health *results from* a change in the normal rhythms of a subsystem incited by stressful experience."[7](my italics). The etiological significance of biological rhythms will be examined later on, for now I wish to draw attention to the slightly different characterizations found here between the "stress theory" characterization of ill health (person-environment transaction and its meaning for the individual) and his later emphasis upon biological functioning. It is the

---

6   Weiner (1992a), p. 93.
7   Ibid. p. 150.

main task of Weiner's theory to integrate adaption, subjective experiences, and physiology. If he has succeeded or not will be the topic of this chapter.

Weiner has two main general points he wishes to make about diseases. First of all, he states that it is important to understand that diseases are heterogeneous. This means that there is no single invariant set of factors which will account for all the subforms of the disease. For example, there are at least 29 forms of human peptic ulcers, over 100 forms of malignant diseases, and several forms of diabetes mellitus.[8] It has been demonstrated that borderline hypertension can be seen in three profiles differing in both physiological and psychological make-up.[9] One can also find 3 different types of functional bowl disorders.[10] All of these examples demonstrate that the pathogenesis of one and the same disease is not invariant. According to Weiner, it is possible that many of the controversies about the different contexts in which diseases manifest themselves, the various onset factors, as well as individual differences in psychological profiles among people with the same disease, can be explained by the simple fact that although diseases are defined anatomically, they are actually heterogeneous in nature. Because of the dominance of the biomedical model, it is still common that one speaks of a specific disease as if it were identical in terms of etiology and predisposition with every other manifestation. But this is not the case. Most, if not all, diseases are heterogeneous.[11] Secondly, Weiner emphasizes that there are different factors which predispose, initiate and sustain disease processes. Psychological factors may be of importance in the initiation of a disease, but not its maintenance, or vice versa. The various factors which predispose to a certain disease fall into many categories, such as genetic defects, per-

---

[8] Weiner (1992b), p. 571.

[9] Weiner (1979).

[10] Weiner (1992b).

[11] A distinction can be made here between diseases conceptualized in terms of their content (a list of symptoms or signs) and those defined in terms of their causes. Diseases are sometimes defined in terms of causes, but this is not always the case. Weiner does not always distinguish between causes and content in his discussion of the heterogeneity of diseases.

sonal habits, social customs, psychological make-up and the historical period in which one lives. There are likewise a variety of factors which may initiate and sustain the disease process. The important point here is that what we traditionally call a "disease" can exist in a variety of sub-forms (e.g. with or without psychological traits, physiological changes), and can also come about through a variety of predisposing, initiating and sustaining factors.

The integrative theory states that there is only one integrated organism in interaction with his/her environment. The strength of this model is that it attempts to build a theory of the entire person - social, biological, psychological, cellular - in his/her context. Disease and ill health are seen as the result of breakdown in adaption, which may occur on any of these levels. But what is adaption? The examples Weiner gives are characterized by being adjusted, mature, content, stable, coping; and finally, adaption is associated with patterned, rhythmic, dynamic biological processes. Thus, for Weiner, adaption is a social, psychological, biological phenomen which can be conceptualized at any level. The examples of adaption given in Weiner's texts most often have to do with what would be called "coping" in stress theory, although coping is more narrowly associated with cognitive processes (see chapter 4), while Weiner's adaption seems to be a wider concept. There is something about the flow of a person's interaction with his/her world which accounts for health or non-health. In citing a study by Hinkle,[12] Weiner writes: "The only factor that differentiated those persons who were repeatedly ill from those who were not was that those who were ill were not adapted to their work, marriages, or everyday lives. Overall, the subjects who were repeatedly ill were the most discontented with their lives."[13]

Finally, Weiner is interesting because he does not avoid the fundamental mystery of psychosomatic theory, that is, how symbolic, non-material events can get "translated" into material changes, such as sustained elevations in blood pressure, alterations in immune processes and

---

[12] Hinkle (1974).
[13] Weiner (1984), p. 256.

so on.[14] Failure to come to grips with this problem has both historical, philosophical and empirical roots, according to Weiner. He protests against the dualistic framework underlying this type of question, and proposes that we need to reexamine our conceptualizations of the relations between mind and body in order to better understand health, disease and ill health. He believes that the neurological phenomenon of transduction may be of some help in this re-evaluation process. Transduction concerns the transformation of, for example, chemical into neural excitations, or neural inputs into hormonal outputs, or of chemical, neurological excitations into experience. According to Delbrück,[15] the phenomenon of transduction is essentially about the point at which a stimuli is converted into its first "interesting" output. Transduction is not the answer to the mind-body problem, but Weiner hopes that it may open up some new ways of understanding these issues.

The ontological questions

According to Weiner, the mind-brain-body conundrum is the major stumbling block of psychosomatic theory. As long as classical Western biomedicine continues to view the mental in non-material terms and the body in material ones, the dualism remains insoluble. Weiner criticizes both psychosomatic medicine and stress theory for reasons mentioned in the previous chapters, namely, that they have been unable to explain how an experience, such as bereavement for example, is translated into struc-

---

14 Weiner: "The chain of events that begins with an experience and ends with a lesion is largely unknown." (1977) p. 611; and: "We do not understand how nerve impulses can achieve psychological representation in the form of thoughts, memories and feelings. And we have no concept to help us explain how feelings bring about physiological changes in the body" (ibid., p. 628); and, "Obviously, light also stimulates the retina to entrain impulses which pass via the classic visual pathways to the visual cortex, and in a way which is not understood, produce the *experience* of light." (1972), p. 372, italics in original; finally: "How can a disturbing event in the life of the patient be linked to the known pathological changes in the disease, such a the immunological or physiological mechanisms? Once again, the answer must be that we do not know" (1977) p. 457.

15 Delbrück (1970).

tural and functional changes in cells. We still do not have an answer to the basic problem of how experience is translated into bodily processes. A practical result of this unsolved dualism is that we have divided health care into two divisions. On the one hand we have clinics and specialists for patients with "pure" bodily diseases, providing reparation for body parts (bodies without minds), and on the other hand special clinics for minds without bodies. According to Weiner, in order to remedy this dualistic misconception, together with its negative consequences for patients,[16] we need to rethink our conceptualization of health, illness and disease. The dualistic mind-body problem lies at the core of this task, and is considered by Weiner to be one of the central questions of psychosomatic theory. What does Weiner propose instead of the traditional dualistic approach? He has written a considerable amount over the years,[17] and I can only attempt to give an answer to this question by examining a selection of his work. The passages of interest here are those dealing specifically with issues related to the mind-body problem, such as the brain, emotions, and the phenomenon of transduction.

In 1995 Weiner writes that a major hindrance to our being able to integrate sociopsychological, physiological and genetic factors into a theory of disease and illness has to do with the fact that "...our ignorance about the relationship of the functions of the mind and the structure of the brain remains profound. Therefore, a large gap exists in truly integrating the mental and the bodily, which goes beyond the use of two languages to describe them." [18] We are not just dealing with parallel descriptions here (cf. Graham's linguistic parallelism, chapter 3), we seem to have to do with two basically different realms, the mind and the brain.

---

16 "Persons in ill-health constitute a major burden to themselves, their families and society. They are at risk for incorrect diagnoses; repeated, unnecessary surgery, and diagnostic procedures, and iatrogenic disease. They puzzle, frustrate and anger physicians" (1987) p. 154.

17 In 1992, Weiner is listed as having written 210 articles and chapters in books as well as being the author or editor of 19 books.

18 Weiner (1995), p. 28.

But although Weiner speaks of the mind and the brain as distinct,[19] he often refers to them together: for example, "The mind-brain can also modify its own intrinsic physiological - not only the body's activities"[20] and "The organ of adaption is the mind/brain" and "...or that the mind (brain) could analyze a threatening situation into separate components."[21] For Weiner, mental and physical occurrences are not identical (cf. identity theory, chapter 1), but rather contemporaneous, and because we have used different techniques to study these two contemporaneous occurrences, we have drawn the erroneous conclusion that such occurrences are always causally related. The usual chain of influence is the idea that thoughts or feelings are imagined to cause various physical occurrences in the body. This is not the case, according to Weiner. There is no necessary causal relationship between mental experiences and physiological occurrences in the body. But what is the relationship between the mind and the brain operating in this theory? Because Weiner does not speak about the nature of the mind or experiences per se, it is hard to answer this question. He has more to say about the brain. For example, the brain seems to be the "place" where the linkage occurs between mental events and physiological/behavioral "output". The brain is the "seat of all adaptive action and the storehouse of experience and self awareness. It occupies, therefore, a central position in the mediation of behavior and bodily processes."[22] Brain processes somehow mediate between the psychological and the physical. This would seem to suggest that the mental event is, after all, another "side" of the physiological brain process, accessible to us via introspection. But this conclusion is not drawn out or clearly stated. Furthermore, since Weiner is concerned with problematizing the relationship between mental events and physiological occurrences, it would hardly be the case that mind and brain

---

19 For example, (1977) p. 638, "Alternative ways of organizing data may provide us with insights needed ultimately to develop an accurate overview that bridges the gap between mind, brain and body in health and disease - a gap that remains a crucial factor in biology and medicine."
20 Weiner (1992a), p. 251.
21 Weiner (1977), p. 630.
22 Weiner (1977), p. 5.

should be understood as two sides of the same coin. Were it so, we would have identity rather than concomitance. One of Weiner's main points is that concomitant mental occurrences and physiological processes are not necessarily causally related to one another.

Concerning the notion of "mediation", it is accepted knowledge today that physiological processes are regulated by brain processes, but the way in which *experiences* and *meaning* relate to brain processes is more problematic. Weiner admits this difficulty, but does not doubt that one day the answer to this difficulty will be found in brain processes themselves. When Weiner does speak of experience and mental events, he refers to them in terms of neurological circuits in the brain, distinct and separate from other neural circuits responsible for physiological reactions. What experience *is* over and above the neural circuit is not defined. In animal experiments it has been shown that experience (e.g. of restraint-immobilization or crowding) produces changes in the animal's behavior later on in life in relation to various conditions, as well as changing the physiology of the animal's biological functioning. However, what *is it* about restraint-immobilization or crowding which gives rise to altered physiology? This is the same problem Selye was confronted with in regards to the first link in the "stress-chain". Similarly, transduction must address the meaning-constitution aspects of experience before it can speak about these various "events" which occur in the brain and the mind, and their eventual relationship to one another. Weiner would agree, but couches his hopes on this point in classical stimulus-response terms, "First I would like to stress that further insight into events in the brain which link a psychologic experience with a series of physiologic events cannot be achieved until there has been careful analysis of the specific constellation of stimuli or events which impinge upon the organism."[23]However, the stimulus-response model is adequate for studying physicalistic occurrences, but not meaning and experience. Experience and meaning are not "responses" to incoming stimuli, only neurological occurrences can be examined in this way. Studying neural

---

[23] Weiner (1972), p. 370.

circuits in the brain does not yield any understanding of experience per se, nor of the first link in the chain (meaning-constitution).

Emotion has been lifted out in my analyses of psychosomatic theories as the hypothesized bridge between meaning/signification (psycho-social reality) and objective body (physiology). The previous theories examined have all found emotions to be of central importance for the understanding of psychosomatic pathology. Emotions partake of meaning and body, and for that reason are comprehensible "double aspect" phenomena. However, Weiner rejects this conceptualization of emotion. Emotions are not necessarily physiological in nature, nor are they translated directly or indirectly into disease. He points out that we do not in fact to this day know how emotions are related to disease and ill health. According to Weiner, it is simply a prejudice to believe that emotions and physiology are inextricably bound up with each other. Emotions and physiological changes in the body may be correlated, as they may happen to arise simultaneously, but they are not causally related to one another. Emotions do not give rise to physiological reactions, nor vice versa (cf. the James-Lange theory of emotions). Weiner states: "Although the emotional response to the signal may appear to be causally correlated with physiological changes, they are usually only associated in time. To conceptualize emotion and the correlated physiological response in any other manner leads to the insuperable conundrum traditionally designated as one aspect of the mind-brain-body problem."[24]Emotions and physiology are both biologically purposive, but they may occur independently of one another. However, Weiner's conceptualization of the traditional view is somewhat misleading, as he presents the position as if emotions were "translated in some unknown manner into bodily changes..."[25] As I have understood psychodynamic theory, psychosomatic medicine and stress theory on this point, emotions are *in themselves* both meaning and body, they are not conceptually split up into two causally related moments. Weiner's contribution to the discussion of

---

[24] Weiner (1992a), pp. 29-30.
[25] Ibid., p. 137.

emotion is the separation of emotion into an experiential aspect and a (not necessarily correlated) physiological concomitant. However, the legitimacy of this move is in itself debatable, as one wonders what an "emotional response" would be apart from its affect, its *drang*, its bodily component. Would it be some special kind of cognitive content, differing in some way from other types of thoughts? Because Weiner is only looking at experience in terms of neural locations in *the brain,* he does not see this problem. A further criticism in this context is that Weiner's examples of emotion, like his examples of experience above, are couched in terms of stimulus-response, which greatly reduces their heuristic value. Signification and psychological meaning as such are not adequately captured in terms of a "response" to a stimulus, described in natural scientific terms.

Weiner's reason for dividing up emotion into experience and physiology is to attempt to get rid of the widespread assumption that mental experiences initiate physiological changes. Leaning on the work of Axelrod,[26] Weiner argues that it has been empirically demonstrated that a stimulus input into receptors (for example, light hitting the optic nerve) travels along different neural pathways to produce the *experience* of light, and along other pathways to produce various physiological effects. According to Weiner, this contradicts the common notion that for example, it is the experience of light which regulates the release of melatonin. These processes are in fact independent of one another. The consequence of this insight for psychosomatic theory is that "one can no longer automatically assume that psychosocial events and external stimuli alter bodily function in health and disease by their initial impact on the mind."[27]However, again we have the problem that experience and mental life have only been discussed here in terms of neurological manifestations. One cannot use Weiner's argument in order to dismiss the notion that events have an "impact on the mind", unless one has shown that the mind can be definitively described in terms of neural functioning. If ex-

---

[26] Axelrod (1971).
[27] Weiner (1972) p. 375.

perience/emotion and the mental life partake of another dimension, as Weiner himself seems to believe, we cannot just get rid of them because the brain seems to have parallel neurological circuits for various cerebral functions. That which is efficacious about the mental life is its motivational power, its constitutive intentionality, its interpretative capacity. For Weiner's point to be relevant, it must be demonstrated that it is the brain which is responsible for these events. As Descartes designated the pineal gland as the mysterious place where mind and body interact, so has Weiner deferred the solution to the brain.[28] We have not answered the mind-body problem, we have simply put it somewhere.

What does Weiner suggest instead of the unsolvable dualistic characterization of mind-body interaction? He advocates the notion of *function* as a theoretical step forward. We must regard the organism as an integrated whole, although it consists of a number of communicating subsystems. The key to understanding the organism's integrated, patterned behavior is to see the human being as a network of information transfer. There is a continuous information exchange going on between cells, between cells and organs, between organs and the brain, and between "the brain and the environment."[29] The "information" which is exchanged between cells, organs and the brain can be understood in terms of peptides and chemical substances, but what about the information exchanged between the person (brain?) and his/her environment? Is this also to be understood in physiological terms? If it is indeed the brain which "exchanges" information with the environment, this process must be explicated further. Using the brain as an icon for the *person* is reminiscent of Daniel Dennett's[30] functionalism. Dennett claimed that the enigma of mind could be solved by the materialistic hypothesis of multi-

---

28 For example: (1992a) "The mechanisms by which stressful experiences such as bereavement, change, and challenge set off a chain of events leading to bodily disease are largely unknown. Implicit in all past and current theories of pathogenesis is the belief that the brain, which regulates every bodily process, mediates in an undisclosed manner the changes that lead to physiological disturbances in bodily systems..." (p. 136).
29 Weiner (1989), p. 630.
30 See Dennett (1991).

ple channels of specialist circuits in the brain. These circuits carry out various functions at various times. There is no one place where it all comes together. For Dennett, this "parallel pandemonium" in the brain is meant to replace the myth of the unified Cartesian Self/Observer/ Witness.

Weiner, like Dennett, seems to use the brain (a material organ) as interchangeable or synonymous with person or self. If this is so, it must be argued for. The problem with this position is to satisfactorily account for the non-material properties of personhood (will, intentions, experience) in terms of brain processes. Weiner has not argued for the symmetry between brain and person, nor has he subscribed outright to an "identity-theory" position. His argumentation for the concomitance thesis is based upon materialistic conceptualizations: for example, his conceptualization of <u>experience</u> is described in terms of specific neural pathways in the brain, and likewise he characterizes <u>emotions</u> in terms of neural responses exhibited in various parts of the brain. These characterizations may be neurologically correct, but it has not been shown that the physicalistic descriptions given can account for the meaning or signification of experiences and emotions. We may have a description of their "outer aspect," to use von Wright's terminology, but the essence of these phenomena, their "inner aspect," is left unaccounted for in Weiner's conceptualizations. Weiner has (like many theoreticians before him) subsumed mental life *as such* under the workings of brain processes, although this move has not been argued for. Since he maintains that the mind-body problem dissolves once we see the organism as a network of functional communicating subsystems, he must demonstrate that the description of neurological tracts and biological phenomena does in fact account for that which we recognize as "mental" phenomena. Is this possible?[31] Weiner claims that as soon as we have understood that the prin-

---

31 Nagel, T. (1994) has criticized functionalism on this point: "In addition to their functional role in the explanation of behavior and their concrete physiological basis, conscious mental states have characteristic of a third type, familiar to us all, namely, their subjective, experiential quality: how they are or how they appear or feel from the point of view of their subjects" (p. 64). On this subjective level, experience and

ciples of information exchange are *the same* on all levels, "The separation between the brain (and its mind) and the body falls away when the organism is seen in such a totally integrated system of information exchange and processing."[32] I would protest that no argument has been forwarded which demonstrates how meaning and signification can be satisfactorily subsumed under the same physicalistic mechanisms which regulate "information" exchange between cells, organs and the nervous system.

Weiner has pointed out that the mind-body problem is still implicit and unsolved, in both psychosomatic medicine and stress theory. His own ontological position on the mind-body issue is unclear. He seems to profess a form of parallelism (concomitance), while at the same time he often expresses himself as an identity theorist (the mind-brain). His overriding emphasis upon neurological and biological functioning places him in the monistic camp, yet he never claims outright that all that there *is* is material. In terms of his own contribution to the mind-body discussion, he has called into question linear causality between experience and physiology, and proposed temporal concomitance in order to understand the relationship between mental events and physiological occurrences, but we find no account of what mental events or experience are as such. He has introduced the notions of function and information exchange as an alternative to the dualistic prejudice that mind influences body. The concomitance idea comes from the experimental work performed on the phenomenon of transduction. Transduction is the process by which the brain translates information in the form of peptides, hormones and transmitter substances from one system to the other within the body. The basic problem for psychosomatic theory is, how do psychological signification and experience get transformed (transduced) into physiological changes which may lead to disease? The mind-body problem is

---

emotion are not analyzable in terms of physicalistic descriptions. One may of course deny the existence of the subjective, as eliminative materialists do, but this is to ignore one of the givens of human life, that we in fact do experience our mental life "from the inside".

32 Weiner (1989), p. 630.

obvious: How does the non-material get translated into material changes? Traditionally (ever since Freud), we are accustomed to thinking that the line of influence is linear causal, going from mental experiences to physiological changes. For example, we believe that fear and joy "cause" increased heart rate. This is the most familiar approach to the transduction of experience into physiology; it is the model used by both psychobiologists as well as psychosomatic medicine. According to Weiner, this is incorrect. Weiner presents 6 models of transduction[33] all of which are attempts to solve the basic problem of how experience is transduced into physiological changes.

Weiner cites a variety of experimental literature in the above discussion of transduction. The most relevant finding for our purposes, according to Weiner, is the discovery that animals in experimental situations respond to different aspects the experimental situation in separate ways. Baby rats separated from their mothers, for example, reacted to the absence of milk with cardiorespiratory changes, while behavioral changes (hyperactivity, increased self-grooming, increased defecation, rearing up on hind legs etc.) were due to the physical absence of the mother.[34] According to Weiner, because the "brain" can apparently abstract elements from a situation and respond to them separately, we need an analysis of behavior and physiology which would take into account the independent nature of their separate neural paths. My first objection is that we suddenly find here a plea for an atomistic analysis, in a theory which is ostensibly organistic and holistic in its approach. Secondly, the same comment can be made here as above, namely, that it is not the brain as a collection of nerve cells which responds and reacts to a situation, it is the whole person in interaction with the meaning of the situation. If the interactive theory "integrates" adaption, experience and physiology by letting the brain be ultimately responsible for everything that happens on all levels of existence, this is hardly an integration. There is something peculiar about an organistic, holistic theory whose primary task seems to

---

33 See Weiner (1977), pp. 624-638.
34 Hofer (1975).

be to first analytically separate that which functions naturally as a whole, and then integrate the same components again, primarily by couching everything (even the "difficult" parts like psychological, social factors, meaning-constitution) in neurological terms. I find it hard to see how this neurological excursion has helped us to solve the mind-body problem. Weiner ends his discussion of transduction by stating that the value of the transduction model is heuristic. We need to think differently about the mind-body problem. This is clear. However, focusing exclusively upon neurological processes, however fascinating, will not integrate what we need to integrate, namely, experience, signification and meaning-constitution with physiological processes. Weiner is correct in pointing out the impossibility of dualism, but on the wrong track if he believes that transduction is going to help us reformulate the psychosomatic field.

Weiner has not given any outright definition of psychosomatic pathology, to be distinguished from other forms of disease. However, his basic position seems to be in line with psychosomatic medicine. He rejects the idea of linear psychogenesis and he affirms multifactorial etiology. Diseases are the result of a variety of factors. Psychical and social factors, among others, play a role in the development of disease and ill health. He has made the general statement that disease and ill health arise as a result of a failure to adapt, which comes close to the concept of not-coping in stress theory. The distinction he makes between disease and ill health is that disease is identifiable by anatomic lesions or clear physiological occurrences, often with genetic or physiological preconditions, whilst ill health is characterized first and foremost by experiences of distress, anxiety and depression, accompanied by changes in basic biological functions such as sleep, body temperature, gastrointestinal motility, menstruation and respiratory rhythms. These latter conditions have been called "the functional disorders", and they have historically gone by many names, such as neurasthenia, hyperventilation syndrome, soldier's heart, spastic colitis, and more recently fibromyalgia. The mistake of biomedicine has been to look inside the body for structural changes in order to account for these conditions. The functional disorders lack clear anatomical lesions, though they are distinguished by psycho-biological disturbance of the organism. Weiner prefers to call these conditions "dynamic diseases" because they are the result of perturbations in dynamic rhythmic functioning. Discovering the mechanisms and causes of ill health and disease is no simple matter. Weiner himself presents a variety of ideas on the etiology issues, to which we now turn.

The etiological questions

Weiner is at home in both psychosomatic medicine and stress theory, as mentioned earlier. He states clearly that it is not an event *in itself* which is stressful, but the meaning an event has for the person in question. According to Weiner, we still have no detailed knowledge of how people successfully cope,[35] nor do we understand how failure to cope gives rise to physiological changes that can, in predisposed (genetically or psychologically) people lead to disease.[36] In fact, the "stress" factor is rather low in correlating to disease. More often than not one finds disrupted biological functions (sleep, respiration, temperature etc.) associated with stress. Stressful events on their own do not produce disease or ill health. The chain of events from stressful experiences, such as bereavement, to bodily disease is unknown. Weiner states that the relationship between stressful experience and disease onset is correlational and retrospective in nature. We do not know what the correlation means (is it causal or merely temporally concomitant?), nor do we acquire any genuine explanatory power with historical-reconstructive theories[37] (cf. Lazarus,

---

[35] "But the fact remains that we still have no detailed knowledge about how most people cope successfully with migration, unemployment, bereavement, marriage, divorce, illness and disease." Weiner (1992a), p. 44.

[36] "It is not known how acute or chronic stressful experiences and the distress they generate, or the failure to cope with them, directly contribute to the onset of one disease or illness. Despite decades of research in autonomic psychophysiology, psychoneuroendocrinology, and now psychoneuroimmunology (Ader 1981), progress in answering this question has been slow" (Ibid. p. 138).

[37] "The physician is predominantly concerned with the relationship of stressful experience to disease onset; if no disease ensues, the experience cannot have been stressful!" Ibid., p. 28.

Ontological Questions, chapter 4). Because Weiner is interested in ill health as a person-environment interaction, he is interested in the experience of stress. At the same time, he perceives the organism as an integrated whole, and he actually seems to be much more interested in biological functioning, especially the disturbances of basic dynamic rhythmic functions. Weiner has two parallel lines of thought on etiology: on the one hand person-environment interaction (which he pays very little attention to), and on the other dynamic biological rhythms. If his integrative theory is to succeed, he must show how these levels of the organism are indeed integrated.

There are a variety of factors which are involved in the development of disease and ill health, such as genetic factors, psychological traits, habits, behavior, social customs, distress, instability, discontentment, coping ability, dynamic biological patterns. As stated earlier, because diseases are in fact heterogeneous, it is possible that some factors are more relevant than others for particular subsets of the same disease.[38] Although we can list all these factors, and even in some cases predict what diseases a person is *predisposed to*, these factors in themselves do not tell us if and when this particular person will fall ill, nor which mechanisms are working in order to produce disease/illness. The difficulty involved with multifactorial theories, according to Weiner, is that we are still trying to model our understanding upon traditional, linear causal thinking. Besides the problem of the heterogeneity of diseases, Weiner has pointed out that the correlations between experience and physiology are most probably concomitant rather than causal. Thus it will be an exercise in futility to try to forge causal links between invariant constellations of factors and disease. If I understand Weiner correctly, we need to study adaption/maladaption in order to gain insight into the processes which mediate between experience and the body, much in the same way that stress theory needs to gain insight into coping/lack of coping in order to understand the disease/illness mechanisms. There is something about

---

[38] Some patients with peptic duodenal ulcers have elevated levels of serum pepsinogen I (about 50%), some have normal levels. Some people may have these elevated levels without an ulcer.

stability and coping/adaption which protects us from disease/illness, and there is something about distress which makes us ill and/or susceptible to disease.

Weiner does not write very much specifically about psycho-social aspects of adaption. He spends much more time on biological issues. However, one of the person-environment interactions he does take up is the phenomenon of bereavement. Bereavement is pathogenic because of its tendency to disrupt adaption. It gives rise to distress, to helplessness/hopelessness[39], to disturbed biological rhythms (*how* it does this is, of course, the mind-body problem again, sneaking around in disguise). As stress theory has taught us, it is not bereavement in itself which is pathogenic, but bereavement which is not coped with. People have a variety of ways in which they may react to separation and loss. The usual response is grief, although one may develop pathological mourning, chronic anger, depression, psychosis, or even physical breakdown. The specific disease a bereaved person may develop depends upon a variety of multiple predisposing factors. However, as has been stated so many times within the stress tradition, the relationship between experience (e.g. of bereavement), physiological changes, and somatic disease is not known.[40] One study has shown that 70 to 80% of disease onset occurs when persons have "given up,"[41] that is, when they can no longer feel engaged in their life, their work, hobbies, relationships and so on. Their sense of continuity is disrupted, they feel out of time and out of place. It seems to me that pursuing this line of inquiry would be much more promising with regard to understanding the person-environment aspects of pathogenic processes than, for example, measuring levels of 17-

---

[39] See Engel & Schmale, chapter 2.

[40] "But we do not know how the physiological changes accompanying bereavement interact with predisposing factors. Nor do we know whether the relationship between the physiological, behavioral and psychological changes is a causal one." Weiner, (1977), p. 617. And again, 15 years later, "The mechanisms by which stressful experiences such as bereavement, change, and challenge set off a chain of events leading to bodily disease are largely unknown." Weiner (1992a), p. 136.

[41] Engel (1968).

hydroxycorticosteroid levels in patients during grieving.[42]It is often the case in the literature that the meaning of a phenomenon (for example, bereavement), the way in which it is lived, what changes it brings about in the person-environment interaction and so on, are neglected in favor of correlating physiological changes with lived situations. Weiner's work on concomitance can be seen as an internal critique of this type of correlation research. We cannot say that physiological occurrences have any causal relationship to experience, and for that reason all efforts to link experiences with physiological changes are of questionable value.

There is a further psychosocial aspect which Weiner discusses in his work, namely that of social stability. Empirical studies have shown that there is something about solid social traditions and customs in a community which protect one against disease/ill health. A well-known study by Bruhn et al[43]examined the inhabitants of two towns in Pennsylvania, and found that the death rate from myocardial infarction per thousand per year (between 1955 and 1961) was significantly lower in Roseto than in Bangor. Roseto was an Italian-American community, whose inhabitants had maintained traditional religious and secular habits. Despite the fact that these inhabitants ate high fat diets and were on average 20 pounds overweight compared to the general population, they had significantly lower mortality from heart disease than the neighboring community Bangor (a normal "mixed" community). In a follow up study, it was found that those second-generation American Italians who moved from Roseto had a mortality rate in myocardial infarction which was the same as that of other Americans. What is it about stability that protects from disease? Weiner would reply that a stable environment with a minimum of adaptive tasks imposes fewer demands upon its inhabitants, giving rise to less "stress". However, as seen in chapter 4, the stress concept is by no means crystal-clear, nor is its relation to ill health and disease established.

---

42 Wolff et al. (1964).
43 Bruhn et al. (1966)

Weiner's definition of stress is organistic, that is, stressful experiences arise inevitably from our physical and social environment, they threaten and challenge us to respond, and we respond to these challenges by integrated behavioral and physiological patterns. Weiner's contribution to stress theory is his conceptualization of stress in terms of perturbations of the organism. These perturbations are disruptions in rhythms. To see disease and ill health as the result of disturbances in the organism's social, psychological and biological rhythms is an interesting idea. Unfortunately, as far as I have seen, Weiner limits his discussion to perturbations of *biological* rhythms. Examining, for example, the phenomena of bereavement and social stability in terms of lived rhythms (psychological, social, temporal) would have done justice to an integrative theory. In fact, this is the type of analysis which Merleau-Ponty outlines in his *Structure of Behavior*.[44] For now, let us see what Weiner does with "disturbed rhythms" in his texts.

The organism is a network of interacting subsystems. The network is dynamic, since it is in an ever-changing interaction with its environment. Communication between systems (neurons, hormones, blood pressure, respiratory rate, muscle tension etc.) can be normal (patterned to a preferred rhythmic oscillation) or perturbed/disturbed, in which case new rhythmic patterns may emerge, which change the function[45] and perhaps even alter the structure of the performing subsystem. Altered rhythms (or "bifurcations" in mathematical language) arise as the result of chaotic or disturbed communication in the network. Communication transpires between cells in the subsystem, as well as between various subsystems. Altered (or failed) communication creates new rhythmic patterns, patterns which may give rise to symptoms of ill health, or even ultimately to disease. All subsystems have a preferred pattern of functioning, which is

---

44 Merleau-Ponty (1942/1963)
45 Changes in function include 1) new periodicities in ongoing rhythmic processes; 2) the disappearance of a certain rhythmic process (e.g. apnea); 3) regularities in oscillations not usually connected to a system (e.g. hiccups, muscle fibrillations). According to Weiner, most functional disorders are characterized by transitions to new periodic rhythms.

dynamic yet stable within certain parameters (amplitude, phase, frequency, wave form etc.). Perturbing the organism is one antecedent of altered rhythmic patterns. On this view, illness and disease can be seen in terms of disorders in communication networks, characterized by perturbations in dynamic rhythm patterns. Altered rhythmic changes may occur with or without structural changes in the body. Dealing with perturbations successfully is adaption, not dealing with them is to succumb to ill health, and perhaps even disease. However, the consequences of perturbation and disturbed biological rhythms are unpredictable and individual, in the same way as we have seen that particular individuals react differently to "stress" (chapter 4). And in the same manner that Selye's stress theory was challenged by the "first link" question, we may ask Weiner the troublesome question, "What perturbs the organism?" What is it about a situation (Weiner would say "stimulus") which leads to altered rhythmic functioning? The mind-body problem has not gone away, it has simply been covered up.

Weiner's ideas on perturbed biological rhythms can be seen as a variation of the psychosomatic theory of psychosomatic medicine (with its feed-back loops) and stress theory (stress leads to physiological changes).[46] That which was to be an improvement on psychosomatic medicine and stress theory, the "integrative theory", aimed to show how experience, adaption, brain, behavior and physiology could be explicated in a holistic theory of the entire psychosocial biological person. This project has not been properly worked out. The "person" in the final analysis is the brain,[47] and that which we have been offered instead of

---

[46] "To repeat, the interrelationship of the subsystems is brought about by a large variety of communication signals emitted in regular, or irregular, rhythmic manner and arranged in a series of feedback loops...Stressful experience perturbs these rhythms... and may result in illness and disease." Weiner, (1992a) p. 249.

[47] "The organism is also embedded into a larger system of information exchange from which it receives, and into which it emits, coded signals of many different kinds. The received signals are...transduced and digitized by receptors at the surface of the body. The brain, like other subsystems, processes the signal in parallel: it is capable of responding both selectively to one aspect of, or in toto to the signal depending on the

mind-body dualism is a physicalistic explication of information communication between subsystems. It has not been demonstrated that the kind of information exchanged between cells and organs is *the same* as those processes in which the person experiences and adapts to his/her situation. That biological rhythms can become chaotic, and that disturbed rhythms may lead to ill health in terms of sleep disturbances, hyperventilation, etc. is interesting, but it does not help us with the mind-body problem or give any mechanisms which allow us to understand the interaction between "perturbation"/stress and physiology. As in stress theory, we need to better understand what it is that "perturbs the organism", and how these perturbations (or "stressors") are lived. Many of the studies Weiner mentions point to meaning-constitution (cf. bereavement, Italian-American life-style etc.), but he has not focused on this aspect. He himself comments that a large body of evidence suggests that the *experience* of adverse situations, social isolation, unemployment, bereavement etc. is correlated with excess morbidity and mortality;[48] however, the investigation of *experience* is not undertaken by Weiner.

As a concluding remark on Weiner's etiological contributions, a word must be said about causation. One of Weiner's main points is that mental events such as thoughts and emotions do not *cause* physiological occurrences. They may do so, in some cases, but this is an hypothesis which needs to be proven. Weiner himself suspects that concomitance is the most common relationship between mental and physical occurrences. If this is so, it is hard to see how Wiener's own professed stress theory understanding of ill health and disease can be comprehensible within his own theory. His critique of the relationship between mental events and physical ones must deal a hard blow to his own theorizing about stress. He says that ill health always concerns the *meaning* of the event for the person in the person-environment transaction (as any good stress theorist will say), and yet this meaning is not considered by him as having any necessary connection to physiological processes. A related

context in which it occurs..." Weiner (1989), p. 608. It is not the brain which selects aspects of the situation, it is the person.
48   Weiner (1992a), pp. 120-121.

comment on causation is that although Weiner rejects the notion of causation in favor of concomitance for understanding the relations between the mental and the physical, he constantly uses causal terms in his descriptions of events and processes.[49] It is hard to pin down exactly where Weiner stands on causality. He seems to glide between concomitance (no causal connection) and contrafactual everyday language causality and a natural scientific Hempel/Oppenheim "covering law" model.

The cure

Weiner has not concerned himself with a detailed theoretical account of health in his writings. Health is the state of the person which is the opposite of ill health. If ill health is the result of maladaption (failure to cope) and disturbed biological rhythms, health is adaption and patterned rhythmic biological functioning. A healthy person is one who can respond to the challenges of life without too much anxiety and discomfort. Routine seems to be a salutogenic factor, as novelty and ambiguity tend to elicit a variety of potentially stressful psychological and physiological reactions. In accordance with this concept of health, treatment will be designed in order to improve or correct the adaptive failure, a procedure which is reminiscent of the stress management programs discussed in chapter 4. Weiner states that successful coping "is more likely when the person possesses personal qualities such as intelligence, problem-solving ability, past experience in mastering the event and having information about it...the capacity to use information, support or advice from others, self-reliance and self-confidence, realism and hopefulness in the face of

---

[49] For example, from the 1972 article on transduction we find a variety of causal terms; "...we know that stressful experiences *give rise* to an *organized pattern* of physiologic change, which includes hormonal and autonomically mediated changes" (p. 356 first italics mine); "Or, stated more precisely, in the course of the transduction of early experience, permanent changes in brain functioning *are produced* which modify later responses to psychological experience" (p. 361 my italics); and finally, "Thus one can conclude from these findings that earlier experiences *determine* later responses to stress..." (p. 364 my italics). These relations are stronger than concomitance, yet nowhere does Weiner give an account of his usage of these kinds of terms.

challenge, and the fortitude to face it if the odds are not overwhelming."[50]

Like his fellow stress theoreticians, Weiner makes the connection between failure to adapt to various life situations and the development of disease. Adaption/coping protects us against breakdown, but what it *is* about coping that is salutogenic is still elusive. Because Weiner has rejected the hypothesis that emotions lead to physiological changes via their mental content, he has little to back up a more traditional stress theory explication of cure (cf. Lazarus chapter 4). In the beginning of this chapter, it seemed as if Weiner was going to show us how the entire organism responded as an integrated being in adapting/non adapting to various situations. We have had high hopes concerning Weiner, and although he has enriched the literature with his distinction between "ill health" and "disease", and has made some interesting and provocative statements about the mind-body issue, he has not addressed the nature of experience, mind and meaning-constitution in his theory, nor has he given us a fully explicated account of the nature of "adaption." He himself has stated that the psychosomatic approach rests upon the study of the person, in his/her human, social and cultural environment,[51] yet he has hardly addressed this dimension of existence at all in his integrative theory. Despite his characterization of ill health as a person-environment interaction, he has remained mute on these issues. It is perhaps for this reason he must admit that: "How to best care for patients in ill health remains unresolved. The solution on the problem is obscured by our traditional and outdated theories and models in medicine and of the nature of symptoms, our value judgments about patients, and our lack of humanity."[52]Unfortunately, the integrative theory has not made us any wiser regarding the holistic understanding of the human being in his her world. We will in fact have to leave traditional medical and psychological theories in order to come further in our attempts to build a truly holistic psychosomatic theory.

---

50 Weiner & Fawzy (1989), p. 29.
51 Weiner (1977), p. xii.
52 Weiner (1987), p. 157.

Summary of Herbert Weiner's integrative theory

The aim of Weiner's theory is to integrate experience, behavior, brain/nervous system and physiological occurrences into an organistic functional whole. He has criticized stress theory and psychosomatic medicine for their dualistic stance as well as for their conceptualization of a linear causation from experience/emotion to physiological activity. According to Weiner, concomitance would be a better way to describe the relationship between experience and bodily functioning, although he himself uses a variety of causal terms in his own descriptions of , for example, the phenomenon of transduction. Weiner distinguishes ill health from disease, and says that we should understand ill health as a disturbance in the person-environment interaction. He actually espouses two concurrent theories of health and ill health/disease in his texts. On the one hand, we find a classical stress-theory understanding of health and ill health, where health is maintained when one can successfully adapt to (cope with) adverse situations. Here, the person-environment interaction is in focus, and he emphasizes the meaning of the situation for the person in question. On the other hand, his most detailed theory about the nature of ill health is biological, conceptualizing ill health as perturbed biological rhythms. He spends little time discussing the nature of experience, mind and meaning-constituting, devoting most of his work to discussions of parallel neurological functioning in the brain. The brain "mediates" between meaning/experience and physiology, although his conceptualization of mind and meaning is not clear. At times, he expresses himself as a parallelist (mind exists, and is not the same thing as the brain) while at other times he uses identity-theory conceptualizations such as "the mind-brain." The brain is often used as an icon for the person, and this is hard to reconcile with his initial stress theory idea of health/ill health as a *person*-environment transaction. He has made the interesting point that diseases are heterogeneous in nature, which challenges our traditional thinking about *the* etiology of, for example, ulcers or diabetes. Some instances of a disease will be due to psychological factors, others to biological factors. Some factors are of importance for the initiation of the disease, others for the maintenence of the disease and so on.

Concerning etiology, Weiner follows psychosomatic medicine in advocating a multi-factorial theory. There are a variety of factors involved in the development of disease and ill health, factors such as genetic make-up, psychological traits, habits, coping abilities, social network, and dynamic biological patterns. Despite the fact that many of these factors come from the psycho-social realm, Weiner does not discuss how they contribute to the development of disease and ill health. His starting point for etiological discussions is the biological organism, and he concentrates on the image of the organism as a functional, dynamic network of interacting subsystems. When information between these subsystems is disturbed, altered rhythms give rise to disturbed sleep, altered menstruation and so on. However, just *what it is* that disturbs the organism is the mind-body question all over again, and Weiner has not addressed this issue. He assumes that the information which is exchanged between nerve cells and muscle cells is the same as the information exchanged between "the brain" and the environment. In general, he does not problematize or discuss mind and meaning but speaks of this kind of "information" in neurological terms. An internal critique of Weiner's theory is that his criticism of research which attempts to find correlations between experience/emotion and physiology must render his own (first) stress-theory understanding of ill health as a person-environment interaction unintelligible. The other psychosomatic theory found in his later work is the idea that illness and disease arise because of perturbed biological rhythms and disturbances in communicating network interactions. However, this theory does not succeed in integrating mind, behavior and physiology, as the terms used and the processes described begin and end at the level of physicalistic description. It is now time to turn to an alternative to the traditional psychosomatic theories discussed in this dissertation. This alternative will be based upon phenomenology rather than psychological/medical theories.

PART II

A Phenomenological Theory
of Psychosomatics

CHAPTER 6

A phenomenological approach to psycho-somatic pathology: An introduction

"Cheshire Puss," she began, rather timidly, as she did not at all know whether it would like the name: however, it only grinned a little wider. "Come, it's pleased so far," thought Alice, and she went on. "Would you tell me, please, which way I ought to go from here?" "That depends a good deal on where you want to get to," said the Cat. "I don't much care where--" said Alice. "Then it doesn't matter which way you go," said the Cat. "--so long as I get somewhere," Alice added as an explanation. "Oh, you're sure to do that," said the Cat, "if you only walk long enough."

--*Alice in Wonderland*
Lewis Carroll

The first part of this dissertation has shown that traditional theories of psychosomatic pathology have missed the mark. Proponents have not done what they claimed they would do, namely to take into account the biological, psychological and social nature of man, and from that holistic ground build a theory which would illuminate the etiology and cure of psychosomatic pathology. This ground should do justice to the complexity of man's existence and provide a way to understand the relationship between various levels of human life. The credo of psychosomatic medicine was clearly to "study in their interrelation the psychological and physiological aspects of all normal and abnormal bodily functions and thus to integrate somatic therapy and psychotherapy."[1] Theorists from psychosomatic medicine themselves agree that this has not been accomplished. The two neuroimmunologists Booth & Ashbridge pre-

---

1 Introductory Statement, *Psychosom Med* 1:3.

sented in chapter 4 have pointed out that there can be no true *psycho*neuroimmunology until one has taken into account the psychological level of existence (meaning as intentional and subjective), which their colleagues seldom do. Weiner (chapter 5) called his approach an "integrative theory" yet ultimately failed to integrate meaning and physiology, opting instead for a form of functionalism which results in materialistic reductionism, clothing psycho-social reality in neurological terms. Freudians still grapple with the "mysterious leap" from mind to body. All of these theories have, in one way or another, tried to formulate a holistic approach to theorizing about psychosomatic pathology, an approach which would be a necessary compliment to the mechanistic, biomedical model of disease and illness.

As the previous chapters have indicated, there are problems with these theories on various levels. Their ontological stand on the mind/body issue is either dualistic (leading to the inevitable dead end pointed out by Weiner), or reductionistic/materialistic, which eliminates the psychical as such, leaving us with a psycho-somatic model which is essentially no different from biomedicine. In the first case, dualistic theories retain a problematic mind-body conceptualization which postulates an objective, impersonal, mechanical (medical) body in some form of "relationship" to a personal, psychological sphere of meaning. There are no comprehensible interactive mechanisms to be found in these dualistic theories by which we could come to understand the relationship between meaning and physiology, except at the very general level of psychophysical causation, whereby physiological arousal or overload (emotions, cathexis) seems to disturb homeostatic functioning.[2] In the case of materialistic reductionism, we have no truly *psycho*somatic theory, taking psychical reality seriously.

---

[2] As I have pointed out in chapter 4, even this very general hypothesis has been called into question by stress theoreticians themselves. Not all stress is pathogenic, and there is certainly no one-to-one causal correspondence between heightened physiological arousal and disease and ill health. It is the *meaning* of the situation which is important, not the mechanical stimulation per se.

It is argued in part I of the dissertation that we need to reformulate the psychosomatic field (mind/body/world) in order to provide a genuinely holistic theory of psychosomatics, a theory which will be able to illuminate the various levels of existence which the biomedical model does not address. This ground will be provided by phenomenology, the science of phenomena (the world as it appears to man), and in particular the phenomenology of Maurice Merleau-Ponty. Using Merleau-Ponty's thinking as a source of inspiration, I will present a plausible mind/body/world position and upon that ground work out an analysis of the psychosomatic mode of being-in-the-world. I will not concern myself with the same types of questions with which the four traditional theories have been confronted, since the perspective I am taking does not begin with dualistic interaction problems or eliminative reductionistic conceptualizations of meaning. Within the phenomenological frame of reference, we may retain mind as mind (but in a new way) and investigate an expressive, communicative, understanding body. A phenomenological theory will help us to understand some of the things which have been difficult to grasp from within the traditional theories, such as: Why is it curative to express oneself? How is the body "used" to maintain equilibrium, what does this process look like, what does it entail? What form of self-understanding is operating when a physical expression replaces a verbal utterance? What is coping/adaption seen from a phenomenological point of view? If we begin with the lived body, alternative ways of thinking are opened up which allow the psychosomatic field to emerge in a new way.

The phenomenological project

"Phenomenology" means, literally, the study of that which shows itself. The philosopher Edmund Husserl (1859-1938) is considered to be the founding father of phenomenology. His writings inspired the first wave of phenomenological thinking (the German phase) up until World War II. The term "phenomenology" had been used before,[3] but it was

---

3 The first documented philosophical use of the term is found 1764 in Johann Heinrich Lambert's *Neues Organon oder Gedanken über die Erforschung und Bezeichnung*

Husserl who gave phenomenology its special meaning as the "first philosophy", the philosophy which would provide a rigorous science of consciousness and experience. Transcendental phenomenology would be the science of the source of all knowledge. Phenomenology is specifically interested in the study of subjectivity. To investigate how man experiences and constitutes the world *as* a world is the phenomenological task. Husserl was absolutely clear about his field of inquiry. He had no quarrel with the natural sciences, but he would make no use of them in his project. The basic methodological question for Husserl was how to study subjectivity. It was clear that the methodology which had been so successfully developed by the natural sciences could not be used, since their object was nature, or the "objective" world. Phenomenology does not concern itself with the objective world as such, but rather, with how the world "appears" to us as a world; its focus of study is the world as *meant* or *intended*. The aim of phenomenology is to discern and describe the world and consciousness in their specific modes of appearance. Some examples of phenomenological questions are: How is it that I experience objects as if they were independent of me? What is it about their way of appearing which leads me to experience them as independent of my own intending acts of consciousness? Or, How is it possible that one can perceive an entire object when only one side or perspective of the object is sensuously given at one time? One never *sees* an entire table, from all sides and possible perspectives, yet we all experience that we have in fact seen an entire object. One cannot answer these kinds of questions by referring to the independent reality character of objects, for example the answer to the question "How is it possible that I experience an entire

---

des Wahren und der Unterscheidung von Irrtum und Schein. Kant also used the term "phenomenology" scientifically in 1786 when referring to the last of his four sciences of matter (dealing with appearances) as well as philosophically, in preparing his *Critique of Pure Reason.* But phenomenology for Lambert was the study of illusion, while for Kant phenomenology became a critique of human knowledge. Hegel wrote *Phenomenology of the Spirit* in 1807, tracing out how Spirit gains consciousness of itself in various concrete, historical stages. None of these usages approximates what came to be the specific Husserlian phenomenology, that is, the science of consciousness. See Spiegelberg (1982) for an account of the history of the phenomenological movement.

object?" cannot be "Because it *is* really there as a whole." This answer does not address the level of experience, and therefore cannot help us to illuminate the phenomenological field of interest. There is something about the interplay between consciousness and the object which accounts for what we want investigate. To study this realm is the phenomenological project.

It was Husserl's insight that in order to be able to approach this very special area of inquiry, we must systematically put aside all our everyday ideas and convictions about the world. We must suspend our belief in the real "objective" world. Husserl called this ordinary, everyday attitude which naturally believes in the reality character of the world, this un-problematized credo of the existence of the world,[4] "the natural attitude." It is natural because consciousness has this tendency to leap into its object and disregard its own contribution to experience. To investigate subjectivity and phenomena, we must put the thesis of the world within brackets, in order to put it out of play. This putting into brackets, or suspension, of the "real world" is the implementation of the so-called phenomenological reduction.[5] It is important to understand that phe-

---

4 Also called the "thetic/positional/existential/ontic reality character of perception". It is the positing of realness, which Ricoeur has poetically called "the vehemence of presence."

5 The phenomenological reduction could be a dissertation topic in itself. It is one of the cornerstones of Husserlian phenomenology, and Husserl himself maintained that it was indispensable for understanding phenomenology. The reduction is also called "bracketing", or up until the 1920's "epoché." Basically, the reduction entails performing a series of steps in order to free oneself from the natural attitude, thereby making possible phenomenological reflection. The reduction entails different moves, or steps, which pertain to different aims. The point of the *eidetic* reduction is to free reflection from contingencies (*this* particular cup) and to move to the essential (cup-*ness*). The aim of the other reductions is not to look for essentials, but rather focus on the presentation of the givenness. One pays attention to that which is absolutely, indubitably given in and through consciousness, in its specific modes of appearance. The different phenomenological reductions have to do with the different levels of analysis involved. The transcendental phenomenological reduction aims at laying bare the absolute, pure constituting consciousness. This level of analysis examines the pure streaming of consciousness, that primordial level of consciousness which makes the perception of objects at all possible. The psychological phenomenological reduc-

nomenology does not deny the existence of the world. The natural sciences do a fine job of investigating and describing the objective transcendent world. Phenomenology does not deny the world, it is simply interested in another realm, namely, the subjective. For this reason it is necessary to understand what the bias of the natural attitude is, and be able to suspend or disregard it, in order to investigate subjectivity. If we cannot perform this move, we will never reach the realm of the subjective. It should be pointed out that the objective world is not lost: phenomenology does investigate the world, but it will be the world *as it appears* which is examined. The objective world is in this way subsumed under the umbrella of subjectivity. If one has not been able to make this basic shift in perspective, one will not understand what phenomenology is all about.

How can we systematically, scientifically study subjectivity? Where shall we start? In good Cartesian fashion, Husserl grounded his project in the certitude of immediate experience. Descartes said "*Cogito ergo sum*" (I think, therefore I am). Husserl's Cartesianism could be expressed in the following way: "I am, just now, conscious of (something in) the world, in just this particular way, and the way in which I, just at this moment, experience this world is given to me with an absolute certitude." The world is intuitively and immediately present to us, we have access to our own experiences in this intuitive, immediate way. One may, of course, have been mistaken about some aspect of one's experience, for example one may have mistaken a paper clip on the sidewalk for a coin. However, during the experience itself there is no doubt about what one experiences. I may even be uncertain if it is a paper clip or a

---

tion, which Husserl later distinguished from the full-fledged transcendental reduction, examines the empirical, psychological ego or consciousness. The difference between these two reductions has to do with the radicality of the bracketing. If one brackets the empirical ego (thus implementing the transcendental reduction), one finds pure constituting consciousness. If one does not bracket the situated, empirical ego (implementing the psychological reduction), one examines the psychological realm of signification. The aim of both of the reductions is to allow for the discovery (intuiting) of essences. See Ballard (1972); Bernet (1991); Kockelmans (1972) on the different phenomenological reductions.

coin, but my experience of uncertainty is, in any case, certain. As Descartes pointed out, when I am in doubt, at least I know that I am doubting. In this certitude of consciousness' own immediate and absolute experience of itself as it is directed towards the world, Husserl reconfirmed Brentano's[6] insight that consciousness is always consciousness *of* something. The technical term used to designate this essential directedness of consciousness is called "intentionality." The phenomenological project is thus the rigorous study of the way in which objects ("objects" understood in a broad sense, including not only physical objects but also imaginary objects, cultural objects etc.) show themselves *in and through consciousness*. There are some differences between Brentano's notion of intentionality and Husserl's, mainly having to do with the status of the object intended. However, for our purposes the important point here is the discovery that consciousness is both immediately self-present and always directed towards its object. For Husserl, "intending" has to do with the capacity of consciousness to <u>constitute</u> the given in such a way that an object is apprehended, to <u>connect</u> various stages of apprehension into a whole, to <u>synthesize</u> the identity of the self-same object unfolding through time.[7] The apprehension of an object is an *achievement* of consciousness, not a passive imprinting from without. Consciousness intends its objects, from a Cartesian center of self-presence. This is Husserl's Archimedean point, it is the given, and from here Husserl begins his phenomenological investigations.[8]

When we perform the phenomenological reduction and set aside all our ordinary prejudices and ideas about how the world is, we must also

---

6 Franz Brentano (1838-1917) was one of the forerunners of the phenomenological movement. His aim was to create a descriptive psychology which would emancipate psychology from the natural sciences.

7 In Spiegelberg (1982), p. 99 .

8 Derrida (1967/1973) questions this "givenness" in his critique of Western philosophy (the metaphysics of presence). He exemplifies Husserl's phenomenological project as the culmination of this philosophical tradition, with the "here and now" serving as the incontestable ground for philosophy. Derrida's project is to deconstruct this certitude and thus question the base of all our philosophical efforts since the ancient Greeks.

suspend all theories we have about the nature of things. In phenomenology, one does not use pre-conceived theories in order to explain that which shows itself.[9] We must place ourselves in a state of radical presuppositionlessness and attempt to describe what we find when we bracket all our ideas and attitudes about the world. The proper phenomenological attitude is to be meticulous and open-minded, as free as possible from natural attitude presuppositions. The phenomenological task is one of suspension, reflection, and intuiting,[10] using no notions or ideas which do not spring from the experience itself. To begin from scratch[11] in this way is very difficult, problematic, and goes against much of our ordinary way of thinking, as we are so accustomed to the natural scientific interpretation of the world. Phenomenology breaks new ground, and therefore needs fresh terms and descriptions which do not, by association, pull us back into the natural attitude, which is where consciousness has its natural home. Husserl discovered that when we perform the reduction and examine the given as it is found in and through conscious experience, we can delimit two poles of experience, each of which can be

---

9   Husserl (1954/1970) has argued that natural scientific theories (and any other type of theory constructed from within the natural attitude) are themselves abstractions from lived experience, and in no way prior to or causally responsible for the life-world (*Lebenswelt*). Thus, it is meaningless to use theories which have been constructed and abstracted *from* lived experience in order to *explain* lived experience. This does not mean that we may not construct phenomenological theories about the nature of lived experience, it just means that such theories must be based upon rigorous reflection under the reduction, using terms, descriptions and concepts which are as free as possible from the prejudices of the natural attitude.

10   Husserl's "intuition" has nothing to do with mystical or inexplicable knowledge. *Anschauung*, the German term, can be translated as "looking at" but there is no exact English equivalent. Intuiting is that certitude with which we can all agree that color is extended in space, to give Husserl's famous example in *Ideas I* (1913/1962). (The insight that color is extended is actually an example of a particular case of intuiting, the intuiting of <u>essences</u> (*Wesensschau*), which Husserl claimed was specific to phenomenology.)

11   The Husserlian notion of presuppositionlessness is controversial, debated both within and outside of phenomenology. A common misunderstanding is that presuppositionlessness entails some point at which we no longer have access to language, logic or ideas. What Husserl meant by "presuppositionlessness" was that no *un-examined* notions and ideas should influence and color the description of phenomena.

analytically examined separately, although the one presupposes the other. These two poles correspond to the dichotomy which was the subject/object division before the reduction, namely the pole of subjectivity, which we now under the reduction understand as *noesis* (the flow of conscious acts), and *noema* which is the object as it is meant or intended by consciousness. Noesis and noema are called the "phenomenological residue" which remains after the reduction. To reiterate, after the phenomenological reduction we find: 1) the real transcendent object in suspension, or "bracketed". This object under the reduction is called the noema, which is not a real object, but an ideal one[12]; 2) the acts of consciousness, usually hidden from view, which posit and, according to Husserl, "constitute" the object. The acts of consciousness are the incessant "streaming towards the world."[13]

According to Husserl, the analysis of the noetic (consciousness) side of experience reveals two different egos. The transcendental ego which is the source of all experience, and the concrete, empirical ego, which is always inserted into the world. The sentence, "I am aware of myself writing at my desk" reveals the transcendental ego as the first "I", that is, the condition for the possibility of any experience at all (I am aware...), while the empirical, psychological, situated ego is the one which sits and types on the computer right at this moment. Merleau-Ponty rejects the idea of the existence of a transcendental ego as a remnant of idealism. He contests the notion of an "I" which would be pure consciousness, and maintains that the "I" is always an embodied ego, always already inserted into

---

12 The real tree may burn up, but the noema "tree" is indestructible. It is capable of endless repetitions, it can be translated into various languages etc.

13 Whereas Husserl could imagine a streaming of consciousness without a world (as an organized, noematic system), Merleau-Ponty (as well as other phenomenologists) rejects this as a remnant of Husserl's idealism. The controversial passage in Husserl concerning this priority of the noetic (consciousness) over the contingency of the noematic is found in *Ideas I* (1913/1962, paragraph 49, pp. 136-139). Husserl argues here that even if the entire noematic system should explode upon deeper investigation into illusion or disintegration, we would still have the streaming of consciousness. To nullify the world is not to nullify consciousness. As we shall see, Merleau-Ponty does not accept such a position.

the world. There is no positing consciousness outside of this being-in-the-world.[14] This leads to a very interesting phenomenological position, namely, that the empirical, psychological, concrete embodied "I" is both constituting (noetic) and constituted (noematic). This is a radical and unusual notion, because it gives the body a status as both subject and object. For Husserl, the body belonged to the noematic side, an object constituted by consciousness. This is not the case according to Merleau-Ponty. The body is neither subject nor object, in the traditional sense. This is why the body is so fundamentally ambiguous. For Merleau-Ponty, our phenomenological investigation begins not with pure constituting consciousness, but with a lived body caught up in a world of meaning and signification. Let us now turn to Merleau-Ponty's phenomenological project, which will provide us with our starting point for a phenomenological theory of psychosomatics.

Merleau-Ponty's phenomenology

Merleau-Ponty belongs to the French phenomenological tradition which has been called the second phenomenological wave[15] after the first German phase initiated by Husserl. French phenomenologists have sometimes been called existential phenomenologists, since they have taken up issues such as the significance of the body, the social, political, aesthetic and religious spheres of man's experience. Existential phenomenologists are deeply engaged in man's concrete existence, rather than investigating,

---

14 The term "being-in-the-world" is a translation of Merleau-Ponty's "*être-au-monde,*" which in French carries the connotation of being *towards* the world, rather than *in* (*dans)* the world. "Towards" conveys the directedness of man better than "in", which easily gives rise to misleading spatial associations. As Merleau-Ponty has shown, we are hardly "in" the world the way that things are in the world. We are rather "hollows" or "nodes in being", places where a world may emerge. Both Heidegger and Marcel have used the term "being-in-the-world" but the specific Merleau-Pontian usage of the term indicates being immersed in the world, engaged in the world, bound up with the world. Because the term "being-in-the-world" is the least clumsy and most well-known formulation in English, I will use it to refer to *être-au-monde,* having made these qualifying remarks.
15 See Speigelberg (1982).

for example, the abstract conditions for the possibility of a world given to consciousness. Merleau-Ponty has been called "the philosopher of the body" due to his interest in the body and his thesis of the primacy of perception. He has also been called "the philosopher of ambiguity", a title not necessarily so pejorative as it sounds.[16]His point of departure is the embodied subject, having replaced Cartesian idealism with being-in-the-world. It may be helpful to introduce Merleau-Ponty by briefly showing in what ways he deviates from Husserlian phenomenology.

Jean-Paul Sartre introduced Merleau-Ponty to Husserl's work during the 1930's. Merleau-Ponty became enchanted by Husserl's phenomenology and he paid an extended visit in 1939 to the Husserl archives at Louvain, where he studied with great interest the later, unpublished Husserl manuscripts. Husserl's later work had turned towards the experience of the life world (*Lebenswelt*). Merleau-Ponty has claimed that his own phenomenology is really just a further development of the later Husserl, a natural continuation of Husserl's own undeveloped lines of thought, rather than a radical break from it. But although Merleau-Ponty was indebted to Husserl, he was also critical of Husserl's idealism. He wanted to rid phenomenology of this Cartesian heritage. According to Merleau-Ponty, there is no Cartesian transcendental subject "behind it all", busy constituting the world. There is no transcendental mind or consciousness which lies *under* perception, making judgments, focusing attention, seeing to it that things cohere and make sense. These functions are performed already at the level of the body. And just as there is no ideal consciousness busy constructing the world, independently of the body, so is there no mind/body unity which could exist independently of the world. Merleau-Ponty builds his phenomenology upon the fundament of embodied, perceptual experience. He does not ask, what are the abstract conditions for the possibility of consciousness, but rather, how does this situated, embodied, psychological ego constitute the world?

---

16 This epithet was initially bestowed upon him by his critic Ferdinand Alquié, but was later on used by de Waelhens (1951) in a positive sense. Ambiguity in Merleau-Ponty's philosophy does not stand for fuzziness of confusion, but rather for the fundamental insight that there are no final answers for philosophical reflection.

This project involves an explication of the ambiguous, lived body. Upon this rock are all things built, all levels of existence take their point of departure from embodied existence. For Merleau-Ponty, this point of departure entails a fundamental ambiguity, an ambiguity which shows itself on all levels, an ambiguity of subject/object, mind/body, perceiver/perceived.[17] Merleau-Ponty writes in his difficult last work, a posthumously published and edited collection of working notes,[18] that man is always inserted into "wild being" somewhere in the middle. If this difficult last work is an attempt to explicate a radical break-up of subject/object as the reversibility of the flesh of the world folding over upon itself, we can already find this neither/nor, third term ambiguity present in his earlier works as the realm of the "in-between".

One can explicate the "in-between" at many levels in Merleau-Ponty's philosophy. I will begin with the body. I stated earlier that the body for Merleau-Ponty is both subject and object, both constituted and constituting. He calls this ambiguous unity a "third term" between the purely psychological and the purely physical. How is this to be understood? The body is a very special form of existence, it is not an object like any other object in the world. In some sense, of course, the body is an object. It is extended in space, it has a continuity and coherence of stability as material corporeality. It can be looked at, touched and investigated objectively using methods of natural science. But what one easily forgets is that it is the (lived) body itself which is looking and touching. Merleau-Ponty points out that an object is an object only insofar as it can disappear from my sphere of attention. The body, however, is always *here*. It cannot be put down, walked around, nor disregarded. It is never really in front of me, since it is *with me* at all times. My body itself is, then, a special kind of "thing" which I cannot really observe. In order to be able to do so, I would need a second body, which itself would be unobserv-

---

17 "Inside and outside are inseparable. The world is wholly inside and I am wholly outside myself." *PP* p. 407.
18 *The Visible and the Invisible* (1964/1968), hereafter referred to as *VI*.

able.[19] I can, however, in a certain attitude, regard my body as a thing or external object. I can pinch my leg or look at my hand, or even look myself in the eyes in a mirror. But I trick myself if I think that I have in this way "caught" the lived body. Even if I, with my left hand, feel my right hand as it touches an object, I cannot with the left hand capture the hand that *touches*. I can feel the bones and muscles of the hand, but this information does not help me understand what the hand is doing. The right hand-in-touching is constituting the world in a specific "hand" way. The hand touching *is* me, and cannot be an object for my consideration *as* touching. The body in its lived relation to the world can never be captured in the objectified impersonal language of natural science. The term "lived body" in French (*le corps propre*) conveys this important nuance, in that it refers to my body, a personal existence, an opening upon the world which is always understood in the first person. The objectified body studied by natural science does not capture this vital aspect of the human body.

The lived body is a living relation to the world. However, it is an ambiguous, unique phenomenon which is both subject and object, yet neither wholly the one nor the other. I *am* this corporeal being which is self-conscious and opens up upon the world. The relationship between the perceiver and the perceived is also ambiguous for Merleau-Ponty. He has extensively criticized both idealism and empiricism[20] for neglecting either the existence of the world or the reality of the subject. Briefly, the classical empiricist theory of perception which Merleau-Ponty criticizes outlines a mechanistic, causal atomistic model, where the world is ready-made and finished "out there", affecting us through excitation of sense organs by sense-appropriate stimuli. These various sensations are taken in and cause us to have certain experiences (of light, color, sound etc.).

---

19 "In so far as it sees or touches the world, my body can therefore be neither seen nor touched. What prevents it ever being an object, ever being 'completely constituted' is that it is that by which there are objects. It is neither tangible nor visible in so far as it is that which sees and touches." (*PP*, p. 92).

20 "Empiricism" for Merleau-Ponty refers to a style of thinking which he calls, interchangeably, "causal thinking", "mechanical thinking", "naturalism" and "materialism".

Merleau-Ponty points out that we never experience these sensations in this way; rather, as soon as we have perceived something we experience it as meaningful, organized, and contextualized. Empiricism must explain this fact by referring to cognitive processes such as judgment and association in order to account for the synthesis of all the diverse "stimuli". However, it is obvious that these processes which empiricism needs to account for perceptual experience occur *after* perception, not before. The world is already understood and organized for us before we start to elaborate with explicit cognitive processes.[21] Idealism has made a similar mistake, according to Merleau-Ponty, although from the other side. Idealism lets consciousness create the world. The world is a product of conscious activity. Merleau-Ponty's criticism here is that one ignores the fact that the world contributes to experience with its own weight and power. There *is* a world, although it does not cause my experiences, neither is it

---

[21] A question one might pose here is whether Merleau-Ponty's criticism of classical empiricism would also apply to modern empiristic theories, such as functionalism, cognitivism and connectionism within AI. These modern versions are built upon the idea that cognition and consciousness are multiple functions of brain processes (or in AI, computer processes). These processes consist of the manipulation of symbols (which are both meaningful and physical) which are physically encoded in the brain or the computer program. Symbolic computation is performed by humans while digital computers operate only with the physical form of the symbols, having no access to their semantic values. The computer's "understanding" of the symbols manipulated is regulated by the syntax of the programming. Both Dennett (1991) and connectionism define "subjectivity" as massive interconnections between self-organizing, non-centralized physical processes in the brain. As I mentioned in chapter 4, Dennett has homunculized the brain into "the person", and connectionism has done away with the symbolic nature of symbols entirely and replaced them with numerical operations. (See Varela et. al 1996.) In all of these cases, I think Merleau-Ponty's critique is valid, that is, we have not been provided with any explanation of the constitution of these elements into meaningful contextualized content. The agent (person) has the experience of meaning, and the problem for empiristic theories is to squeeze meaning out of physical brain processes. How do symbols acquire meaning? What principle is responsible for the organization of the physical brain processes? How does this physicalistic level of description apply to lived phenomena? The very project of trying to construct a mechanical model of cognition could be subjected to Merleau-Ponty's critique, namely that there is no one there to think or perceive.

a product of consciousness.[22] For example, take the experience of attention. Attention is not created *ex nihilo*. Attention is set into motion by the world. There is something *there* which interests me. How can one thing be more interesting than another if everything is created by consciousness? Idealism has missed the world, while empiricism has ignored the subject. Empiricism has turned man into one object among many, resulting in perception without anyone there to perceive, and intellectualism sees the world as an achievement of consciousness, thereby depriving us of the world.[23]

What we need instead of these two classical positions is an "in-between", where we can see the collaboration between man and world (consciousness and nature). But here man is not just a constituting consciousness, and the world is not merely a kind of container of objectively existing physical things. We discover instead an interlocking system, a primordial relationship where the subject and object are born together (*connaissance* in French means knowledge, but it also literally means "born together"). [24] When we redefine the relations between man and

22 "The world is not what I think, but what I live; I am open to the world, I have no doubt that I am in communication with it, but I do not possess it, it is inexhaustible." (*PP*, xii).

23 Merleau-Ponty has been criticized (Madison, 1981) for being un-phenomenological in his conceptualization of a kind of "pre-world" which exists prior to the dialectical body-world interaction of human beings. The "world" can be said to have several meanings for Merleau-Ponty, 1) the constructed world of thought (the objective world as conceived of from within the natural attitude); 2) the correlate of our incarnated life (the perceived world); and finally, 3) a world of Being, prior to subjectivity. It is obvious that Merleau-Ponty concerns himself for the most part with criticizing the bias of the constructed world (1), and laying out an explication of the incarnate world (2). But his implicit ontology (which becomes explicit in *VI*) has caused debate as to whether his work is really phenomenological (see Zaner, 1964).

24 Some quotations to illustrate this point: "Reality is not a crucial appearance underlying the rest, it is the framework of relations with which all appearances tally. If I hold my pen near my eyes so that it shuts out almost the whole scene before me, its real size remains small, because the pen which hides everything is also a pen *seen at close quarters*,..." (*PP*, p. 300) and "This apparatus is the gaze, in other words the natural correlation between appearances and our kinesthetic unfoldings, something not known through a law, but experienced as the involvement of our body in the typical structures of a world. Lighting and the constancy of the thing illuminated, which is

world, we find an ambiguous "in-between" which is precisely the nature of our embodied existence, concretely illustrated in the nature of perception. To give an example, take the experience of foreground and background. This perceptual phenomenon does not *exist in the world*. Foreground and background only arise in relation to a subject who has interests, focuses of attention and a point of view. In the same way, the phenomenon of depth is not a quality of the *thing* itself. Depth exists only in-between the subject's bodily position and the position of the object. Depth is not a product of consciousness, it exists with respect to things, but to things in their positional relationship to the subject. We need both the subject with his/her point of view and the world in order for these perceptual phenomena to exist. We call the area where this meeting occurs <u>the world</u>, and the world can only arise due to our bodies. Human existence, embodiment and the world are thus bound up in an indissoluble unity. To exist as human beings is to belong to the world in this special way.

Merleau-Ponty was just as concerned about the influence of the prejudice of the natural sciences as he was with Husserl's idealism. His concern with natural scientific thinking was that it had deeply influenced our ways of thinking about ourselves and our relationship to the world, sedimenting the natural scientific interpretation of the world. We have learned to consider our bodies as "objective bodies", that is, as a collection of physiological and biomechanical processes. Likewise, we are con-

---

its correlate, are directly dependent on our bodily situation. If, in a brightly lit room, we observe a white disc placed in a shady corner, the constancy of the white is imperfect. It improves when we approach the shady zone containing the disc. It becomes perfect when we actually enter it." (ibid., pp. 310-311) and "Taking up our abode in a certain setting of color, with the transposition which it entails, is a bodily operation, and I cannot effect it otherwise than by *entering into* the new atmosphere, because my body is my general power of inhabiting all the environments which the world contains, the key to all those transpositions and equivalencies which keep it constant. (ibid., p. 311) and "How are we to understand both that the thing is the correlative of my knowing body, and that it rejects that body? What is given is not the thing on its own, but the experience of the thing, or of something transcendent standing in the wake of one's subjectivity, some kind of natural entity of which a glimpse is afforded through a personal history." (ibid., 325). All italics in original.

vinced that the world is "really out there" exactly as natural science has described it, and for that reason we constitute our experience in objectivistic terms, i.e. our experiences of the world are held to be the result of external excitation in terms of stimuli (mechanistic, atomistic elements) which impinge upon our sense organs and cause experience. This way of thinking is so ingrained that it is difficult for us to think in any other way. The phenomenological tradition has always pointed out that however interesting and valuable these natural scientific theories may be, they are *constructions* and in no way causally responsible, for nor temporally prior to, experience. Because they are *derived* from the life world and experience, they cannot be logically placed causally prior *to* experience.[25] Following this critique, Merleau-Ponty's ambition is to clear phenomenology of both idealism and the remnants of empiricism which he felt exerted too strong an influence upon philosophy and psychology. He gave some credit to Gestalt psychology for coming up with the notion of form, but he criticized the philosophical realism underlying Gestalt psychology, which maintained that the forms are "really out there". Merleau-Ponty found this naturalism unsatisfactory, and therefore felt compelled to further develop the Gestalt discovery of form himself. His notion of form, which he called "structure," is neither "out there" (*really* in the world) nor "in here" (entirely constituted by the subject). Structure is another ambiguous dimension of reality which is neither thought nor thing, but the meeting between the two. Structures are "in between" in that they can only exist for a subject situated in a world: the one cannot exist without the other. Merleau-Ponty's notion of structure is an important concept which I will discuss at length further on. At this point, however, I will wind up the general introduction to Merleau-Ponty's phenomenology by discussing briefly his thesis of the primacy of perception.

Merleau-Ponty gives perception a primordial status as the foundation of all knowing and experiencing. Why perception? Why not thinking or reason (the ancient Greek ideal)? Or today we would perhaps prefer to

---

25 See Husserl (1954/1970) and footnote 8.

imagine the neurophysiology of the brain as providing the basis of human existence. Why is perception primordial for Merleau-Ponty? The answer has to do with his grounding of phenomenology in <u>embodied</u> existence. The world which is given to us in perception via our bodies is the primary reality, the true access to Being. Perceptual experience offers us the most telling account of what it is to be a human being; to take a perspective on the world (to *be* a perspective, a point of view), to stand opposed to Otherness, to have immediate access to things - in short, to live the world through the medium of the body. Perception is the level of human experience which opens up upon the world. All higher levels of existence such as imagination, rationality, language and culture are built upon the fundament of perceptual experience; a more fundamental level of existence than this cannot be reached. Perception is, for Merleau-Ponty, an existential act whereby we, at one stroke, commit ourselves to a past, a future and a world. In perception we come into contact with something which is not us, but we also take up this "something" and relate to it, which is an essential moment of perceptual experience. Perception, is then, neither completely passive (mechanistic, causal) nor completely active (constituting).[26] We live the world, and the world lives in us. The world needs our participation in order to be, and we exist only insofar as we have a world.[27] The "in-between" character of perception is not the result of some kind of imperfection in ourselves or in the world, but rather constitutes the concrete conditions of our existence, as embodied, thinking creatures. However, this does not mean that we should

---

[26] "Thus a sensible datum which is on the point of being felt sets a kind of muddled problem for my body to solve. I must find the attitude which *will* provide it with the means of becoming determinate, of showing up as blue; I must find the reply to a question which is obscurely expressed. And yet I do so only when I am invited by it, my attitude is never sufficient to make me really see blue or really touch a hard surface. The sensible gives back to me what I lent to it, but this is only what I took from it in the first place." (*PP*, p. 214).

[27] "True reflection presents me to myself not as an idle and inaccessible subjectivity, but as identical with my presence in the world and to others, as I am now realizing it: I am all that I see, I am an intersubjective field, not despite my body and historical situation, but on the contrary, by being this body and this situation, and through them, all the rest" (ibid., p. 452).

reduce every level of experience to perception. Merleau-Ponty has not denied the existence of such "higher order" levels as cognition and social reality. He is often misunderstood on this particular point.[28] Merleau-Ponty simply means that perceptual experience is the original relationship between man and world (consciousness and nature), the relationship upon which all further articulation of ourselves and the world is built.[29] For example, cognition is built upon perception, although it is not reducible to it. They partake of similar structures, they are both human ways of being open to the world. Both perception and cognition are ambiguous and unfinished by nature. We never stop perceptually experiencing the world once and for all. Our perceptual experience flows continually with further nuances, details, sides and shades.[30] In the same way, we never think a complete, finished thought. Thought and perception are both in motion, always on the way towards further articulations and developments. They are also both sedimented (have a tendency to repeat themselves) as well as spontaneous, in that we can always see something new/think a new thought, even though we prefer to let sedimented ways of perceiving and thinking guide our orientation in the world. Merleau-Ponty summarizes in his article "The Primacy of Per-

---

28 See e.g. the discussion at the end of his address to the Société francaise de philosophie given shortly after the publication of *PP*, preserved as the essay "The Primacy of Perception" (1947/1964).

29 "By these words 'primacy of perception' we mean that the experience of perception is our presence at the moment when things, truths, values are constituted for us; that perception is a nascent *logos*, that it teaches us, outside of all dogmatism, the true conditions of objectivity itself; that it summons us to the tasks of knowledge and action. It is not a question of reducing human knowledge to sensation, but of assisting at the birth of this knowledge..." (ibid., p. 25 italics in original), and "I never claimed that perception...has a monopoly on truth. What I mean to say is that we find in perception a mode of access to the object which is rediscovered at every level...Consequently, I do not detract anything from the more complex forms of knowledge; I only show how they refer to this fundamental experience as the basic experience which they must render more determinate and explicit" (ibid., p. 34).

30 "I say that I perceive correctly when my body has a precise hold on the spectacle, but that does not mean that my hold is ever all-embracing; it would be so only if I had succeeded in reducing to a state of articulate perception all the inner and outer horizons of the object, which is in principle impossible" (*PP*, p. 297).

ception", "Should we now generalize and say that what is true of perception is also true in the order of the intellect and that in a general way all our experience, all our knowledge, has the same fundamental structures, the same synthesis of transition, the same kinds of horizons which we have found in perceptual experience?"[31]

Merleau-Ponty's phenomenological project was intended to eventually encompass more than a philosophical explication of embodied existence. After his study on perception, he wished to take up phenomenological analyses of language, culture, rationality, ethics, aesthetics and politics. During his lifetime, he was unable to do more than begin some of these preliminary studies. For the purposes of this dissertation, I will be concerned with his work on the lived body (*le corps propre*) as it is here I find interesting points of departure for my phenomenological reflection on psychosomatic pathology. I will now look specifically at some of the ideas which will be of interest for the coming chapters.

Merleau-Ponty and the mind-body problem

"...the notions of soul and body must be revitalized: there is the body as a mass of chemical components in interaction, the body as dialectic of lived being and its biological milieu, and the body as dialectic of social subject and his group...The body in general is an ensemble of paths already traced, of powers already constituted; the body is the acquired dialectic soil upon which a higher 'formation' is accomplished, and the soul is the meaning which is then established."[32]

"...the relations of the soul and body - obscure as long as the body is treated in abstraction as a fragment of matter - are clarified when one sees in the body the bearer of a dialectic."[33]

"...the psychophysical event can no longer be conceived after the model of Cartesian physiology and as the juxtaposition of a process in itself and

---

[31] Merleau-Ponty (1947/1964, p. 19).
[32] Merleau-Ponty *The Structure of Behavior* (1942/1963), hereafter referred to as *SB*, p. 210.
[33] Ibid., p. 204.

a *cogitatio*. The union of soul and body is not an amalgamation between two mutually external terms, subject and object, brought about by arbitrary decree. It is enacted at every instant in the movement of existence."[34]

"We said earlier that it is the body which 'understands' in the acquisition of habit...But the phenomenon of habit is just what prompts us to revise our notion of 'understand' and our notion of the body. To understand is to experience the harmony between what we aim at and what is given, between the intention and the performance - and the body is our anchorage in a world."[35]

"...the objective body is not the true version of the phenomenal body, that is, the true version of the body that we live by: it is indeed no more than the latter's impoverished image, so that the problem of the relation of soul to body has nothing to do with the objective body, which exists only conceptually, but with the phenomenal body. What is true, however, is that our open and personal existence rests on an initial foundation of acquired and stabilized existence."[36]

The quotations above hopefully give a flavor of the Merleau-Pontian line of argumentation on this issue. As I have pointed out earlier, Merleau-Ponty was no idealist. He wanted to clear phenomenology of Husserl's constitutive phenomenological bias, which gave consciousness sovereignty over the constituted world. Merleau-Ponty wanted to create a new center for phenomenological investigations, a center which would replace the Cogito ("I think") with Existence, with being-in-the-world. Getting rid of both the transcendental cogito of Husserl's idealism and the prejudice of natural scientific thinking (empiricism) allowed for the discovery of the "in-between" which I have tried to present in the previous section. In order to formulate a new mind/body position, Merleau-Ponty will once again make use of the "in-between" metaphor. We are always already this concrete being who *is* both mind and body in a natural unity. Mind and body are not one and the same, they are not interchangeable, but neither are they as distinct from one another as Carte-

---

34 *PP*, p. 88.
35 Ibid., p. 144.
36 Ibid., pp. 431-432.

sian dualism has led us to believe.[37] Merleau-Ponty prefers to speak of mind and body as different "planes of signification"[38] rather than different sorts of being or orders of reality. The dizzying discussion of how material, physiological processes relate to meaning (the psychological/social realm) is both fascinating and essentially insoluble, as illustrated in part I of the dissertation. Merleau-Ponty quips in *PP*: "How signification and intentionality could come to dwell in molecular edifices or masses of cells is a thing which can never be made comprehensible, and here Cartesianism is right. But there is, in any case, no question of any such absurd undertaking."[39] The mind-body problem has its origins in faulty conceptualizations of both mind and body. The constructed "objective" mechanical body which we stubbornly try to vitalize with meaning is in fact already brimming with "mind", with phenomenal intentionality and meaning. To find this subjectivized, lived body, we must again and again remind ourselves that we are not concerned with the body as a collection of objective, third person-processes (although one can of course speak of the body in this way). The body we are interested in is the lived body, the psychosomatic body, *my* body. This body is always engaged in a lived relation to the world, anchored in perception, cognition and social reality. Likewise, the "mind" which consistently refuses to settle into the material is the Cartesian "I think" which has been cut off from its lived roots in embodiment. However, as mentioned earlier, Merleau-Ponty has not denied that there is a reflective level of existence. Neither has he contested the reality of our corporeal existence. The physiology and materiality of the body are important, as they set the frame for *possibilities*; however, he is against the idea that our experience is ever causally physically determined.[40] Our concrete exis-

---

37 "The ego as a center from which his intentions radiate, the body which carries them and the beings and things to which they are addressed are not confused: but they are only three sectors of a unique field." (*SB*, p. 189.)

38 Ibid., p. 201.

39 *PP*, p. 351.

40 In *SB* Merleau-Ponty writes of the painter El Greco: "If one supposes an anomaly of vision in El Greco, as has sometimes been done, it does not follow that the form of the body in his paintings, and consequently the style of the attitudes, admit of a

tence as beings who live in a significant, meaningful world is never the product or result of physiological processes. We are psychological, cultural beings. The materiality of our body is a fundament which is taken up and transformed into levels of existence which lie over and above our brute physicality.

If the mind and the body are not distinct regions for Merleau-Ponty, understood in diametrical opposition to one another, what is their relationship? One could say that the mental and the physical overlap, show themselves as different levels on a continuum from body to mind. We can think of the mind/body continuum as describing different levels of existence which emerge in response to that which meets us in the world. Take the example of driving a car a familiar route. We are not consciously aware of having anything to do with this task, it is something which just seems to happen between my body, the car (which I have incorporated into my body), and the road. It may happen, amidst this habitual driving, that I suddenly realize that I am already home, or I may need to deal with some unexpected traffic situation on the road. At such a moment "I" emerge from my daydreaming and become "mentally" involved in the scene, and my body, which has been habitually performing the driving task, becomes a highly vigilant, concentrated body. What this example illustrates is that in lived experience it is difficult to locate "mind" and "body" in strict Cartesian terms. Mind is being towards the world through the body. The thinking body and the embodied mind are always *there,* although how these levels of existence appear and to what extent they are active in the present moment depends upon the situation.

'physiological explanation.' When irremedial bodily peculiarities are integrated with the whole of our experience, they cease to have the dignity of a cause in us. A visual anomaly can receive a universal signification by the mediation of the artist and become for him the occasion of perceiving one of the 'profiles' of human existence" (p. 203). A similar comment on Cézanne, "Heredity may well have given him rich sensations, strong emotions, and a vague feeling of anguish or mystery which upset the life he might have wished for himself and which cut him off from humanity; but these qualities cannot create a work of art without the expressive act, and they have no bearing on the difficulties or the virtues of that act." (Merleau-Ponty, 1964/1993, p. 69).

"I" am always somewhere on this mind/body continuum, existing at the level which blends harmoniously with that which is given in the world, or put in another way, blending together with that which corresponds to my intending (mind/body constitution) of the situation at hand. That which we traditionally call "mind", comprising the cognitive processes associated with conscious thought, is just one level of meaning, one level of mind. We also find "mind" operating at the level of the body, in perception. For example, my eyes focus upon a scene which I wish to see, and it becomes foreground, while everything else fades into background. This task is not accomplished reflectively/cognitively, nor is it the result of automatic, causal processes. We need our eyes to see, but we don't see with our eyes, we see with sight. Sight is a lived relation between the lived body and the world. Merleau-Ponty writes, "The eye is not the mind, but a material organ. How could it ever take anything 'into account'? It can only do so if we introduce the phenomenal body besides the objective one, if we make a knowing body of it, and if, in short, we substitute for consciousness, as the subject of perception, existence, or being in the world through a body."[41] In this very basic perceptual way, the body is already an instrument of comprehension. Neither the eye as retinal structure nor thought as cognitive processes is responsible for being able to *look* at something. To "look" is to orient oneself in the display of the world, and this task is performed instantaneously, before reflective thought. There is no mystery in this, but we need a phenomenological attitude in order to understand it, and as well as a non-dualistic way of describing it.

Psychological motives and bodily activity go into each other. The body is not an inert mass or thing which we must orchestrate into action but rather the "living envelope" of all our actions and intentions. We are a body-subject, living a mind/body/world unity.[42] In order to under-

---

[41] *PP*, p. 309, footnote.

[42] "Man taken as a concrete being is not a psyche joined to an organism, but the movement to and fro of existence which at one time allows itself to take corporeal form and at others moves towards personal acts. Psychological motives and bodily occasions may overlap because there is not a single impulse in a living body which is en-

stand what this means, we need to examine in greater depth Merleau-Ponty's notion of the lived body, and in connection to this, the "tacit cogito". One could say that the lived body and the tacit cogito are revealed as the phenomenological residue after Merleau-Ponty's bracketing of "the body" and "the mind", as they are normally understood from within the natural attitude.

The lived body and the tacit cogito

That which has been said thus far about the lived body is that it is not to be confused with the objectified body described and studied by natural science.[43] The lived body is someone's lived relationship to the world. It is an ambiguous unity, both subject and object, both mind and body, participating in perception in an existential "in between" manner. In a polemical fashion, Merleau-Ponty has dismissed both idealism and empiricism as being inadequate to the task of illuminating man's existence as being-in-the-world. He grounds his entire phenomenological project in the lived body as existence. This lived body as being-in-the-world is the source of all experience and knowledge. However, Merleau-Ponty does make some distinctions in his discussion of the lived body. At the most fundamental level, he speaks of an anonymous pre-personal bodily

---

tirely fortuitous in relation to psychic intentions, and not a single mental act which has not found at least its germ or its general outline in physiological tendencies." (*PP*, p. 88).

43 It is interesting to note that the German language has two words for "body," the one *Leib* bearing a resemblance to the English "life". Both terms are derived from common roots in old Saxon and Teutonic *leip,loip,* or *lip.* This term referred originally to "life" "person" or "self". The other term, *Körper,* comes from the Latin *corpus* and refers to the objectified or dead body. The term *Leib* emphasizes the lived, person quality of being a body, while *Körper* refers to the thing aspects of the body. In English, we have only "body", with its roots in old English *bodig* and present-day German *Bottich* which means "barrel" (container to be filled). Thus, the term for body has become divorced from its original connection to life and person. The terms "lived body" and "embodiment" are attempts to reinvoke the connection between life and body. *Körper* is a good term for the objectified, lifeless (person-less) body studied by natural science, that which we have, in English, come to regard as "body." From Ots (1994), pp. 116-117.

existence (*le moi naturel*). Here, we find a level of existence which is meaningful, intentional and significant, although it concerns a *lived* meaning which is not thematic nor articulated in higher orders.[44] This level of meaning is anonymous, pre-personal. This lived, body meaning provides us with stable, habitual functioning which is the general outline of that which (always) gets taken up and transformed into the personal, psychological/cultural existence. What is this level of meaning? For example, take the everyday experience of moving about in one's home. My body knows its way around the apartment, it is a knowledge of the legs. Merleau-Ponty gives the example in *PP* of the woman who has a feather on her hat which she manages to keep at a distance from her surroundings so that it doesn't break off. She does not calculate this distance, she has incorporated the feather into her body. This kind of body knowledge is our bodily understanding of the world, a kind of harmony between that which we aim for (to get to the kitchen) and that which is given (the particular lay out of the apartment). This level of meaning is not a mental content nor is it a stimuli-bound reflex. It is neither thematic knowledge nor involuntary action. It is a form of life which places us in a situation which we already understand. Merleau-Ponty refers to this quiet life subtending our thetic consciousness as an "intentional arc", which projects around us our past, our future, our current setting, our being situated. On the most basic level, I never have to *think* the unity of the object, the coherence of my own body, the spatiality of the world and so on. Here one may speak of a body-intentionality, a life of the

---

44 Merleau-Ponty is criticized on this point by Zaner (1964), who denies the Merleau-Pontian assertion that the body can "know" anything in any comprehensible fashion. According to phenomenology, the level of the lived (body experience) and the level of the known (the reflected upon) are not interchangeable. Zaner's point is that if the body "knows" anything, whatever is "known" in this way could no longer be understood at the level of non-thematizing experience, it would no longer belong to the experience of the body. A bodily meaning is, according to Zaner, incomprehensible. Indeed, the notion of the constituting body is an idea which goes against our usual patterns of thought. Merleau-Ponty claims that the lived body is meaning-bestowing, although meaning at this level is not to be understood in terms of conscious thematic content.

body which is not yet thematic, personal existence. However, this anonymous life of the body is never purely present as such. Just as we can only imagine what it was like not having language as an infant, so can we only simulate or approximate this general body life, since we have already appropriated the higher levels of existence.[45] We may from time to time temporarily withdraw into the anonymous life pulsating in our ears, but we are never completely given over to it.[46] We may fluctuate around this level of existence from time to time, but our personal, psychosocial life which rests upon this pre-personal level of existence can never be totally absent, once established. At any given instant this seemingly anonymous body may suddenly transform into personal existence, as something unexpected intrudes onto the scene, and "I" must resurface in order to face challenges, threats and so on. We thus move to and fro on this continuum from general body life to highly personal acts. The important point for Merleau-Ponty is that the body remains the general instrument of comprehension, it is that base from which all higher meaning (cognition, language, culture) will emerge.

Merleau-Ponty's further explication of the lived body in *PP* is presented in terms of the spatiality of the body, the synthesis of one's own body, and the body as expression and speech. It would take too much

---

[45] "It is impossible to superimpose on man a lower layer of behavior which one chooses to call 'natural', followed by a manufactured cultural or spiritual world. Everything is both manufactured and natural in man, as it were, in the sense that there is not a word, not a form of behavior which does not owe something to purely biological being--and which at the same time does not elude the simplicity of animal life, and cause forms of vital behavior to deviate from their pre-ordained direction, through a sort of *leakage* and through a genius for ambiguity which might serve to define man." (*PP*, p. 189). Italics in original.

[46] "But precisely because my body can shut itself off from the world, it is also what opens me out upon the world and places me in a situation there. The momentum of existence towards others, towards the future, towards the world can be restored as a river unfreezes...I never become quite a thing in the world; the density of existence as a thing always evades me, my own substance slips away from me internally, and some intention is always foreshadowed" (ibid., p. 165). Or, earlier in the same discussion, "..in this sense the sleeper is never completely isolated within himself, never totally a sleeper, and the patient never totally cut off from the intersubjective world, never totally ill" (ibid., p. 164).

space to present these chapters in detail here, but the body as expression and speech will be discussed in chapter 9 in connection with psychosomatic pathology. Suffice to say for now that Merleau-Ponty wishes to show that the lived body is the source of every layer of meaning, from simple perception to complex forms of psychological and social existence. The form which meaning constitution takes on in Merleau-Ponty's phenomenology could be described in terms of a question-answer dialectic. The world asks me vague, diffuse questions which I feel compelled to answer, just as I continually interrogate the world. There is a tension introduced, a beckoning from the world which invites us to respond (in our bodies, our psychological make-up, our social relations) in order to reduce the tension. Bodily, I automatically adjust my posture to accommodate the incline; perceptually, I squint my eyes and take a closer look over in the shadows in order to see if it is a man standing there or just a shadow. On a psychological level, I try to fit new facts into previously known categories.[47] Meaning is that which emerges from the concrete meeting between the array which meets me and those tasks, interests and attentions which I bring to the scene. Meaning is virtual for Merleau-Ponty, it is not real, like a thing, nor ideal like a thought. It emerges as the world and the subject carve out each other "somewhere towards the middle". This is by now a familiar theme.

I have said that the tacit cogito is what is discovered after the bracketing of "mind" under the reduction. For Merleau-Ponty, although we do have access to levels of existence which are highly abstract, cognitive and reflective, we also live "mind" at a much lower level. We find a deeper life already going on within us which partakes of meaning, although it precedes thought. This "thinking" he calls the tacit cogito. The tacit cogito is the fundamental experience of oneself, the silent, unspoken

---

47 Although harmony and equilibrium is the preferred "answer", one may, in certain situations, prefer tension and incoherence, e.g. in artistic creation or drug experience. People who systematically prefer tension and disorientation are sometimes called "thrill seekers" in psychological literature, and there are different theories (biological/psychological) about why certain people seem to prefer these disharmonious states.

cogito which is simply the power of existing.[48] Because perception and existence are primordial, thinking for Merleau-Ponty is a transformation of perceptual experience, a representation at a higher level of the organization of that which we already experience perceptually.[49] Before we think, we are. We are a field of experience, a directed point of view, an orientation already situated, before reflection and thought. According to Merleau-Ponty, thought does not constitute existence, it is itself parasitic upon it. The experience of existence, this being present to oneself and to the world simultaneously, is the tacit cogito. It is the initial upsurge of meaning where subject and world are born. This primordial faith in and openness to the world, prior to reflection, is, for Merleau-Ponty, a form of consciousness, a form of transcendence (being always *beyond* oneself, always further on). Without this level of existence, there could be no thetic consciousness. A thing can never begin to think, only an animated, directed, situated life can develop such a talent. Reflection and thought are considered to be second order functions which allow us to further articulate and explore our experiences of the world. And just how does this process of articulation and exploration come about? This brings us to the important notion of structure, which I will be using in my analysis of psychosomatic pathology.

---

[48] "Behind the spoken *cogito*, the one which is converted into discourse and into essential truth, there lies a tacit *cogito*, myself experienced by myself. But this subjectivity, indeclinable, has upon itself and upon the world only a precarious hold. It does not constitute the world, it divines the world's presence round about it as a field not provided by itself..."(*PP*, pp. 403-404).

[49] It has been suggested that Merleau-Ponty before his death began to doubt if he had been correct in grounding human existence in perceptual experience. The difficulty he grappled with concerned the philosophical legitimacy of grounding reason and rationality in the factual contingency of embodiment. Merleau-Ponty has been quoted later on as calling his *PP* a "bad ambiguity" (Madison, 1981, p. xxvii). His last work, *VI*, which he never finished, was considered by some to be an attempt to remedy this problem. Whether this last work is in fact a repudiation of the themes of *PP* or a logical continuation of them is still a matter of debate.

Structures

Merleau-Ponty's notion of structure was first introduced in *SB*, where his primary aim was to criticize the causal, mechanistic thinking which had infiltrated philosophy and psychology. As mentioned earlier, he considered the Gestalt psychologist's notion of form to be a step in the right direction, but not radical enough. Structure was his own development of the concept of form, freed from Gestalt psychology's naturalistic bias. Structures are neither out there (*really* in the world, objectively) nor in here (completely constituted by consciousness). Merleau-Ponty's structure is another "in-between" phenomenon. Structures are the signification of the lived, there is no antimony between structures and signification. Structures are the bodily, psychological, socio-cultural patterns which lead us in our experience of the world, but they are also formed by our encounter with the world.

Structures are an attunement to the world, on all levels, whereby we take in "something" which is other than ourselves, come to terms with it (achieve a harmony) and then return towards the world, using these very structures then in order to further delineate and articulate what is there. Structures are thus modified by the world, yet they are that by which we can organize and understand the world, on all levels. This process is described by Merleau-Ponty as "circular" in *SB*, "dialectical" in *PP* and "reversible" in *VI*. In all three works the point is to illustrate a dialectical give and take, question-answer pattern, which both develops and constrains our understanding of the world. Structures allow us to feel at home in the world, to recognize and implement habitual ways of perceiving and thinking, freeing us thereby from the concrete towards the possible. We do not need to relearn our mother tongue every time we use it, nor do we thematically visually examine our apartment or our partner unless there is something special going on which prompts us to do so. However, structures are not only stable and sedimented,[50] they are

---

50 "But the word 'sediment' should not lead us astray: this acquired knowledge is not an inert mass in the depths of our consciousness. My flat is, for me, not a set of closely associated images. It remains a familiar domain round about me only as long as I still have it 'in my hands' or 'in my legs' the main distances and directions involved, and

also spontaneous, mobile and capable of transformations. No structure will always and in every way fit every possible situation. Structures are initially formed in response to a particular concrete lived situation, and we constantly find ourselves in new situations, however familiar they may seem. A final, important characteristic of structures is that they seek harmony, or tension reduction. A successful structure is one which resolves the tension which inevitably arises between man and the world. For example, when confronted with an intellectual problem, one searches for a structure (a higher order, cognitive one) which will enable one to understand what is presented. When one is surprised by something, one immediately tries to fit the new and different into something already known, or if this cannot be done, one is cast into the tumult of "making sense" (creating a new structure) out of what has occurred. The dialectical process is the following: something appears (presents itself), that "something" is either familiar (responded to with sedimented structure) or not (tension arises and structures are transformed).When structures are transformed in this way, they then become part of sedimentation. The world presents me with a rudimentary organization, unfinished and beckoning, which calls for my participation or response. The world is inexhaustible in that it is always transcendent or beyond that which is for the moment manifest. There are always further perspectives or views. This means that I am continually challenged by the world to further articulate, modify and deepen my understanding of it. The more I deepen and articulate my understanding of the world, the more of the world is shown to me. This is the human condition, to be a subject, already in the world, directed towards it, continually asking questions of it, being questioned, sedimenting the world in layers of "ready-made" significations, but also always prepared to overturn comfortable structures and transform the world (through the creation of new structures) when necessary.

---

as long as from my body intentional threads run out towards it. Similarly my acquired thoughts are not a final gain, they continually draw their sustenance from my present thought, they offer me a meaning, but I give it back to them." *PP*, p. 130.

To illustrate this rather difficult notion of structure, let me take some examples from Merleau-Ponty. In *SB* he shows how animals can respond in various ways to the world, at various levels of intelligence. This intelligence can be understood in terms of structures. For example, at the lowest level of animal existence, we find simple reflex responses.[51] Higher up, there are animals who can respond to a variety of situations which could not be handled by reflex behavior. These animals respond to a type of *configuration*, a level of reality which has been disengaged from material properties. It is this openness or ambiguity in the perception of the situation which allows for a certain degree of flexibility in the animal's response. A monkey can learn to pick "the lighter color" or is able to understand that the chocolate is always under "the last box" and so on. The higher animals can understand *the form or structure* of the situation. They have succeeded in discerning the structure of signals from their material properties (not this or that particular box, but the box which happens to be *the last one*.) The more complex the configurations are, and the higher the degree of freedom in the animal's response, the more "intelligent" we wish to call the behavior.

Merleau-Ponty recounts an interesting experiment concerning primitive animal behavior in *SB*, where fish who had learned to eat both white and black bread were fed white chalk mixed together with the white bread. It was observed that the fish could only very slowly and arduously learn to ignore the chalk and eat only the bread. What was interesting was that when these same fish were then fed black bread mixed together with pieces of black rubber, they learned very quickly to ignore the rubber. Merleau-Ponty comments, "It is not to a certain material that the animal has adapted, but to speak a human language, to a certain kind of deception...It is an aptitude of choosing, or a 'method of selection'

---

51 Even simple reflex behavior is critically examined by Merleau-Ponty in *SB*, where he demonstrates that even these seemingly automatic behaviors are never completely indifferent to both the internal and the external situation. The rhythm and location of the stimulus, for example, will determine whether or not the reflex is released. The classical account of reflex as blind automatism is called into question, in favor of understanding reflexes as behavior which tends to balance itself in accordance with preferred patterns of distribution. See *SB*, pp. 10-33.

which is established."[52] A very rudimentary structure had become sedimented for the fish, and as structure they were able to apply the lesson from the initial situation to a similar one. The structure "some particles which look like food are in fact not food" had found its way into the world of the fish.

Although higher animals can respond to the world with a certain degree of free variation, they are nevertheless concretely bound to the stimuli. They may be able to discern a structure, but they cannot *create* a structure. Experiments with chimpanzees have shown that although the chimps could learn to use a rod to knock down some bananas which were out of reach, they could not use the rod in this way unless it was within the same view or visual array as the bananas themselves. In other experiments, chimps could not learn that the box in their cage which they sat on could *also* be used to stand on to reach something. The box-as-something-to-sit-on was never transformed by the chimp into the box-as-something-to-stand-on. This means that the box-as-seat and the box-as-potential-stepping-stone remained two different things, they were never two aspects of one and the same thing. In short, the chimpanzee was not capable of assuming a *point of view* in relation to the box. They could not freely choose which aspect of the thing would emerge in a particular field or situation. Man is the only animal who has a point of view, who can transform the signification of the scene, who can have a *possible world*.[53] It is this ability to continually transform the significance of the scene which constitutes man's special way of being in the world. This dialectic of meaning goes on at all levels continually, on the social, the cognitive as well as the perceptual level.

Merleau-Ponty gives some examples of transformation of structures pertaining to the specifically human, symbolic order. For example, in the

---

[52] Ibid., p. 97.

[53] Merleau-Ponty points out that man is the only animal who initiates revolutions and commits suicide. This is because both revolution and suicide "presuppose the capacity of rejecting the given milieu and of searching for equilibrium beyond any milieu" (ibid., p. 97, footnote).

essay "The Child's Relations with Others"[54] he relates how the child's jealousy over the newborn sibling rival must be resolved by creating a new structure, wherein the child's own position in the family can be experienced in a new way. The old structure says something like, "I was alone and loved, the center of the universe for my parents, now I am that no longer, someone else has taken my place". The new structure, the solution to the jealousy, is to be able to understand familial relationships and temporal dimensions in a new way. To remain static in the old structure, where there is *one place*, and that one place is now occupied by another, is not a structure which can obtain harmony in the present situation. To stick to it would be to live a permanent tension or disharmony. According to Merleau-Ponty, the new structure will be something like "I *have been* the youngest, but I *am* the youngest no longer, and I *will become* the biggest."[55] The child has understood that roles are changeable and that temporal relationships are not static. There is more than one place in the family to be loved, and there may now even emerge new possibilities from being the oldest, which were not even conceivable as long as the child was an only child. This transformation of structure is interesting because it involves cognitive development (understanding of temporality) and social relations (family dynamics). Mallin[56] refers to the higher orders of cognition and cultural understanding in Merleau-Ponty's philosophy as "metastructures", which emerge out of and refer back to more "basic structures" such as openness to being and fundamental perceptual articulation (that *there is* something, which is not me, which I experience as de facto given). Cognitive structures which are given to us through language have a direct impact on how we experience and respond to the given. One language may emphasize or delineate some detail of an experience, which will have the result that those who speak the language will more readily experience this detail than other people. The main characteristic of cognitive-linguistic structures is that they are extremely precise and thereby make possible the complex and

---

54 Merleau-Ponty (1964).
55 Ibid., p. 110.
56 Mallin (1979).

sophisticated communication which results in culture and human societies.

A final example of the transformation of structures comes from Merleau-Ponty's *The Prose of the World*,[57] where Merleau-Ponty describes how Stendhal's outlook or point of view can take root in the reader and so transform his understanding of the world. The words of Stendhal open up fresh, new meanings, since he gives familiar words an interesting new twist. As one follows Stendhal's thoughts, one finds more and more cross-references which develop and point towards an entirely new direction of thought never before encountered. The new signification may have hovered on the margins of the reader's thoughts, it may have been vaguely felt, but it would have never taken its place as forcefully in the foreground, unless Stendhal put it there. Because one was open to this new meaning before it was fully articulated, it is easy to think afterwards that one could have understood it oneself, without Stendhal. Merleau-Ponty says that the way we tend to take possession of new ideas is an illustration of the way in which we allow ourselves to become transformed by new meanings. They immediately become a part of us. As human subjects in the world, we are continuously enacting this transformation of significations on all levels. The story of one's life is co-authored together with the world and with others. It is a story which is in the making, never finished, never transparent to itself. The only certainty of self which one actually ever possesses is that of a certain preferred style. For example, it is perhaps easier for someone to daydream about food when s/he gets bored, rather than sex. But this is not to say that some day this person will not daydream about sex. Our habitual, preferred structures are never causal, only motivational. One day, for some reason, one can master the inertia in order to allow a new structure to arise and make itself known. This is a typical theme for literature, when, for example, the most quiet, cowardly member of the group suddenly makes a brilliant counter-attack in some oppressive situation, or the bold hero becomes "weak" in some way, etc. In conclusion, to use the language of Merleau-

---

57   Merleau-Ponty (1969/1973).

Ponty, being-in-the-world is the dialectical process between the subject and the world, in a dynamic transformation of significance through the creation of new structures, resulting in meaning or "sens" (direction) which is characteristic of the human order.

An outline of the phenomenological theory of psychosomatics

"Being ill is before all alienation from the world."

--F.J.J. Buytendijk

In this section I will briefly present my phenomenological theory as a whole, before the following chapters (7-9) provide illustrations of the various constituents which make up the psychosomatic way of being in the world. As stated in chapter 1, I am in this dissertation looking at a specific group of patients whose lives have been transformed in such a way that their bodies and bodily sensations have taken the place of living in the world. They attend to their bodies with a "cognitive attentionality" [58] instead of living towards the world as embodied intentionality. This way of living one's body and one's situation is an experience of being-in-the-world which differs from our "normal" everyday experiences of the body as background and the world-attended-to as foreground. This way of living entails suffering, but a suffering whose nature we must penetrate phenomenologically. The psychosomatic way of being-in-the-world will be described in the following chapters. I will in chapter 10 subject my own theory to critical examination in line with the previous categories of ontology, etiology and cure. For now, I wish to merely provide an outline which will be fleshed out, argued for and scrutinized in the chapters to come.

The previous section in this chapter has provided the philosophical point of departure for the phenomenological theory about to be pre-

---

[58] I would like to thank Gunnar Karlsson for the suggestion of the term "cognitive attentionality" (personal communication).

sented. I have chosen this perspective because Merleau-Ponty has given us a radically new way of conceiving of the body and mind-body relations. The perspective of the lived body is especially appropriate for my purposes because we find here a truly holistic ground which will be able to illuminate those issues which are of importance for understanding psychosomatic phenomena (see part I of the dissertation). Merleau-Ponty himself has not specifically investigated pathology in his own writings[59] and all of the applications of his perspective to psychosomatics are my own.

Let us begin with my <u>definition of psychosomatic pathology.</u> As stated in chapter 1, I am using the term "psychosomatic pathology" in both a wide and a narrow sense. According to the wide definition, psychosomatic pathology is when symptoms (with and without lesions) and diseases, coming from any and all parts of the body, are *used*[60] in such a way that they take the place of a symbolic, verbal utterance. The first wide definition is functional, it describes a particular way of using the body as a means of expression. Secondly, the more narrow definition of psychosomatics refers to the specific psychosomatic *etiology*. Here the body is likewise used as expression, but in addition the *meaning* component (psycho-social reality) is necessary for the initiation and maintenance of the pathology. Without it, there would be no symptom or disease. Thus, according to the narrower definition, the bacterial ulcer is not a psychosomatic condition, although according to the wider definition it *could become* one, if the person in question were to use the ulcer in place of utterances. When the symptom or disease is initiated and maintained by a disturbance in the psycho-social world of the patient,

---

59 He does refer to brain-damaged patients from time to time, but this is a pedagogical strategy in order to show us, by contrast, the normal non-disintegrated being-in-the-world. His discussion of the brain-damaged patient Schneider in *PP* is the most well known example, but he has also made some disparate remarks on illness as a new signification of behavior in *SB*.

60 The term "used" should actually be placed in quotation marks, since this process is not a matter of willed, conscious choice, but rather takes place at a lower, non-thetic level, rather like the Sartrian "breakdown" into emotion (see chapter 7 on the analogy between Sartrian emotion and the psychosomatic "choice.").

we have psychosomatic etiology,[61] in the narrow sense of psychosomatic pathology. In short, those patients who have something to "say" with their bodies have psychosomatic conditions. The boundaries of this definition, determining what falls inside and outside of the definition, have to do with the way in which one lives the body, the way the body is "used", and the way the world is transformed for the patient because of this experience.[62] The nature of this transformation will become clear in the following chapters.

The <u>relevant concepts</u> which will be used in the phenomenological psychosomatic theory are: the lived body, structures, transformation of structures, dialectic of meaning, sedimentation, transcendence and the notion of self-becoming. I am using these terms, which have all been presented in the previous section (with the exception of self-becoming), because they provide a richer, more nuanced picture of the world of the psychosomatic person than the dualistic/reductionistic ones described by traditional theories. The relevance of these terms for my theory is as follows:

---

[61] See chapter 10 for a discussion and examination of the issue of etiology in my theory.

[62] It is difficult to compare the extension of my definition with the previous theories examined in the dissertation, since we are looking at symptoms, diseases and body functioning from very different perspectives. In order to compare my definition with the previous ones, we would have to find a common point of reference from which the comparison would make sense. This is not so easily done. I am concerned with the transformation of the being-in-the-world of the psychosomatic patient. Other theories have other criteria and definitions of what is "psychosomatic" based upon their theoretical positions. As I pointed out in chapter 1, definition and theory are bound up with each other. However, to make a general statement, I would say that if the condition described by the theory as "psychosomatic" (conversion hysteria, vegetative neurosis, stress reaction, perturbed rhythms) entailed the being-in-the world transformation which I describe, we would have an overlapping definition. For example, conversion hysteria is seen as a converted, convoluted bodily expression of an unconscious meaning. This could qualify as an overlap, since meaning is, in this case, lived/expressed at a lower body level. However, Alexander's vegetative neurosis does not, according to his theory, have any meaning content. So, a vegetative neurosis could only overlap with my definition in the wide sense (could be used as an expression), but not in the narrow sense. Because the phenomenological theory entails a radically different perspective from the previous traditional theories, it is best to suspend traditional thinking in order to take in the phenomenological perspective.

*The lived body circumvents the interaction problems which arise when one has to try to bring together impersonal, third-person processes (adrenaline levels, muscle tension, blood pressure etc.) with the psychosocial realm of subjective meaning constitution (the meaning of the situation for the subject). The person who gets a sore throat just when she is about to give a speech which she feels ambivalent about is therefore no problem for the phenomenological theory, since the person is always to be found somewhere on the mind-body continuum. The *lived* body is perfectly capable of expressing this meaning on a bodily level. "Meaning" is to be understood as the lived relationship between the *embodied* subject and the concrete life situation, which are simultaneously born together. The sore throat is the subject (as mind and body together) *living* her ambivalence towards the speech about to be given. From within the perspective of the lived body, other types of questions arise than the traditional ones, for example *why the sore throat* instead of anxiety symptoms, or long telephone calls to friends concerning fears about giving speeches, or psychotherapeutical sessions about forbidden exhibitionistic fantasies and so on. That the throat is the bodily channel for speaking is the "reason" for the symptom. Whether or not there is a bacteria or virus in the throat is of less importance than to understand that the sore throat is an expression of a lived situation which has demanded a response, and in this case the response is a "psychosomatic" one.

*Structures will be used here in order to account for the psychosomatic patient's "choice" of body expression. To understand my usage of structure in this theory, it must be kept in mind that structures are *lived,* they do not exist outside of being-in-the-world, in the same way that depth or perspective do not exist independently of the embodied subject and the perceived world. For this reason, it would be inadequate to speak of structures in terms of objective, third-person processes, like hormone levels and muscle tension, nor can they be adequately expressed in terms of conscious, thematic reflections (a repudiation of both empiricism and intellectualism, following Merleau-Ponty). Rather, a structure is a lived relation to the world, a relation between an embodied, psychosocial subject and a <u>situation</u>, a meaningful, significant context. A description of a structure is the articulation of the lived level of experience, as it can be explicated at the level of the known (thematized). The psychosomatic structure, this particular way of living the symptom/disease, is the way in which the person in question tries to keep everything in equilibrium, which is, as we recall, precisely what structures are supposed to do. The symptom/disease is an attempt to achieve harmony between what is given (the current life situation) and the subject's response to it. For example, problems at the work-place create a tension or disharmony which must be resolved, just as an itch must be scratched, an object must be moved closer in order to be seen clearly, or a conflict between friends strives towards an anticipated reconciliation. The psychosomatic patient attempts to solve the difficulties at work by applying a lower level body response (e.g. back pain). But these somatic responses are not satisfactory ones, because they are incapable of achieving a true harmony with that which has triggered them into being. As low level body signification, they cannot help to transform the higher order levels of meaning, which is the level where the problematic situation has arisen. No matter how often and to what extent one pays attention to one's back, it will have no real effect upon the current problematic situation, it is no real "answer".[63] It creates a semblance of equilibrium, but the somatic structure is nevertheless inadequate to the task, because it is a lower level body response to levels of existence (psycho-social reality) which *require* psycho-social structures for true resolution.

*The transformation of structures and the dialectic of meaning are terms which illustrate the insight that <u>meaning</u> is always in the making, never finished once and for all. Meaning is virtual, as Merleau-Ponty writes. It comes to be through a continual lived process wherein the subject meets the world with structures, structures which are both stable and capable of transformations. Meaning evolves in the dialectical ex-

---

[63] True, the back pain may result in so-called "secondary gains" such as eliciting attention and care from others and diminished responsibility. But these types of consequences are not a solution to the tension, they are, in fact, a sedimentation of the original problem, which the following chapters will try to show.

change between man and his situation. For example, we may have a close friend whom we feel that we know quite well, who one day tells us that he is a homosexual. We suddenly find that we must adjust our picture of our friend to accommodate this new information. A new meaning is born, a meaning which casts all that we have previously known or thought about our friend into a new light. The old structure, or way of understanding and relating to our friend, is transformed, and we have a slightly new and different perspective which enriches and furthers our understanding of him. The problem for the psychosomatic patient is that s/he is no longer able to transform his/her structures in order to meet the new and the challenging. When a person is unable to transform his/her structures, and thereby create new meanings in accordance with the new and different, a stagnation in the flow of life occurs. The world becomes less articulated and more stereotyped. The solution to the tension which the new situation has created is to turn the intentional arc towards the experience of the body, a maneuver which further impoverishes the patient's experience of the world. As Gestalt psychologists have shown, when the body is in the center of the field of attention, the rest of the field is correspondingly transformed. The "silent ground" becomes figure, and that which would have been figure becomes ground. Only when the patient is once again able to participate in the transformation of higher order structures can the attention which was focused upon bodily experiences become re-directed towards the world, which then becomes the arena for structure transformations and the emergence of new meaning.

*Sedimentation is used in the Merleau-Pontian sense, that is, sedimentation is the way in which structures (body structures, perceptual structures, psychological-cognitive structures, social structures) have a tendency to repeat themselves in preferred patterns. We economize by allowing privileged ways of moving, perceiving and thinking to anchor us in the world. Sedimented structures give us the stability we need in order to experience the enormously rich human world. If we always needed to give our entire attention to our perceptions or our body movements, we would never have become free to develop language, and if, in turn, language did not itself sediment into stable patterns of meaning, we could never develop it beyond the sign-level of representation. Finally, the sedimentation of social stability (customs and habits) allows us to move freely in the intersubjective world without difficulty[64]. For the psychosomatic patient, lower level body responses and expressions of lower level "body meaning"[65] have become the privileged way of experiencing the world. Somatization *is* precisely the sedimentation of somatic structures, which in turn transforms the patient's experience of the world.

*Transcendence is our specifically human capacity for going beyond the given towards the possible. It is this existential condition which differentiates human structures from animal structures. Humans are always *beyond,* both perceptually and temporally. In perception, one goes through the given perspective of the object (e.g. of the table) towards the experience of the whole object (thematically perceived as such), which is actually never sensuously given except in and through perspective. A further human attribute is that we know that we stand in relation to a world which is not ourselves. We go out of ourselves towards a world, which is Other. Transcendence manifests itself temporally as well. Just as we are capable of imagining a perceptual horizon beyond the given, so do we understand that we are temporally moving towards the hour of our death. That we "point beyond" is a fundamental structure of our being.[66] As Merleau-Ponty puts it, we are continually "having it out"

---

[64] Anyone who has had the experience of living in a culture which is not one's own realizes how we take this cultural "ease" for granted. It is surprisingly hard to navigate oneself in a new culture, especially if it is very different from one's own, since the correct interpretation/understanding of words, gestures, body language and so on does not occur automatically. We find that we need cognitive processes in order to correctly understand what is going on around us. Our own culture, on the other hand, has been sedimented so that we do not need to take a detour via thought in order to smoothly get about and know what is going on.

[65] Because we are always dealing with a mind/body unity, the body is also imbued with meaning, but it is not yet a personal, symbolic, social meaning. We could call it a nascent meaning, or a rudimentary meaning. See chapter 9 on psychosomatics as expression and rudimentary speech.

[66] See Heidegger (1927/1962) for a good explication of this *ek-stasis.*

with the world.[67] Transcendence is the specifically human ability to be able to take a stand and orient oneself towards the given, which is the definition of (conditioned) freedom which Merleau-Ponty argues for against Sartre's notion of absolute freedom.[68] In my theory, transcendence is that dimension of human life which sustains the experience of self, centers the narrative of the life story, and motivates the responsibility of the adult. Without this dimension intact, we indeed become "thing-like", or rather, as Sartre would say, we *pretend* to be things. The psychosomatic patient has lost contact with this dimension of transcendence and finds himself living at the level of the body as quasi-thing, thereby successfully avoiding his subjectivity and freedom in a form of Sartrian "bad faith". I would say that the deepest description of "ill health" is losing contact with this transcendence, with the self as becoming, with taking responsibility for one's own life. And if we use the body in order to enact this flight, we will call the illness "psychosomatic."[69]

*Self-becoming is not a term which comes from Merleau-Ponty, but I find it to be a good one, illuminating an important aspect of human existence. Self-becoming, in my theory, is tied to the notion of transcendence above. What the "self" is, is of course a enormous question and it has been written about extensively.[70] I am by the term "self" referring to

---

67 "One day, once and for all, something was set in motion which, even during sleep, can no longer cease to see nor not to see, to feel or not to feel, to suffer or be happy, to think or rest from thinking, in a word to 'have it out' with the world...The event of my birth has not passed completely away, it has not fallen into nothingness the way that an event of the objective world does, for it committed a whole future, not as a cause determines its effect, but as a situation, once created, inevitably leads on to some outcome. There was henceforth a new 'setting,' the world received a fresh layer of meaning." (*PP*, pp. 406-407).

68 In *PP*, pp. 434-456.

69 In no way do I mean to suggest that it is only psychosomatic patients who are in ill health. There may be a variety of ways to lose touch with this transcendent dimension of human life (e.g. compulsive gambling, workaholics, alcoholics etc.) However, I am in this dissertation interested in investigating the psychosomatic solution, and for that reason I do not address possible other ways of being ill.

70 See Taylor (1989).

the complex unity of human embodiment which includes specifically human higher order levels of psycho-social reality, engaged in a concrete life world. The self, or "personal existence," is the lived subjectivity of the specific person in his/her concrete life situation. That the self *becomes* is the insight that we are not finished until our last moment. We are always in the process of defining and becoming who we are in the course of our concrete life situations. We are possibilities until we die, when we become once and for all the sum (actuality) of what has been.

Now I will briefly take up the <u>dynamics</u> of the psychosomatic process as I see it in my theory. Because my theory is phenomenological, it must be remembered that I am describing a lived phenomenon, which can only be understood in terms of the "in-between" of being-in-the-world. I am neither focusing on objective bodily processes, psychological processes, external "stimuli" nor hypothesized relations between these different levels of description. The object of study is the lived body and the world as constituted by the subject in this particular psychosomatic way, which will be described and developed fully in the following chapters. My characterization of this process is as follows. There is an event or situation in the current life of the patient which s/he cannot meet with sedimented structures. Neither can this situation be adjusted to by the transformation of current structures. There is thus a meaning in the life of the patient which is denied "higher order" articulation. Because the patient is always both mind and body, the signification of this situation finds expression at a lower body level. The patient is triggered into applying somatic structures (body symptoms and experiences) in those situations which would otherwise (in other people) have elicited thoughts, feelings and perhaps actions. The symptom/disease is an attempt to achieve a harmony with the tension created by the situation, but as lower level body signification it cannot adjust to the new and challenging situation, which is formulated at the higher level of psycho-social reality. The breakdown of the dialectic of meaning in the life of the patient is lived as a reversal of figure ground, where the body and its sensations take the place of directed intentionality towards the world, more specifically towards the impossible situation which cannot be articulated at higher level structures. I have called this reversal "cognitive attentionality." The person-situation dialectic of meaning breaks down, and as long as the situation persists in the life of the patient, and s/he is unable to achieve a harmony with it through transformation of higher order structures, the symptom/disease will remain.

The validity[71] of the phenomenological theory of psychosomatics presented here, like any human scientific theory, rests upon the plausibility of its proposals, the coherence of its logic, the descriptive accuracy with which it addresses the empirical territory under investigation, the successful argumentation against viable alternatives, and finally, its ability to provoke and stimulate further reflection upon the phenomenon in question. It is a theory generated from within a specific perspective (phenomenology), as all theories are, and it must therefore be evaluated according to the interests and goals formulated from within the perspective. I am describing a reality (phenomenon) which is made comprehensible through the application of a theory which elaborates non-empirical components into a coherent system. Clinically, I have, in retrospect, found the theory useful in trying to understand the process of the cure which I was privileged to witness during the course of my work with patients in psychiatric health care. Whether or not the theory has met the validity criteria presented above will be examined in chapter 10.

The following chapters focus upon three different aspects of the psychosomatic way of life, which could be summarized as "being-in-the-world as being-towards-the-body". This psychosomatic way of being will be illustrated in terms of 1) psychosomatics in relation to the self; more specifically, psychosomatic pathology as a retreat from the self-world dialectic (chapter 7); 2) psychosomatics and temporality, which I have called "psychosomatics as frozen time" (chapter 8); and finally 3) psy-

---

71 The concept of "validity" should not be understood here in the positivist sense of accurately measuring that which one intends to measure, but rather in the qualitative sense of choosing among competing knowledge claims based upon the hermeneutical practice of interpretation and argumentation. We are concerned here with a validation based upon communication (human science) rather than observation (natural science). See Kvale (1989) and Ricoeur (1974; 1981a) on the issue of validation in the human sciences.

chosomatics and the relation to others, which focuses upon psychosomatics as expression and rudimentary speech (chapter 9). These aspects have emerged as essential because they address basic aspects of human life; namely, our experience of ourselves, our existence as temporal beings who have histories and futures and our relationship to others. The aspects examined in chapter 7 (retreat from self) and chapter 9 (expression and rudimentary speech) are related internally to each other since the retreat from self *is also* a breakdown in communication with others (and vice versa), while chapter 8 (frozen time) refers specifically to body-memories, which may or may not be involved in the psychosomatic condition. In other words, the psychosomatic way of being-in-the-world always involves a retreat from the self-world dialectic, which manifests itself in various ways, one of which is the primitive body expression of a meaning which cannot be expressed or communicated at a higher level. Whether or not the psychosomatic process originates because a frozen body memory has hindered the transformation of structures, or whether the current incapacity arises from something in the current life situation, will vary from case to case, although it could be argued that every present difficulty has some connection to the past. The latter question concerns psychosomatic *etiology*, which will be discussed finally in chapter 10.

CHAPTER 7

Psychosomatic pathology as a retreat from self

"*I am born*. Whether I shall turn out to be the hero of my own life, or whether that station will be held by anybody else, these pages must show."

-Charles Dickens, *David Copperfield*

Patient : And then when I came home from having dinner with Martin, I had such a pain in my back, I had to lie down. I lay down all evening, and the next day, when I woke up, I had such a pain, I was so stiff I just couldn't get up...

Therapist: I was wondering what happened when you had dinner with Martin? Did it go well?

Patient : Go well? I don't know. I had such a pain in my back, you know. I just can't stand it, it drives me crazy! I never have a moment's peace, all the time it stabs and aches. It feels like a ton of bricks.

Therapist : I understand that having pain all the time is very tiresome, but I can't help but notice that you pay so much attention to your back, that there isn't much room for anything else, like, for example, how you feel about other people, what happens to you, what you would like to do or say in various situations. Do you understand what I mean?

Patient : You think I concentrate on my back to avoid things, but I can't pay attention to anything else!!! What am I supposed to do?

The imaginary dialogue above could be going on in any consulting room today within primary health care or psychiatrics. The patient is thought of as somatizing her difficulties in life, and the task of the clinician/therapist is to help her come to grips with her problems for which the pain in her back is an inadequate solution. The patient experiences her main problem as her back pain. This clash of perspectives is well-known. As seen in the first part of the dissertation, various theories have different ways of understanding the patient's symptom. The psychodynamically oriented therapist believes that unconscious ideas, wishes, fantasies and fears are being defended against by somatization. Something from the mind has escaped into the body. Unconscious thoughts are imagined to be, in principle, unavailable to the patient until the repression and resistance have been undone through psychotherapy. A cognitive therapist sees the patient's difficulties in terms of false, maladapted beliefs and insufficient coping strategies. A socially oriented case worker wonders about the patient's relationships and social network. A biologically oriented doctor may wish to give the patient medication in order treat a presumptive underlying (endogenic) depression. Traditional models focus either on the objective body (chemical imbalances to be corrected) or the disembodied mind, conceptualized either as universal intrapsychical mechanisms (psychoanalytic constructs) or thematized cognitive content (appraisals and beliefs). None of the theories examined in this dissertation take into account the experience of lived embodiment nor the intentional, contextualized nature of meaning. The phenomenological approach I will be developing in this and the following chapters understands the above patient's back pain as a lower level expression/communication of a life situation which the patient cannot (yet) articulate in terms of thoughts and feelings.[1] The symptom is a rigid,

---

[1] Those familiar with the work of the existential psychotherapist Medard Boss may see some similarity between my theory and his *Dasein analytik*. I read Boss and Binswanger at a later stage of my own writing and was both pleased and annoyed to find thoughts similar to my own expressed in their work. Boss' existential psychotherapy is based upon Heidegger's philosophy, especially Heidegger's notion of *Dasein* (being-there) and related ideas on attunement, being-towards-death, anticipatory resoluteness and so on. Although Boss criticizes both Freudian theory and psychosomatic

stereotyped "language" which is not thematically understood by the patient him/herself nor the interlocutor. The nature of this expression/communication will be examined in detail in Chapter 9.

In order to understand the characterization of psychosomatic functioning as a retreat from self, we must first take a look at what a "self" is, and then see in what way psychosomatic illness is a departure from self-becoming. What does it mean to be a self, to have a world (live a situation), to have a past and a future, to communicate with others? All these dimensions of existence are so taken for granted that we don't usually explicitly wonder about them. However, the notion of "self" has not always been as evident as it is for modern Western man. Van den Berg[2] has historically traced out the emergence of what he calls the "inner self" primarily during two epochs, associated with two thinkers, Martin Luther (1483-1546) and Jean Jacques Rousseau (1712-1778). For Luther, the inner man was the religious self, while for Rousseau the notion of the self was an affirmation of individuality. Thus the evolution of the modern Western concept of self has both a religious (15th century) and individualistic (18th century) background.[3] What is our modern Western meaning of the self?

By "self" we generally refer to some idea about the continuity and coherence of personal existence. One could say that I am a narrative[4] (story) which I tell myself and others, which I myself understand. The

---

medicine for reasons similar to my own, his alternative to them is different from mine. We are both concerned with being-in-the-world and the experience of the body, but the concepts and categories of understanding used by Boss diverge from my understanding of these phenomena. See Binswanger (1964; 1975), Boss (1979), and von Uexküll (1963) for literature from this tradition.

2 van den Berg (1961).

3 In Pollio et al. (1997), pp. 265-267.

4 The importance of narrative (the life story) has gained some ground in contemporary psychoanalysis (see Schafer 1976;1983; Spence 1982). The term "narrative" has its roots in the Sanskrit "gna" which means "to know" and the Latin "narrare" which means "to relate". In opposition to narrative conceptualizations of man we find the post modern de-construction of the self. I am in this dissertation aligning myself with the narrative tradition, and assume that there is a unitary narrative self, which is lived and experienced as such.

continuity of self through time is lived as a fundamental ground for all experience. I am, in some very basic way, the same person I was 10 years ago. I may have changed some attitudes, even radically, but it is nevertheless *I* who have changed my mind about various things. Furthermore, there is a harmony or coherence, for the most part, between different aspects of a person's life. For this reason, one can say that it was typical of Peter to do something like that, or the reverse, that one is surprised that Peter could do something like that. The surprise is itself a testimony to the belief in the consistency of personal identity. The self is supported through time by the general availability of memory, and the projection of an imagined future. My*self* is experienced concretely in the world in terms of the efficacy of volition (I can...), the surge of desires and wishes (I want...) and so on. A self is capable of being open to moods and atmospheres, and on the highest, most thematic level, the self as personal identity is related to a network of attitudes, values and opinions. But this self is not created *ex nihilo*. To be a self or person is to continually define and shape oneself in relation to the world, in response to various situations which arise, and in interaction with the people who inhabit one's world. We continually carve out our personal existence in this meeting with others and the world, in concretely lived situations. A person <u>becomes</u> through continual interactions and transformations.[5] The self is the sum of that which has been (experienced as a coherent narrative), pointing towards possibilities, which are understood as such.

The essence of self or personhood, then, is *process*. As long as one lives, one is never "finished", we are always on the way. This fundamental tending beyond oneself is *transcendence*. We take up our lives, our situation, and continually renew and transform the meaning which we find there, a meaning which we ourselves have co-authored, together

---

5   The people of Sierre Leone have a concept of "the witch" which is interesting in this context. For them, a witch is not a person. Personhood *(morgoye)* has to do with collective values, such as being mindful and responsible, open and straightforward. The unsociable person, like the witch, is "bent," "devious," "broken down," "crooked," "useless," or even "unwell." Anyone who sets him/herself apart from others is simply not a person *(morgo ma)*. In Jackson, M. (1989), p. 90.

with others. It is this continual, dialectical transformation of structures which allows for the self to become. I am the same person who was once 8 years old, yet that which I am now was not yet there when I was an 8-year-old child. What has occurred between then and now is the unfolding of my life, which is "myself." Of all the possible worlds which could have been, it has become, up to this point, *this* world, this situation, and I take up this life in my own particular way. It is the *meaning* which I ascribe to my life which is me. Perhaps I had a serious illness when I was 6 years old, or a traumatic childhood, or have at this moment a bodily dysfunction which causes me pain and discomfort. These "facts" about me are a part of my facticity, my history, but they can never be *causes* for me to develop in a certain direction or to become the person I am, they can only serve as motivations for me to do so. The foundation of selfhood is our capacity to transcend the given, to ascribe personal meaning and signification to our facticity, to change our life projects and points of view.[6] The realm of personal identity depends upon this transcendence. Without it, we would not be human beings (existence). Traditional theories of psychosomatics have missed this important insight. As shown in part I, dualistic/reductionistic tendencies have unfortunately aligned themselves together with the natural scientific paradigm, so that the focus of psychosomatic investigations is a mechanical, impersonal, causally influenced body, divorced from subjectivity as embodied existence. To grasp the significance of the psychosomatic symptom, we need to reinstate the idea of personal embodied existence and transcendence. It is the dialectic of meaning between self and situation which is disturbed in psychosomatics, not the mechanical dysfunction of a somatic objective body.

---

6 Merleau-Ponty: "But here once more we must recognize a sort of sedimentation of our life: an attitude towards the world, when it has received frequent confirmation, acquires a favored status for us. Yet...my habitual being in the world is at each moment equally precarious, and the complexes which I have allowed to develop over the years remain equally soothing, the free act can with no difficulty blow them sky high" (*PP* pp. 441-442, my translation from the French ed p. 504).

As existence (persons/selves), we *are* this fundamental relationship between our facticity (our history, gender, class, life events etc.) and our freedom (how we take up and understand our lives). It is in this special combination of the given and the possible, facticity and freedom, that we find the existential ground for what it means to be a self. We are certainly constrained in our freedom (just as we cannot perceive whatever we would like), but within the framework of our facticity we are always free to orient ourselves towards it in terms of possibilities.[7] I would say that it is precisely the exercise of this freedom in relationship to various "facts" which the psychosomatic patient wishes to avoid by becoming ill. The retreat from self is a retreat from the dialectic wherein meaning and personal signification emerge.[8] The patient has replaced the self-world dialectic with the experience of the obtrusive body, the body as quasi-object. Transcendence, self-becoming and the transformation of structures are replaced by a form of body intentionality, which effectively removes the patient from the arena where the self can become. Another way of expressing this idea appears in traditional literature as the "sick-role", which refers to the identification of the sufferer with the suffering body.[9] Let us now attempt to construct this somatization process, with regard to this first aspect: retreat from self.

Instead of speaking about "normal" and "pathological" functioning, I would prefer to speak of higher order and lower order structures. The

---

[7] Levinas (1947/1987) writes that the hero never misses the last chance to take advantage of some possibility, rather than accepting death (the end of all possibilities). I am reminded of the last scene in Cyrano de Bergerac where he takes his sword out of his sheath when death approaches him, fully aware that the gesture is futile, but the sword is drawn, nevertheless.

[8] Rudebeck (1991) has expressed himself similarly on the nature of the psychosomatic symptom, "The symptom expresses that a person who is in fact quite capable has been brought to a stand-still" (p. 46).

[9] Jackson, J. (1994) on the sick role: "For the most part chronic pain patients see their problem as one of 'matter over mind' because their intractable pain makes them feel that their bodies are powerfully influencing their minds...Their lives, their emotions, their spirituality, their personalities, their destinies are dominated by their painful bodies, and their role as sufferer has shunted aside previous roles as caregiver, provider, lover, companion, parent, friend, citizen" (p. 207).

238

higher structures are those which are developed during the maturation/socialization process and refer to levels of existence such as cognition, language, and cultural competence. To call them "higher" is not to evaluate them as better, but to indicate that they are built upon lower functions, and that they bring a higher degree of clarity, articulation and nuance to experience. The lower functions are perception, sensations, moods, and different forms of body experiences. It will be recalled that the higher and lower functions are integrated with each other, and one cannot speak of a body sensation which is pure and separate from cognitive, cultural aspects, nor can one speak of a realm of meaning which is not conditioned by our embodiment. But although this intertwining is a reality of our existence, it is also the case that, as indicated earlier, we may find ourselves positioned at either higher or lower levels at a given time in a given situation. When giving a lecture, the higher order structures are most salient, while in the case of dancing or falling asleep we are farther down at lower levels of body structures. It is our ability to immediately place ourselves at the proper level which is responsible for the flow of life, for the way in which we, for the most part, find ourselves at home in various situations. My clinical experience with psychosomatic patients is that instead of moving up and down on this continuum from higher to lower levels of structure, they are stuck at one level, the body level. This low level body response is activated in life situations which awaken in them a tension or disharmony in their sedimented structures. The psychosomatic response is to exist as body, which I have called "being-towards-the-body", instead of being-in(towards)-the-world. Patients place their bodies in the foreground, and life situations in the background, which is the reverse of our usual orientation. They direct attention and care to their bodies in situations which require a higher level of structural response in order to harmonize and result in new structural transformations. This psychosomatic intentionality, instead of disclosing something "in-between," displaces this something from the center of attention to the periphery, and replaces it with body sensations and experiences of body symptoms. The experience of meaning is then no longer higher order, but lower order (body). The work of the existentialists as well as the psychoanalysts teaches us that human beings cannot tolerate lack of meaning. To live without meaning, at any level, is anxiety-provoking. Because we human beings are creatures of meaning, the "speaking body" expresses meaning which is, at the present time, impossible to grasp or articulate higher up. Low level body meaning thereby provides a buffer against the anxiety of meaninglessness, which we abhor.[10]

According to my theory, psychosomatic patients cling tenaciously to the experience of their body, instead of activating and developing higher order structures. This could also be called a "body solution" to some kind of tension which has been introduced into their present situation. The patients have been triggered into somatizing by something in their world which they have not been able to incorporate into present structures. They seem equally unable to transform their structures in order to accommodate the new and challenging experience. Empirically, we know that when patients are eventually able to formulate themselves at a higher level of articulation (e.g. expressing thoughts and feelings), they become cured of their bodily symptoms. I now ask once again the question posed in part I of this dissertation, what is curative about thinking and feeling? My answer is that it is through the higher order levels of thought and feeling and verbal expression that we have access to ourselves as persons and to others as other selves. Only through the higher orders of psychosocial reality can the self be reintroduced into his/her own meaningful context and situation. Only then can one once more become "the hero of one's own life." At the lower bodily levels, we are not in contact with personal existence. It is virtually impossible to engage in a meaningful dialogue with a headache (if one is not a Gestalt therapist), as one cannot

---

10 A well-known empirical finding supports this idea, namely that when psychosomatic patients begin to let go of their body symptoms they will often experience anxiety, which they had not previously experienced. The anxiety phase eventually recedes when the patient succeeds in establishing what I call "higher order level signification", that is to say, when they can think and reflect about their lives. "The cure" can thus be conceptualized in terms of meaning evolution from body meaning (buffer against meaninglessness), through anxiety (meaninglessness) to psycho-social levels of signification (personal meaning).

speak to a headache, and a headache cannot give any answers. A headache can just be a headache.[11] But if the headache is understood as the bodily expression of a lived situation, and this lived situation eventually becomes thematic (known), one can begin to speak. A conversation with someone who feels overburdened and expresses her desire for relief and assistance in her current life situation may lead to a transformation of her situation, a situation which was badly expressed as a headache, but adequately expressed (at the proper level) as complaints and needs. Let me give a clinical example.

Mrs. A. was referred to our psychiatric out-patient clinic because she had hypochondriacal fears, combined with aches and pains which alternated from stomach pains to back pains to headaches. Her GP had convinced her that he couldn't do anything for her, and that she should look for help on a psychological basis. She arrived for the consultation relatively open and curious about therapeutical treatment. She was an intelligent, middle-aged, divorced mother of two, working part-time as a secretary. Her home life had been traumatic, with an unstable mother and abusive father. The details of her life emerged slowly and laboriously. During the first five months of her therapy she focused exclusively on her body problems, describing them in great detail and complaining bitterly about not getting any relief. The most prominent feeling I had towards her during the first year of therapy was that I needed to get an idea of *who* this person was. Although we spoke together week after week, she remained a stranger to me. I did not get any picture of her life, although she filled the sessions with talk. I knew that she had children, but they did not become real people of flesh and blood in therapy. There were also work colleagues, but neither did they appear in any real way. The few times she brought up actual life events in the session, they were reported without feeling, as if she were speaking about someone else. This was in contrast to the care and attention with which she related her

---

11 A headache may also have non-psychosomatic causes, such as a blow to the head or a tumor. Whether the headache then is used psychosomatically (the wide definition) is an empirical question from case to case, while the etiological question of the "cause" of e.g. the tumor (the narrow definition) will be discussed in chapter 10.

body symptoms. She seemed basically uninterested in what was happening around her. Care was reserved for her body, discussing it, wondering about it, worrying about it. This was the preferred topic. When other topics came up, usually through my questioning, such as "What did you think about that?" or "How did that make you feel?", she more often than not responded by relating a somatic symptom. It seemed that there was in fact no person there who could answer my questions, only a field of body sensations and experiences.

The first step in therapy was to try to help her see some connection between her symptoms and her life situation. In Merleau-Ponty terms, an attempt was made to activate or set in motion the intentional threads which connect a subject to her world. In the case of Mrs. A., it became apparent to us both during the course of the therapy that it was primarily in situations in which an aggressive/assertive response would be called for that she "fainted" (her term) into her body. The challenge which the world addressed to her could not be responded to by the structures available to her. Another way of putting it is that she could not transform *herself* in such a way that these situations could be mastered. In the course of therapy, the process of transformation occurred first with me, in imagination, safe from the threatening presence of reality. She could imagine herself as someone who would say this and do that, someone who could do something about what was going on in her life. By having a safe haven in the therapy hour, Mrs. A. could gradually put into practice some of her imaginary exercises in self-assertion and anger. According to the theory being presented here, the cure was to help Mrs. A. create new structures, structures which could articulate for her herself and her situation in such a way that she could meet the challenges in her world. The *meaning* of her experiences became articulated in the therapeutical dialogue. Before therapy, Mrs. A. had a hard time to even perceive situations *as* threatening: the only thing she was thematically aware of was that her body dominated her field of attention and demanded her total concentration. With the help of several years of therapy, the world gradually became more specific, e.g. and she understood that there are situations in life which are not so pleasant. She herself be-

242

came more developed and articulated, that is, she saw that she was a person who could be both nice and angry, and that anger did not exclude her appraisal of herself as nice as well. Mrs. A. paid less and less attention to her body as the world and her own reactions to it dominated her field of attention. After several years of therapy, she rarely spoke of her body, and the worry and attention she used to give to her sensations were transferred to life situations.

What happened during the therapy of Mrs. A.? A psychoanalyst would say that unconscious conflicts concerning aggression had been made conscious, preferably though a reconstruction of past experiences of aggression directed towards parents and significant others. Cognitive therapists would say that the patient developed new coping strategies and corrected her false beliefs about herself and others. A biomedical opinion might be that the placebo effect was the curative factor, the fact that someone listened to the patient and cared about her year after year. These are plausible explanations when seen from within their own theoretical frameworks (although the theoretical difficulties surrounding these explanations have been presented in part I), but the main problem with these theories is that they do not address the question which is phenomenologically the most interesting, namely how does the patient *live* her world now, and in what way does it differ from her experience of herself and her situation before "the cure"? What is missing in traditional characterizations is an understanding of the nature of the relationship between the patient and her world. The phenomenological theory presented here focuses upon this factor, emphasizing the lived, embodied person who constitutes the meaning of her life and her world.[12] It is here

---

12 A similar characterization from Boss (1979): "Psychic causes and psychodynamics cannot exist, because the psychic part of them is concerned exclusively with a person's way of relating - emotional, rational, hopeful, active, perceptive, and so on - to what matters to him in his world, and in his dimension there are only comprehensible motivational contexts. Any psychological theory that translates a motive or motivational context into a psychic cause or a psychodynamic causal chain destroys the very foundation of human beings. Recognition of the unbridgeable chasm that separates causes from motives lets us see how fundamentally unhuman are all psychologi-

we find the psychosomatic disturbance, in the lived being-in-the-world of the patient. There is a meaning in the world of the patient which is "stuck" in the body, and this being stuck at the level of the body prevents the patient from developing herself and her life. When Mrs. A. could begin to think and feel specific thoughts and feelings about her life situation, she got back on track and her body symptoms disappeared. The cure is to let the process of becoming move forward. The meaning which is nascent in the body becomes fully developed when higher order structures are formed which make possible its articulated expression. Through therapy, Mrs. A. regained access to higher order structures which enabled her to experience her life as transcendence, as a constant project which she herself was responsible for. One of the breakthrough sessions in her treatment occurred when she returned to her first session after a summer break and told me that she had been sitting in her kitchen one morning and suddenly realized that she herself and no one else was responsible for her life. This thought had struck her as extraordinary, and during the months that followed, this insight led to important discussions about the different ways in which she had managed to evade responsibility for herself and her life over the years. One of the ways she had avoided this responsibility was to use her body. She behaved as if she were a body and not a self, and gave the responsibility for herself and her life to others. Her psychosomatic symptoms were clearly a way for her to retreat from the (at the time) overwhelming task of becoming herself.

But one may protest, what is this process of "becoming oneself"? Surely Mrs. A had some idea of *herself* throughout her illness? The answer is yes, if an <u>idea</u> of oneself is all that is meant by "self". Mrs. A's idea of herself throughout her first year of therapy was that she was someone afflicted with various bodily dysfunctions. But if we mean by "self" something more dynamic, interactive and transcending, the patient did not experience her*self* during this time. She experienced, for the most

---

cal theories which, allegedly for the sake of being scientific, try to force motivated human behavior into the dimension of the principle of physical causality" (p. 152).

244

part, her own body, in rigid, sedimented somatic structures. Somatic structures (responding to the world as body) fail, because they do not transform either the subject or her situation. Psychosomatic symptoms sediment the subject in lower level body experiences, rather than leading to the development of self in the world. To become oneself means to partake in the enactment of personal meaning and signification, which is that moment of freedom and transcendence whereby one takes up and transforms the "facts" of one's existence into a personal narrative. Mrs. A described her experience of herself in the therapy process as gradually becoming "sharp and defined", whereas before therapy she had felt "diffuse" and "unreal". She had the feeling that a great fog had lifted, and inside herself she discovered a core which was real, a thought which made her feel happy and proud. However, this process was not an easy one. The relationship between self (personhood), anxiety and responsibility is a well-known theme in existentialist literature. To ascribe personal meaning to one's life and to take responsibility for it is anxiety-provoking. When this task is too difficult, we evade it in various ways. One way of evading is to become entangled at the level of the body. To live as body is, of course, a way of life, and one may ask, well, why not just accept this "psychosomatic" way of life as one mode of human existence, one way of living human life? The answer to that question would be to refer to the patients themselves. It is they who have in fact asked for help. It is my clinical experience that psychosomatic patients are not satisfied with living their lives at this level, although their dissatisfaction has not yet been directed to the source, only to the symptom.

The enactment of self-becoming requires the capacity to travel up and down on the (mind-body) continuum, from high order structures such as cognition and reflection to lower level ones. The patient who responds to difficulties at work by concentrating upon her back will not be able to develop her "work-place" structure in accordance with the new which inevitably arises.[13] Conversely, to respond to lower level situations

---

13 A specialist in occupational and environmental medicine related to me that in many cases, patients who develop an oversensitivity to electrical equipment often experience the debut of their illness shortly after they have been given new work tasks which

(e.g. a sexual encounter) with cognition and reflection would be equally inappropriate. The point is that there are natural correspondences of levels between ourselves and our situation (the question-answer pattern of structures) which allow us to initiate or respond to a seduction, enjoy a sauna, read a difficult text, solve mathematical problems and so on. To be at the right level at the right time is something which occurs spontaneously, in the natural flow of life. We do not normally start to do calculus during a sexual encounter, nor do we pay any attention to our body sensations when we are engaged in a political discussion. It is obvious that something has happened to the psychosomatic patient's ability to move freely on this continuum. The body and its sensations and aches and pains dominate the field, regardless of what is going on in the patient's world. To be flexible in terms of which level one enacts is one aspect of transcendence, it is our ability to transform ourselves and our understanding of the world at one fell swoop. This the patients cannot do. They have riveted themselves to their bodies. How does this come about?

The psychoanalysts[14] spoke of psychosomatic pathology in terms of "regression" to an earlier stage of functioning. Regression implies moving from a later to an earlier functioning. I would rather compare the repetitive usage of somatic structures to Sartre's analysis of emotions as a "spontaneous and lived degradation of consciousness in the face of the world."[15] For Sartre, emotion is an *assumed* (in the sense of "taken up") form of organized human consciousness. His provocative thesis is that emotion is chosen, an idea which runs contrary to most other theories, where emotion is something which "just comes over us". Sartre's basic characterization of emotion is that it is a specific transformation of the world into a *magical world*. When our path becomes too difficult, when we are confronted by insurmountable odds, we "break down" into emo-

---

they have difficulty in mastering (personal communication). A similar finding from Hellström et al (1998b) has shown that the onset of fibromyalgia is often precipitated by a problematic self-image.

[14] See Schur (1955).
[15] Sartre (1948, p. 77).

tion, which is a lower form of consciousness. We find ourselves no longer in a world where the connections between oneself and the world are constituted by determinate causation, but rather by magic. And as Sartre points out, in order to believe in a magical world, one must be very disturbed. Sartre gives the example of the patient who felt that she should confess something to her doctor. She wanted to speak to him, but she also wanted him to be moved and compassionate. His attitude, however, was rather one of impassive waiting. The patient, in order to obtain the quality she wished in the doctor, began to weep, while at the same time she succeeded in putting her body into a state which made her confession impossible. Choked by tears and sobs, she could not utter a word. In this way, she managed to deliver herself from the painful (and impossible) feeling that the act of confession to this impassive doctor was within her power. She gave up dealing realistically with the world, and magically transformed herself and her doctor, without having to take the usual arduous paths of higher consciousness (reflection, verbalization, responsibility etc.). For Sartre, although emotion is a way of reacting to and apprehending the world, it is essentially non-positional consciousness. We are not completely, reflectively aware of what we are doing. We escape without thematically deciding to do so. In a similar way, I would say that the psychosomatic patient "chooses" to relate to the world via impersonal, lower level bodily responses. It is an attempt to avoid the tension which arises when a situation cannot be mastered by any sedimented structures. Instead of transforming structures, and thereby dissolving the tension, the answer is to withdraw into the world of body sensations.

Thus, in place of a question-answer dialogue involving higher level structures, we find the blunt expressiveness of symptoms and somatic functioning. But because we are a always a mind/body unity in some relation to our world, this symptom or bodily experience will be expressive, although it is inadequate to the task at hand. Because the body expression does not enter into transformations,[16] the initial situation which triggered the tension will continue to disturb the equilibrium of the patient. Since the patient has left the higher levels of expression and articulation, she is incapable of taking in that which is new and challenging. That which was a vague and threatening "something" between the patient and her world becomes a menace from within. The problem becomes the body. Situations are no longer situations (an invitation to the transformation of structures and self-becoming), and personal meaning and signification (transcendence and freedom) fall away. The world stands still, and challenging situations are understood in terms of body problems. This is why it is so difficult for, and even insulting to the patient when the therapist/doctor insists upon hearing about what is going on in the patient's life. In order for there to be a world, there must be a self, and in order for there to be a self, there must be higher order structures engaged in situations, capable of transformations. When the psychosomatic patient is seeking help for her symptoms, she has chosen to withdraw into her body, and for that reason cannot be reached by proddings about her world - not initially, in any case.

But what has been illuminated by the notion of psychosomatic pathology as a retreat from self? How does the introduction of the notion of somatic, rigid structures allow us to better understand the psychosomatic patient? What is the advantage of this picture? First of all, in this theory, the focus is upon the rupture *between* the patient and his world. Before the modern cleavage of man into a mechanical body and a sover-

---

16 It has been called to my attention (seminar group "Conversations about the Body") that rituals in various cultures often use the body as a means of expressing, affirming and passing on collective meanings and values. That which is interesting here is that in cultures where body expression is ritualized, codified and understood, the one who uses the cultural body expression finds "an answer" on the social level, and is thus not alone and mute, but rather understood and affirmed. An interesting thought is that if our modern Western culture offered more avenues of ritual (body) expression, it is quite possible that we would enjoy better psychosomatic health. We would have the possibility of dialogue on the lower levels as well, which would incorporate body expression into the psycho-social reality of the group. Dance as an art form is an example of this kind of codified, ritualized body expression.

248

eign mind, the idea of ill health as a disturbed relationship between the subject and his world was quite widespread and well-known. Traditional Chinese Medicine, the ancient Greeks, as well as many other cultures, have viewed illness first and foremost as a disturbance between man, his/her society and the cosmic order. My theory is in line with this age-old insight, and introduces the notion of structure transformation and the dialectic of meaning as a way of understanding these relations. The psychosomatic condition is a disturbance which testifies to the breakdown of the patient's ability to transform structures and integrate new meaning into his/her current life situation. Psychosomatic pathology is always *about* something in the patient's life, although what it is about is, for the time being, incapable of being expressed in terms other than body symptoms. The psychosomatic patient has chosen a body solution to her difficulties, a solution which unfortunately cannot solve the tension which has been introduced into the patient's life. The rigid and repetitive application of somatic structures tells us that the dialectical process of meaning transformation has ceased for the patient at this time. Whether this retreat is a temporary reaction to some overwhelming event, or a chronic way of life, is not important in this context. The constituent "retreat from self" describes the stagnation which has occurred in the flow of the patient's life. A vicious circle arises, since the more the patient uses body responses to higher level situations, the more sedimented this behavior becomes. In turn, the more one uses lower level structures in order to "see" and understand the world, the less of the world one is able to see. The less one sees, the less motivated one is to activate higher level orders. The answer to this dilemma is to find a way to leave the body and (re)discover the self.

The second advantage of the "retreat-from-self" characterization of psychosomatics is that it introduces the important notions of freedom and transcendence, factors which have not been taken into account in the traditional theories examined in part I. There is a kind of baffled acquiescence within these theories about the importance of the individual in the etiology of symptoms and diseases. People seem to cope differently with hardships, and think differently about their lives. But instead of putting this interesting insight into the center of their theories, traditional writers rather hope that one day these idiosyncratic differences may be traced to some general set of factors which can then be tested and verified (a certain enzyme, a specific coping strategy etc.). I would rather say that the salutogenic factor is not this or that particular coping skill, but rather the act of transcending itself, i.e. that the self is actively engaged in a dialogue with the world, and that one manages to both sediment structures and allow new structures to take form. As recounted in chapter 3, Moss[17] found in his study that the Zulus who were able to understand their new urban environment in terms of rural habits remained healthy, while those who experienced what Moss called "information incongruity" suffered from hypertension. It is not hard to see that one can understand these findings in terms of transformation of structures. Indeed, it is hardly conceivable that rural experiences could be applied directly to Big City life. The Zulus had to make their old patterns of thinking and behaving *work* in the new environment. The healthy group succeeded in transforming their rural structures in such a way that they could continue their lives in the city, despite the fact that they must have felt challenged and slightly disoriented in the new city environment. To put it in terms of the phenomenological theory being presented here, the healthy Zulus could continue the question-answer dialectic and, via transformation of structures, continue to become themselves, despite an entirely new situation. Those who were unable to do this reacted with their bodies. Whether those Zulus who developed hypertension became psychosomatically ill according to my (broad and/or narrow) definition is not possible to say here. For the present discussion I only wish to suggest that remaining healthy has something to do with being actively involved in the transcendence of self-becoming and the dialectical transformation of structures.

Let me wind up this chapter on the constituent "retreat from self" with a clinical example. While working at the psychiatric out-patient center, I received a referral from my team to try to "do something" for a

---

[17] Moss (1977).

250

young immigrant woman. She had been in a minor plane accident the year before, and since that time had become completely incapacitated. She had problems sleeping, anxiety and hypochondriac fears. Her most prominent symptom was an obsessive concern for her body. She went to different doctors and various healers several times a week, in order to get "checked out" and confirmed as healthy. There was nothing physically wrong with her. The plane accident had been fairly undramatic, from what I could understand. They had been forced to make an emergency landing a short time after take-off. However, for this young woman the event had precipitated a personal disaster, to the extent that she had been on sick leave for almost a year. During that time, she had received various treatments, to no avail. Her first contact with our psychiatric center had been with a psychiatrist, who found her to be depressed. She took antidepressive medication which did not provide any relief. She then went to a psychologist who tried to find out if the accident had activated early trauma. She went dutifully to the psychologist and spoke of her childhood, but continued to experience her life as a black hole. She could think of nothing but her body and her doctor's appointments. Because this was her main concern, she was eventually referred to me, since I worked specifically with psychosomatic conditions.

During her first appointment, she spoke of the incident with the plane. Her description was interesting, since she placed emphasis on the fact she found it extremely disconcerting that she had not been able to *see* from the outside of the plane that anything had been wrong with it. She had been impressed by the size of the plane, the efficiency of the all the personnel, all the procedures and safety routines, and yet, the plane was not airworthy. The way she described her body formed a parallel with this. She *looked* healthy, certainly, but one never knew. She could not herself see what faulty parts might be inside of her, she may herself not be in shape for living her life. Her concern for her own body was a metaphor for feelings she had about her ability to handle her life.[18] If the impressive plane could turn out to be dangerous and life threatening,

18 See chapter 9 on the expressiveness of the psychosomatic symptom.

how much more precarious it must be with her own body. If we look at the behavior of the patient, what does it tell us? She had an experience which threw her into a radical *doubt*, a doubt which turned upon her own life vessel, her body. She had trusted the plane, and could have died. Could she really trust her body? She now experienced her life as reduced to one task, securing the "airworthness" of her own body. It was impossible for her to perform any other tasks (going to work, meeting friends, reading, watching TV) before this ground had been reestablished. How did it come about that this doubt should become so sedimented? Why did she not accept the verdict of her doctors, that she was physically sound? Was there something else she doubted, something which she couldn't think about, but only represent in a psychosomatic metaphor: "my body is an untrustworthy vessel"?

If we apply the "retreat-from-self" picture here, the question becomes, who would this patient *be* right now, if she did not have her symptoms? She was in fact going to doctors *instead* of doing something else. I became interested in *when* she went to the doctors. My idea was that there was something in her life situation (vague and inarticulate) which prompted her to apply her somatic structure, something in her life which touched upon the theme of doubt and not being airworthy (being able to fly/able to live). I found out that she tended to schedule her various doctor's appointments and other treatments on Tuesdays and Thursdays. I wondered why these days? She told me after some time that there had been a course which her employer had wanted her to attend on Tuesday and Thursday evenings, in order to keep her updated in her field. She had only just begun the course when the plane accident occurred. Because of her sick leave, it was no longer possible for her to attend the course. She was not aware of feeling or thinking anything special about the course, nevertheless there was undoubtedly some connection between it and her concern about her physical status. The phenomenological question is, why did she use her "body solution" to relieve tension on these days? There was something about this course which could not be handled by her higher order structures. Eventually, prompted by my questioning, she related how terrified she actually was of working life, and how ambivalent she felt about it. She doubted that she could make it. Her ideal from her own country of being a woman was that she should marry and have children. Back home she would not have had to worry about either educating or supporting herself. But here in Sweden, she felt forced into a situation where she had to be like other European women, do what they do and like what they like. She had been unaware of her intense dislike of this situation, and was rather surprised to find that as we discussed her fears and feelings about her experiences as an immigrant woman in a foreign country, she forgot about going to the doctor. When she was able to find *herself* in her current life situation, she could forgot about her body. Together with me she developed a way of thinking and reflecting about her experiences which had been impossible for her earlier on. It would seem that the plane accident had opened up a line of retreat, a strategy which, although it imprisoned her in her body and caused her quite a bit of suffering, helped her to avoid the situation which she could not handle with her structures, namely, going to night classes and finding herself with an impossible project ahead of her, a project which she could neither avoid nor carry through.

One may wonder what would have happened to her if she had not experienced the plane accident. Perhaps she would have developed symptoms in any case, something else could have activated her intense fear and doubts about her ability to live her life in Sweden. On the other hand, she might have been able to find a way to articulate herself in her situation by transforming higher order structures. She could have said no to the course, or changed her attitude towards working life. Perhaps she would have married a compatriot and had children. All we can know is that at this particular time, the experience of the plane accident precipitated a retreat into a body solution, in order to solve problems of which she was only vaguely aware. Because somatic structures are general, diffuse and inarticulate, they will not be able to further the development of higher order structures. As long as patients speak only of their bodies, their self in their situation remains hidden. The constituent "retreat-from-self" underlies the importance of the self. Where there is a self, there is a situation. Where there is a self in a situation transforming structures, there is psychosomatic health (even if the person in question may have pain or discomfort). When the patient withdraws from the task of becoming, the body-solution answers all questions, reduces all situations and gradually effaces the beckoning of the world. This is psychosomatic ill health.

CHAPTER 8

Psychosomatics as frozen time

"All the same, that one day should follow another, Wednesday, Thursday, Friday, Saturday; that one should wake up in the morning; see the sky; walk in the park; meet Hugh Whitbread; then suddenly in came Peter; then these roses; it was enough. After that, how unbelievable death was!-that it must end; and no one in the whole world would know how she had loved it all; every instant..."

--Virginia Woolf, *Mrs. Dalloway*

"Then one day, suddenly, it ends, it changes, I don't understand, it dies, or it's me, I don't understand that either. I ask the words that remain--sleeping, waking, morning, evening. They have nothing to say. *(Pause.)* I open the door of the cell and go. I am so bowed I only see my feet, if I open my eyes, and between my legs a little trail of black dust. I say to myself that the earth is extinguished, though I never saw it lit. *(Pause.)* It's easy going. *(Pause.)* When I fall I'll weep for happiness."

--Samuel Beckett, "Endgame"

I once had a patient who had a reoccurring unpleasant sensation around his mouth and tongue. He had the distinct feeling that this area was growing larger and stinging, as if he had been hit on the mouth. He could not recall ever being physically hit, but it became clear during his therapy that he was symbolically "punched in the mouth" by several members of his family systematically during his childhood. When he spoke up in his family, he got verbally beaten up. Why should this memory from the past show itself in terms of a body sensation? It is my experience from working with psychosomatic patients that the body is often used to enact or express something which cannot be thought about. This "something" can be difficulties in a current life situation, or, as in the cases to be examined in this chapter, a memory from the past which refuses to fade away.[1] The constituent dealt with in this chapter, "psychosomatics as frozen time," will show how the body sensations found in some psychosomatic symptoms can be understood as nascent, non-thematized body memories. "Frozen time" refers to the standstill in the dialectic of structure transformations which occurs when experiences from the past are not taken up into the higher orders of cognition and reflection. Although they are denied thematic, conscious articulation, un-remembered memories continue to announce themselves as body experiences. A "body memory" is not what we usually mean by "memory", that is, a conscious, thematic content, but neither is a body memory some strange form of forgetting. A body memory exists *now* as an ambiguous "something" which disturbs. Were these past experiences which the body "remembers" allowed to form themselves in higher order structures, the patient would be able to grasp their significance, and weave them into the life narrative. When certain experiences are denied higher order articulation, these meanings or aspects of life never reach thematic articulated levels. In this way, meaning becomes "frozen" in body expression.[2] But because we are always in contact with the world, even inarticulate body meanings are a *response* to something in the life world of

---

[1] There is an overlapping between difficulties which arise in current life situations and problems from the past, since difficulties in mastering present problems most often have connections to past experiences and sedimented ways of thinking, reacting and understanding. However, psychosomatic conditions can be either *more or less* related to past experiences and memories. In this chapter, I will be looking at psychosomatic symptoms which stand out as being strongly connected to past experiences (memories) which have not been integrated into structures. Not all psychosomatic symptoms are body-memories in this particular way.

[2] The "frozen" metaphor is often evoked in various body oriented therapies (Rosen therapy, bioenergetics, body oriented psychotherapy see footnote 44, chapter 1). The idea is that meaning (memory) is preserved unknowingly at a body level in terms of muscular tensions, body postures and so on. These meanings or memories are then "released" (made thematically available) in the therapy setting through the stimulation/provocation of them via various body techniques combined with therapeutical dialogue. "Frozen" is a particularly apt metaphor in this context, since a block of ice is unmoving and unchanging.

the patient. Body memories are activated, that is to say, announce themselves as symptoms, when they are triggered into being by something in the current life situation. Where another person would remember something, the psychosomatic patient experiences her body. We find once again a body response rather than higher order signification. This is not hard to understand, when we remember that *meaning* is to be understood broadly as the dialectical give and take between man and the world which goes on at all levels, although we are accustomed to attributing "meaning" only to the higher orders. Body meaning is a form of meaning,[3] and body memories *are* memories, but they are embryonic memories, not yet thematic, not yet known.

My patient eventually discovered that he experienced these unpleasant mouth sensations when he had felt the urge to speak up, but quickly suppressed the impulse. What does this tell us? Something in the world was experienced by him as an invitation to speak. But because of his past experiences, he dared not open his mouth. A mouth which would like to formulate words, but cannot, is not just a fleshy piece of skin. The mouth partakes in a lived relationship to the world. The patient's desires and intentions could not yet be formulated on a reflective level, but his mouth could remind him of the entire complex from the past (wish to speak--speak up--suffer the negative consequences). His stinging mouth was not only an aborted attempt at speaking, it also testified to his traumatic family background, a situation which he could not thematically remember nor reflect upon using higher order structures.

How are we to understand a past experience, or memory, which manifests itself at the level of the body? What is our relationship to past experience, after all? We have access to the past both thematically (as explicit memories) and in a general sort of way. The past as a whole is incorporated into our lives as a certain style or set of habits, according to which we imagine the future to emerge. We have both explicit memories and general patterns of signification which originate in our past experiences. One could say that the past is just one more layer of sedimenta-

---

[3] See chapter 9 on body meaning.

tion, one more way in which we find ourselves situated in a world which we already understand. Our past gives rise to privileged attitudes and ways of being, thinking, perceiving. Experiences from the past get sedimented into the standard habitual ways we have of going about in the world. Despite this sedimentation of experience, we are usually open to the spontaneous creation of new meanings, which may in turn leave traces as new structures, thereby transforming our habitual sedimentation. We may come to reevaluate our past and our ideas about things in accordance with new experiences. Thus, the past as *style* or habit is itself in a process of continual transformation. Between the past and the present we find a "give-and-take" dialectic wherein meaning is transformed and evolves. However, something has happened in this flow when the body "speaks" about an experience which has never been formulated at a higher order level. Some aspect of experience, some meaning or signification, is not available for transformation. Something is stuck at the body level. How is this to be understood?

It may be illustrative here to look at the phenomenon of the phantom limb. Merleau-Ponty gives an interesting account of the phantom limb in *PP*. The phantom limb is the sensation of the amputated limb, which no longer exists. Merleau-Ponty's position is, as usual, to dismiss both purely psychological explanations, as well as purely physiological ones. His characterization of the phantom limb is the ambivalent presence of an arm, a refusal of mutilation, a way of being-in-the-world which corresponds to the way it was before one lost the arm. One stubbornly retains the perceptual field one had before the mutilation, refusing to re-orient oneself in the world in order to conform to the new situation without the limb. But this is not a denial on a purely psychological level, according to Merleau-Ponty. It is existential. The phantom limb is a quasi-presence: "The phantom arm must be that same arm, lacerated by shell splinters, its visible substance burned or rotted somewhere, which appears to haunt the present body without being absorbed into it. The imaginary arm is, then, like a repressed experience, a former present which cannot decide to recede into the past."[4] The body memory is analogous to the phantom limb. To have a body memory is to be captivated by a past experience which should have been taken up into higher order transformations in order to dissolve itself into the life narrative. The disturbing event from the past, like the lost arm, is something which one can neither get beyond (integrate) nor leave behind (forget). It is not remembered, yet neither is it forgotten. It is a quasi-presence of a past which is lived bodily, and it is lived in such a way that it disrupts the now.

The psychosomatic symptom thus "reminds" us of a past which has not been integrated into the higher orders of personal, psycho-social meaning. An experience becomes integrated when it becomes a part of our life story, a part of our narrative. And in order to become a part of our life story, experience must reach the level of thematic cognition/reflection. It is only at the higher levels that we go beyond the anonymous life of the organism to the human life of existence. The meaning our lives take on depends upon the way in which we constitute, take up and understand our situation. We are able to form a narrative life story about ourselves because we are conscious of ourselves and we constitute the world in terms of possibilities. To experience the world in terms of possibilities requires both self-consciousness, and the willingness to exercise our freedom in relation to various situations which arise. These two criteria require the ability to think and reflect. Experience is thus integrated into my personal life-story when I have thematically taken into account both my self and my freedom in relation to what I experience. This could also be called the *significance* of experience. The signification which our lives take on is formed and articulated in psycho-social, higher order structures, and our capacity to continually transform these structures is the basis of our personal existence. It is an empirical fact that patients stop somatizing when they can remember and communicate thoughts and feelings about themselves and their lives. It is curative to be able to remember, express, appraise, cope and adapt. Thinking

---

[4] *PP* p. 85.

259

and reflection are salutogenic, as witnessed in the first part of this dissertation. There is something about having access to higher order levels of meaning which prevents somatization. What could this be?

Cognition, as mentioned earlier, is a very precise articulation of the world. We greatly expand the horizon of the object when we can hold on to various details of it through language and thought. Cognition separates and differentiates, but also brings together and integrates. We can distinguish various colors as well as subsume a variety of different objects under classes. For Merleau-Ponty, cognition is grounded in perception, it is not before or behind it. Reflective thought is born in and through a concrete lived situation. It is "parasitic" on perception, since it emerges from the perceptual conditions which are given (such as figure/ground and temporal synthesis). Cognition manifests the world for us in such a pervasive way that it is impossible to "get back" to a pre-linguistic, pre-verbal world. Most importantly, cognition is responsible for our not being overwhelmed by the world. Thanks to linguistic and cognitive functions, we can pick and choose the objects for our attention, organize or ignore large sectors of the world. So in a way, the world becomes more specific (differentiated) while at the same time less overpowering, thanks to our ability to think. Although there is already a primordial world of meaning for Merleau-Ponty, ("something to be understood"), the structures of language and culture are responsible for the structuring of this primary openness to Being on a higher level. It is specifically through thought and language that we find ourselves in human situations. The difficulty for the psychosomatic patient is to allow certain experiences to gain access to and become a part of these higher order structures. The patients are *overwhelmed* by experience, instead of gaining mastery over it through reflective articulation. Cognition and reflection place us in the human world, but they also provide us with the anchors we need in order to successfully root ourselves in this world. Without these anchors, anxiety and somatization are not far away.[5] We are able to orient our-

---

[5] Arieti (1974) has written an interesting book on schizophrenia where he writes that the cognitive alterations in schizophrenic patients, such as losing grasp of, for example, logic, rationality, teleology and attention lead to a bizarre and terrifying experi-

selves in the psycho-social human world thanks to cognition and reflection, and as long as we can handle the constant challenges to our understanding of our world, we continue to experience ourselves and our world in an unproblematic way. However, when we become so challenged that we can no longer take in and come to grips with the meaning of what we experience, we find ourselves overwhelmed and out of ourselves. The options available to us then are the psychotic solution, the body solution, or anxiety. All of these options are "breakdowns" from the higher orders, although they are different sorts of substitutions, each in its own way attempting to regain mastery over experience. The psychotic structures the world idiosyncratically, the psychosomatic patient - bodily, the anxious person - without meaning. The issue of how these different solutions are chosen will be discussed in chapter 10.

In the case of psychosomatics as body memories, there is some disturbance in the relationship to the past which exhibits itself in a bodily symptom. The flow of life is stagnated or frozen, because some meaning (memory) is not taken up into dialectic transformations. The metaphors "flow of time" and "frozen time" should perhaps be examined. I have called this constituent "frozen time" which implies that time usually flows. Merleau-Ponty[6] has called the "flowing river" metaphor into question since it gives the impression that there *is* a river which is time, and that we find ourselves somehow within this flowing stream. The flowing river metaphor is correct in one sense, as it illustrates the important quality of time as both constantly flowing yet always the same. However, the river metaphor is incorrect in that it suggests that there is someone off sides watching it flow. There can be no such perspective whereby we could place ourselves outside of time. Time *becomes* through our participation in life.[7] It is through existing as we do that time comes

---

ence of the world, an experience which non-schizophrenic people have difficulty in even understanding.

6 See *PP* pp. 410-433 on temporality.

7 "Time is, therefore, not a real process, not an actual succession that I am content to record. It arises from *my* relation to things." (ibid. p. 412, italics in original).

to be.[8] It is the subject who is time, and time is the subject. The unfolding of time is experienced as the way in which ever new horizons open up for us, blending harmoniously together and continuously pointing further on. The present is a constantly new field towards which we find ourselves always oriented. Time pushes onward (another inadequate metaphor) and we follow, or rather, we are the pushing forward of time. Just as the perceptual object "hides" further views which are implicit (I need only to turn the object or move my body and they will "appear"), so does the present contain both the past and the future. As human existence, we are oriented towards the unfolding of the object through further perspectives and the "flowing" of time towards the future. This tending beyond the given and the now is transcendence. If we were not this basic pointing beyond, e.g. if we were only immersed in the actual now and the present view, we would have no experience of time, nor would we perceive a human world. It is through our way of existing (as transcendence) that there is both time and human world.

Continuing the analogy between perception and time, we can understand the past through a horizon metaphor. We have the past just on the fringe of the present, similar to the way in which the perceptual horizon continues just out of sight beyond the present view. The past, as well as the future, exists as a beyond (stretching both backwards and forwards) which completes the present moment, just as the (spatial) perspectival view trails off into that which is perceptually out of view for the moment. The past is a kind of quasi-present. If it were actually present like the present moment, it would not be past. But if it were completely absent, like some event unknown to me which occurred in China 3000 years ago, it would not be *my* past. I may have the past thematically available to me, and in such a case, it can be retrieved as easily as the way

---

8 "If we separate the objective world from the finite perspectives which open upon it, and posit it in itself, we find everywhere in it only so many instances of 'now.' These instances of now, moreover, not being present to anybody, have no temporal character and could not occur in sequence...We should, then, gain nothing by transferring into ourselves the time that belongs to things, if we repeated 'in consciousness' the mistake of defining it as a succession of instances of now." (ibid. p. 412).

in which I can move my body in order to get another view of the scene. This thematic reaching back, which we call memory, entails a summoning up of moments and experiences which were my present *then*. The immediate past is easily found, while remote memories must be first unraveled from all the threads which have been spun out from them since they were the present. However, we also *live* the past, in an unreflected, non-thematic way. We do not need to constantly remind ourselves of past experiences in order to assure ourselves that we are the same person we were yesterday, last month or last year. We own our past as we own our bodies, in an immediate, natural way. Time flows in and through us, and we take up this flow and live it in accordance with structures which we create together with the world. Our past is part and parcel of these structures, which is why the past is both familiar (sedimented) yet distant (not present any longer).

Certain psychosomatic patients do not have access to various threads from their past. This lack of coherence backwards leads to blind spots and holes in their experience. They are unable to respond to certain situations with thematic memories, feelings and thoughts. It is as if these levels of experience are not available. Instead, it is the body and body sensations which come into the fore. Where another person might have explicit memories or thoughts, the psychosomatic patient responds with his body. This is, in fact, a kind of memory, but it is a non-thematic memory, a reminder from the past which has never reached cognitive, reflective levels. The low level body experience testifies to a past experience which has been lived through, but not thematically known. And the past which has not been known, if it is a past which disturbs, lives on as body. This is not hard to understand when we realize that we are always bodily involved in our experiences, and lower levels of existence (body, sensation, perception) are the fundament from which higher order levels emerge. We must remember that our experiences are not only present to us in terms of thematic cognitive content, although our modern Western society tends to focus upon this level of experience. Experiences/situations are lived on all levels, as we are a mind/body continuum. Going back to my patient mentioned in the beginning of this chapter, during his past he had experienced situations where he was roughly silenced and humiliated, but he *lived* these situations without letting them acquire higher order signification. How is this possible? A Sartrian hypothesis would be to see this lack of higher order integration as a *refusal* of the reality of his suffering and his responsibility (e.g. if I don't know about it, it didn't really happen, and if it didn't really happen, I don't have to do anything about it). A Freudian would say that he repressed both thoughts and feelings *which he had at the time* to the unconscious.[9] I do not believe that he ever formed any thoughts or feelings about these situations. The higher order signification of his lived experiences came into being for the first time in the therapy situation. They did exist previously as unconscious ideas, lying perfectly formed behind the scenes, awaiting to be discovered. Their status before therapy would be rather that they were embryonic "un-thought thoughts", which had only a rudimentary kind of existence as body meaning. Lower level structures cannot articulate the world precisely or personally. It was not until the patient "found his tongue" and could begin to speak about his past that he discovered what his body was trying to tell him, namely, that he, in certain situations, would have liked to speak up but felt unable to do so. He learned how he could think about and reflect upon events from his past. His body had remembered the trauma, he had lived through it, but his higher level structures had never taken in these experiences and allowed them to take part in the dialectic of meaning transformation. It was first when he could think about what he had experienced in the past

---

9   A Freudian could also try to use the concept of *Nachträglichkeit* in this case, and claim that the meaning of these experiences did not in fact become traumatic for the patient until much later on. At the time at which they occurred, the experiences were not traumatic. However, as soon as the patient forms a symptom, the question becomes, does the patient have a traumatic memory, and if so, why does he not remember it? Or if he does not have a traumatic memory, why does he have the symptom? For Freudians, either the memory is traumatic, and then we have a meaning, although it is unconscious, or the memory is not traumatic, and in such a case there is no reason for the symptom. My position is that we have a meaning, although it is a lived, lower level meaning which takes on body signification. It is a meaning which is lived rather than known.

that his body stopped remembering. After a period of therapy, his mouth symptoms disappeared.

The body *lives* meaning, just as thought and reflection also live meaning, but this meaning is lived differently on the different levels. The cognitive level of meaning for my patient was, "I *have been* badly hurt when I tried to express myself, and because of this, I *now* dare not try, even though there are situations in my life where I would like to speak and be heard." This complex was not available to him when he came to us with his burning mouth and unsatisfactory life. What his body expressed was the generalized condensed experience of "mouth-- something-- yet nothing". The mouth and tongue move and are engaged when one speaks, and when one is silent they rest.[10] It was this in-between speaking and being silent where the patient's mouth made itself known, in the aborted speech which was neither speech nor true silence.

The body symptom, as frozen time, is the expression of a past which has not been incorporated into sedimentation (nor faded away as irrelevant). It is a past which is unavailable to the patient, he cannot simply reach back for it and possess it as memory. Body memories are activated by the world (current life situations) when the higher order functions are not there. Why psychosomatic patients do not initially find ways of thinking and reflecting about certain experiences in their lives is an interesting question. The fact that they can often do so later on, in therapy, would suggest that it has something to do with the safe environment of the therapy setting. It is a difficult process to allow body memories to develop and infiltrate the higher orders. The patient moves from the general to the particular (mouth sensations to personal, thematic meaning), from the passive (I am overwhelmed) to the active (how do I feel about X?), from distortion (the others will mock me) to the real (I don't know how they will react until I try). That which is pathogenic about body memories and lower level responses to the world is that the body is mute,

---

10 There are a variety of expressions which illustrate the relationship between mouth/ tongue and speaking; "Has the cat got your tongue?" "My mother tongue" "Shut up (your mouth)" "A loose tongue" "You really put your foot in your mouth" "Tongue in cheek" "Bite your tongue" "Zipper your lip" "Button up (your lip)" etc.

impersonal and general, and as such, cannot develop or transform our-selves or our understanding of the world.

The body stands in a privileged relation to the "now". I can at any time let my body sensations fill my attention of the moment. The way in which the body offers a permanent haven for attention at any given time makes it especially appropriate for what cognitive theorists have called "self- focus." The concept of "self-focus" comes from two cognitive theo-rists Duval and Wicklund[11] who have described a dichotomy of atten-tion between self and environment. They proposed that attention could be directed either towards the self or towards the environment, but never towards both simultaneously. Attention may oscillate from the one to the other, but at any given time will be focused either upon the self or upon the environment. An increase in self-focus, then, actually refers to an increase in the amount of time spent in self-focus, at the expense of paying attention to the environment. What is interesting about this idea is that it illustrates how paying attention to, for example, body sensa-tions, will automatically lead to a diminished capacity to pay attention to the environment. A hypothesis concerning the development of body memories could be that during the original traumatic experience (or any experience, for that matter, which does not take on higher order mean-ing, for whatever reason) the person is not capable of responding with the higher order transformation of structures, as previously described. Instead of paying attention to an overwhelming field of experience which cannot be taken in, the patient turns instead towards the experience of her body.[12] She may also become psychotic, which is one of McDou-gall's insights regarding the similarity between psychosis and psychoso-matic (see chapter 2). The body is, after all, always *there*. A clinical find-ing is that self-focus has been associated with both stress vulnerabil-

---

[11] Duval & Wicklund (1972).

[12] In certain cases of extreme traumatization, such as incest or torture, it is not uncom-mon that one rather has the experience of leaving one's body. The reason for this could be that the body itself is so centrally involved in these particular traumatic ex-periences.

ity[13]and states of anxiety and depression.[14]Within the theory being proposed here, the focus upon self (in this case, the focus upon one's own body) is the result of the patient's inability to respond to current life situations with higher order levels which would correspond to the demands being made upon him/her. When one turns away from the world, one will always find the body.

The somatization process in the case of body memories could be understood in the following way. In some initial situation, the patient has turned away from a field of overwhelming experience towards her body sensations. These sensations become sedimented as responses to situations and experiences which would have required higher order levels of structure in order to become resolved/transformed. Because certain meanings are denied access to higher order structures, the patient has no way to think about or reflect upon certain specific life situations. But because one is never completely cut off from the dialogue with the world, meaning will show up in a rudimentary body form. These responses, which have here been called alternatively "body memories" or "lower level structures" or "body meaning", take the place of articulated higher order structures. The lower level body response is an attempt to achieve a harmony with that which has elicited it (e.g. wanting to speak), but because the level of the body is mute and impersonal, the tension which has been introduced into the patient's world will not be reduced, and the patient's structures will not be transformed in these situations. Body sensations cannot transform either oneself or one's understanding of one's current life situation. That which is thematically available to psychosomatic patients when they seek medical assistance is often a gnawing sense of dissatisfaction, and a body symptom. It is understandable that they tend to associate their dissatisfaction with the body symptom, and in this way a powerful alliance is formed between the inadequate body solution (the symptom), and the reality of the patient's dissatisfaction with his/her life. The patient is convinced that if only she could get rid of her

---

13 Matthews & Wells (1988).
14 Ingram (1990).

headache, backache, etc. everything would be fine. But these patients do not find relief for their symptoms in the biomedical health care system. They cannot be cured of their symptoms through somatic treatments since the symptoms are an indication of a larger problem, the lack of higher order structures. It is not until the patient is able to move from body meaning to personal, higher order levels of signification that s/he will be able to get rid of the body symptoms. When the patient has succeeded in integrating the past in this way, new meanings can take form, the world opens up new horizons, and the patient's sense of dissatisfaction is remedied as well.

I asked earlier on why the patients turn away from overwhelming experience towards the body. One wonders what it is that prevents them from being able to integrate experiences into higher order structures? There is no causal relationship between certain types of experiences (or emotions) and the development of specific symptoms, as the so-called "specificity research" has shown.[15] Freud hypothesized that patients who experienced overwhelming traumas were not able to "bind" these experiences with psychic energy, and were for that reason subject to free-floating anxiety and symptom formation until these experiences could be "bound."[16] McDougall has hypothesized that disturbances in individuation from mother play a part in the psychosomatic line of development. Stress theoreticians and cognitive theorists emphasize appraisals and coping strategies. The theory being presented here, a theory of structures, would fall in line with the idea that that if one has access to higher order levels of signification, one is protected from psychosomatic symptoms. However, the reason why one person will develop a body solution (psychosomatic symptoms), another will become psychotic and a third will find a way to integrate traumatic experience, cannot be definitively answered here. Qualitative empirical and clinical research focusing upon the lived body is needed in order to trace out possible factors of importance. The fact that patients can, as adults in therapy, gradually create

---

15 See part I of this dissertation, especially chapters 2-3.
16 Freud (1920), Beyond the Pleasure Principle, *SE* XVIII, London: Hogarth Press.

higher order structures using language and reflection, and thereby become cured of their symptoms, would indicate that something in the therapy setting is conducive to this process. This "something" could be feelings of security and trust towards the therapist, or the careful introduction of new thoughts, attitudes, feelings in this safe environment, or the therapist's interest in the body symptom as body-meaning etc. When the patient has integrated "un-thoughts" about the past, the body loses its signification as messenger, and the patient finds that he is able to handle a more complex world than before. This is the cure. When attention is released from lower levels, the patient has more interest in his current life situation, and in the future as well.[17] This ties in with the constituent from the previous chapter, retreat from self. When the patient can get back on track (or on track for the fist time) of the process of becoming himself, experiencing a complex, nuanced changing world, taking responsibility for himself, there is no need for the body to express anything. The body fades back into instrumentality, passed over in silence, like language, to be used rather than paid attention to.

I'll give a clinical example here to illustrate the tremendous tenacity of the psychosomatic symptom, as well as its inadequacy as structure (transforming meaning and reducing tension). The patient presented in this case "suffered from remembrances," as Freud used to say of hysterical neuroses, but these "remembrances" were not conscious, nor were they unconscious. They were body memories lived at a lower level body structure, and their hold on the patient nearly destroyed her. Mrs. T. was a middle aged-woman, referred to me after her second unsuccessful slipped disc spinal operation. She had had her first operation several years before, but her symptoms of pain and irritation in her back and leg had gradually returned, which was the reason for her second operation some 7 months before her referral to the psychiatric clinic. Mrs. T. had felt better immediately after the second operation, but her pain symp-

---

[17] An interesting finding from a qualitative study of fibromyalgia patients (Hellström et al. 1998b) was that when fibromyalgia patients were asked to comment upon how they saw their future, none of them answered by saying anything about the future, but rather described in detail the many ways in which they were incapacitated.

toms became worse as time went on, contrary to what would be expected. She had been thoroughly checked out somatically, and no indication for further surgery had been found. She was advised to continue her rehabilitation program and to be patient. This was out of the question for Mrs. T., and she insisted vehemently upon getting a third operation. She refused to accept the conclusion of her surgeon, that nothing more could be surgically done for her. In fact, a third spinal operation would be absolutely counter indicative, as the increased scar tissue around the disc would only aggravate her symptoms of pain and discomfort. She was convinced that another operation would cure her, despite all arguments to the contrary. Her physicians were alarmed at the intensity of her reaction, and her inability to "cope" with her situation, and accordingly referred her for a psychiatric consultation. Mrs. T. was, in contrast to previously mentioned patients, completely uninterested in the psychiatric consultation. She was, in fact, insulted by the referral, and the only reason she came at all to her first appointment was the fact that she knew I had a medical background, which had given her some hope that I could perhaps be persuaded into agreeing with her that she was in need of further surgical treatment, and write a letter of recommendation to that effect.

Mrs. T. related that her life situation around the time of the second operation had been turbulent. She had just been promoted at her job, when her youngest child came down with diabetes. So, at the same time as she needed to involve herself intensely in her work, she also needed to be equally intensely involved with her sick child. This situation would be taxing for anyone, and the fact that she broke down physically at this time at the very place where her back was weak (previously operated on) is not surprising. That the back (spinal cord) can also be seen as a symbol for one's coping ability (to stand "upright", "stand up for yourself", don't be "spineless" etc.) has its roots in the embodied level of lived meaning. In euphoria and exhalation we stretch upwards, in depression and sorrow we are bent. Our higher orders of meaning have an embodied basis. The physiognomy of body symbolism has been studied by a variety of thinkers including Gestalt psychologists, philosophers and cultural anthropologists.[18] According to the phenomenological theory presented here, Mrs. T.'s situation was too overwhelming to be taken in and transformed by the structures available to her at the time. Someone else may have handled it (not broken down physically), but she could not. On the other hand, another person, in a similar situation, might have instead developed an anxiety neurosis. Mrs. T. had a physical reaction (pain and irritation from a previously treated injury) and she was accordingly given surgical treatment. As we shall see, there was a "reason" for her relapse, but it was yet not manifest at this time. Thus far in the story of Mrs. T, we do not yet find a "psychosomatic way of life", we have only a psychosomatic breakdown, understandable but not yet devastating. What more was happening with Mrs. T. which threatened to reduce her life to a somatic project, and eventually threatened her very life?

When the patient volunteered these bits of information about herself during our initial meeting, it was with the express purpose to provide me with the background information I needed in order to write the letter of recommendation for surgery. When I explained to her that my role was not to write such a letter for her, but to try to help her understand her predicament and find a way out of it, she closed up. It was obvious that there were no paths open for any kind of dialogue about the meaning of her situation for her. She thanked me politely for my time, and made herself ready to leave. With a feeling of having nothing to lose, I said that she might in any case be interested in something which I myself found interesting and rather unusual, the fact that she had felt better after the operation (when most people feel pain) and that she had felt worse during her period of rehabilitation (when most people feel better). I wondered if she had any thoughts about that? She did not. I asked her if she wanted to know what I thought about that. She smiled slightly and motioned with her hands, well yes, go on. I told her that it would seem that she felt fine when she was not expected to be able to do anything,

---

18 See Arnheim (1958); Buytendijk (1974); Csordas (1993); Jonas (1966); Lakoff & Johnson (1980); Straus (1980).

and worse when she felt that she should do something, but felt unable to do it. This was, I added, a completely understandable reaction, given the enormous burden she had been under prior to her second operation. She looked blankly at me, and replied mechanically that everything was fine now with her diabetic son, who had adapted well to the routines around testing his blood sugar counts and taking his shots and so on, and as for her job, well, she was sure that when she got her third operation she would be fully capable of performing her work tasks satisfactorily (she was still on rehabilitation leave from the second operation). She thanked me again for my time, and I told her that she could feel free to call me at any time if she wished for a new appointment. She left, and I had an uneasy feeling about her, but put it out of my mind and wrote up the session as well as a referral answer. I didn't think about her again until a month later, when I was informed that she had been admitted to the psychiatric hospital after threatening to jump out of the window at her home if she did not get her third operation. She had mentioned my name at the hospital, and asked to come and see me at the out-patient clinic.

During the month or so between our first and second appointment, Mrs. T. had found herself in an ever intensifying spiral of desperation, trying to get her operation by any means possible, and having these various plans dashed to the ground. Finally, she had decided that she could no longer live with her situation, it was absolutely intolerable. She would either have her operation, or she would kill herself. While in the hospital, Mrs. T. became less panicked and easier to communicate with, during which time she asked to come and speak to me about her back and her situation. That her back had become a part of a "situation" was a step forward, and she and I agreed to meet on a regular basis to see if we could together try to work out a solution. Where to begin? In a way, her obsessive concentration upon her back pains and her operation reminds us of the young immigrant woman described in the previous chapter. Mrs. T's back problems definitely kept her busy to the extent that she her*self* had faded into the background. But it turned out that her symptoms were not only a response to a *present* situation, even if it would have been understandable considering all the pressure she was under from both home and work. We could gradually see that the way in which she lived her back pains and her obsessive demand for the operation was a body-remembrance or re-enactment of a very difficult situation from the past which the patient was triggered into "remembering" because of her current life situation. Instead of remembering and thinking about the incident from the past and all that went with it, she could only live it as a pain in her back.

What was it that the back symptomatology was expressing so inadequately? It turned out that when she was a young child, Mrs. T.'s parents divorced, and the three children were asked by their parents to choose the parent with whom they wanted to live. Mrs. T. was 9 years old at the time, and although she had loved her father, she felt that she should stay with her mother, while her two brothers went to live with the father. Making this choice had been an overwhelming experience for her, something which she had not been able to integrate into her higher order structures. Instead of finding some way to accept and understand what she had done, she lived these meanings as a poorly specified general structure, which could be described as something like "choosing is dangerous, it will destroy all that you know and love". During the period after her parents' divorce, she had not had back problems, but she had become depressive and withdrawn, preferring to lie on her bed (recline the spine, lying down) and read rather than playing with her friends. Her response to her overwhelming situation was to give up her upright position (symbolizing "I choose"), voluntarily as a child, aided by a physical injury as an adult. She bore this traumatic experience with her into her present life situation as a structure, a structure which could be described on a lived level as "choice-danger-lie-down-give up". It was this structure, referring to her latent past, which triggered her into somatizing as an adult.[19] Later on in life, when she was placed in a similar situation

---

[19] It is important to remember that that which makes the symptom "psychosomatic" is not the slipped disc in itself (or any other specific symptom or illness per se). Many people have slipped discs and continue to live their lives in one way or another.

273

where she was forced to choose between two very important things, her job (her father) and her child (her mother), she found herself thrust into the same overwhelming experience, and instead of choosing to prioritize the one or the other, she gave up (got herself admitted to the hospital for her second operation). She could not "take a stand" in this very important choice, she could only apply the structure she knew, which had seemed to work for her as a child, namely to lie low and not think about what was going on. This may have worked for her as a child, but it would not solve her situation as an adult woman with a family and a responsible job. Her frantic attempts to get a third operation could be seen as her effort to get herself back on her feet, to get back into her life. Because of her past, the path back to her life could only be thought about in terms of an "it" (back pains to be mechanically repaired) rather than an "I". As long as she was faced with her overwhelming choice, to give up time from work for her child or give up time from her child for work, she could not think about her life or her situation. It was not until she could remember and think about her first catastrophic experience of this kind, that she could begin to transform her present situation. After about a year of therapy, Mrs. T. was able to reflect upon and consider her life and the choices she had to make, without panic and without symptoms. She did not get another operation, and her symptoms receded in importance for her, although she did continue to experience some discomfort from her back. However, discomfort in itself is not necessarily a psychosomatic symptom. Her back pain ceased to be psychosomatic when she was able to remember the past, and get on with her life.

Let us now take a look at an example which is not as easy to follow as the previous example. This case is an unsuccessful one, but by examining it we may be able to say something further about the relationship between expressed bodily symptoms and non-thematic, "unthought" memories. A young man in his early 20s was referred to me for consultation because of a bizarre symptom which caused him great suffering.

Rather it is the specific way of living this bodily experience which makes it psychosomatic (see definition "psychosomatic" in chapter 1).

He reported that he had a strange sensation in his throat and nasal canal, and the only way to alleviate this sensation was to make a "clucking" sound with his tongue. After he had made this sound, the irritating sensation would disappear for a while, only to return after a short time. He most often felt this sensation and the urge to make the noise in the company of other people. Besides the compulsive nature of his urge to "cluck", the patient expressed how he suffered because he felt that he should not produce this sound when together with others. Consequently, he felt that he had to give up all forms of social contact. He simply could no longer be together with other people. He described how after he had been with others for a period of time, he felt forced to remove himself from their company, whereupon he then engaged in a very intense and drawn out clucking, as if he had built up quite a bit of tension which had to be relieved. As a psychodynamically oriented therapist, my first thought was that his description of his clucking was reminiscent of masturbation, and that the clucking could be seen as a substitution for his desire to masturbate, presumably in conjunction with homosexual oral fantasies (he had "something in his throat"). He also told me that he had found a doctor abroad who had agreed to replace his teeth in order to "fix" his problem, and he had up to date spent over 2000 dollars on these dental operations, without any symptom abatement. His next idea was to try to get his jaw operated on. The obvious Freudian association to these bits of information was that this young man suffered from enormous castration anxiety, and he attempted to remove his own penis (teeth) before anyone else got the chance to do so. None of these thoughts were conveyed to the patient, but I wondered about the relationship between his symptom and his current/past life situation.

This patient (call him Mr. B.) worked as a hairdresser, and lived at home with his parents. He said that he had no problems in his life, and if it were not for this disturbing symptom, everything would be just fine. He had no girlfriend at the time, nor did he say anything which would indicate that he was homosexual. He was at the present time completely at the mercy of his throat sensations, and his only wish was that I should help him to get rid of them. After the initial 3 interviews, Mr. B. and I could not find anything in his current life situation which this symptom would seem to be related to. The symptom had started about 6 months before the consultation, and Mr. B. could think of nothing going on in his life, then or now, which would have provoked it. One thing I noticed about Mr. B. was that he himself did not seem to consider the clucking behavior to be especially bizarre; rather, his criticism was often directed to others who noticed and commented upon his behavior. I felt that there must be something from the past which he was acting out or "remembering" in this bodily form, but what could it be?

Shortly after the initial sessions, Mr. B. and I lost our therapeutical alliance. He felt that I had nothing to offer him and wondered what the point of our sessions could be. My understanding of this was that as soon as I started to show an interest in his past, he became afraid and wished to terminate our contact. It was as if my questions and interest in his past somehow threatened his precarious balance. Whereas the patient presented in the beginning of this chapter was willing to follow me in examining what his mouth sensations might be trying to say about his past, Mr. B. did not believe that his past experiences had any bearing on his throat symptom or his compulsive clucking. He had been cooperative enough when we looked at his present situation, but as soon as the past became a topic, he was no longer interested in therapy. It was my intuition that Mr. B. needed his throat symptom in order to keep himself together, so I agreed with him that therapy did not seem to be the answer to his problems. We terminated our contact, and I did not hear from him again. However, some time later I saw his name on the list of hospitalized patients, with the diagnosis "psychosis".

Without any patient material, it is rather difficult to hypothesize about the meaning of Mr. B's symptom. After the fact, it seems clear enough that because of his psychical instability he could not tolerate any probings into his psychosomatic solution which allowed him to function, albeit with a bothersome symptom. His symptom (the nose/throat sensation together with the compulsive clicking) kept everything in balance, whatever "everything" was for him. He managed to work at the beauty parlor and live together with his parents as long as he could find relief in his symptom. When the symptom no longer worked for him, his world fell apart and he could no longer function at that level. I will try to construct a story around Mr. B., in line with my theory, without having any actual material on hand. But his case *could* be understood in the following way.

Let us say that Mr. B. had felt extremely abandoned as a child. Let us say that a large family and economic burdens prevented his parents, who were themselves disturbed, from giving him the attention and care he needed in order to feel welcomed and loved. He grew up without forming any real ties to other people. He often felt adrift amongst strangers, and even people whom he knew quite well did not awaken any feelings of closeness or affection in him. This feeling of being a stranger amongst strangers was his everyday, sedimented experience of others. He never questioned it, nor wondered about it. When this boy becomes a young man, he feels both sexual urges and a vague feeling that something has been denied him, something which has to do with other people and the quality of relationships with other people. For this reason, he experiences something disturbing when in the company of others. After a time he feels forced to remove himself from their presence. He has no way to think about what he lacks or to reflect upon his experience, but he has an inkling that he has been excluded from something very wonderful and important in life. When he finds himself in this situation, he feels a strange sensation in his throat (perhaps sorrow? a "lump in the throat" meaning feeling "all choked up"?). He cannot weep, because he is not sad, and he is not sad because he does not know what to grieve for. He only feels "something" which is in his throat, which has to do with being in the company of others. To get rid of this something, he makes a sound with his tongue, and finds some relief. Why does he do this? His clucking could be understood as a very small infant's attempt to get mother's attention, or it could be calling out to a pet animal. We will recall that he was disturbed by the fact that people did not let him cluck, that is, they did not let him try to communicate as a baby, or to call out to an animal. His clucking was a way of saying, at a primitive, rudimentary level "I feel lonely, will someone/some animal, pay attention to me?" The symptom complex, like the example in the beginning of this chapter, is both an illustration, at a lower level, of an experience which had not been thematically known or thought about, and a communication in the present life situation. Mr. B. "remembers" with his throat how abandoned and lonely he has always felt in the company of others, and he tries to remedy this loneliness by calling out at the level where he is at home, the level of the small child. That he became psychotic would tend to support this story, since he apparently did not have a good solid foundation in his early relationships upon which he could build up the psychic stability needed in order to live a satisfactory life together with others.

My interpretation of Mr. B's choice of career is that he wanted to be around women (mother), specifically, women who take care of other people. That he chose to be a hairdresser instead of a hospital worker had to do with the fact that he wanted to be around healthy, happy people instead of needy sick ones, who reminded him of himself. Because of the impoverished nature of his early relationships, Mr. B. had no higher order structures which would enable him to articulate his situation in terms of lack and grief, and thus no way to express his longing and disappointment, except with his body. It was this meaning, at a low level, which he brought to me in the consulting room. That we were not able together to translate his symptom into a life narrative was unfortunate. Why some patients take up this challenge and others do not, will be discussed in chapter 10.

CHAPTER 9

Psychosomatics as expression and rudimentary speech

"I must speak to find relief..."
--Book of Job 32:20

This chapter will be dealing with vital aspects our relationship to other people. The constituent "retreat from self" also dealt with the intersubjective world, but from the point of view of the subject. The constituent "psychosomatics as expression and rudimentary speech" focuses upon the aspect of *communication,* which is our mode of access to the Other. Because higher order level structures are not functioning in psychosomatic patients, we are dealing with a level of expression which is rudimentary, a lower level, body meaning. The patient is not thematically aware of the message of the body, and the Other cannot respond to this meaning, at least not on higher order levels.[1] The significance of the illness/disease/ body sensation is the way in which the body attempts to express and communicate something which has not yet formed itself on personal higher order levels of meaning. Let me give a clinical example.

Mr. S. was a middle-aged man who had been referred to our psychiatric clinic because he had been diagnosed as suffering from psychosomatic symptoms, which he himself experienced and reported as intolerable muscular back tension. His GP was baffled, as he considered Mr. S. to be a perfectly healthy man, and yet this man was completely unable to

---

[1] Psychological research has shown how we often react to each other on a bodily level (synchronizing breathing, imitating body posture etc.); however, these "conversations" are subliminal and normally not thematic for the persons in question.

return to work due to the inexplicable "spasms" in his back musculature. These spasms were clearly felt by Mr. S., but his physician had not been able to verify them nor find any reasonable physical explanation for them. Mr. S. was convinced that his muscle spasms indicated that he was in the first stage of a very serious degenerative muscular disease. At the time of his referral, he had seen a variety of doctors, but none of them had been able to reassure him that he was in good physical health. He was obviously in very ill health, but his difficulties were not to be found at the level of the medical, objective body.

Mr. S. was married and the father of three children. He had a skilled job which he seemed to enjoy. He spoke of his children and his job freely, and he had no problems verbally formulating ideas, thoughts and feelings around these topics. However, when he started to speak about his wife, his face contorted, and he reached for his back, making a grimace of pain. "It's doing it right now!" he cried, and began to hyperventilate. I felt a rising feeling of panic in myself as he became more and more agitated in his chair, and I wondered if he was trying to communicate to me his own panic about something which had to do with his wife. I asked him to describe the pain and tell me about his sensations while he was having them. Because I regarded the spasm as communication, I wanted to hear if he could formulate anything verbally about this body meaning. To palpate it, or try to "localize" it in the body, would not be of any particular help. He was in such a state, gasping and writhing, that it was almost impossible for him to speak. I suddenly got the distinct impression that he was acting out a pantomime of sexual intercourse. He showed me something which he could not tell me. He gradually calmed down, told me that it had "gone over" and looked inquisitively at me to see what I would say. It seemed obvious that there was some connection between his spasms and his wife, yet I felt it was too early to speak about it. Mr. S. was waiting for some reaction from me to his dramatic symptom display. I said that he certainly had a difficult problem with his back, but that I was sure that if we were both patient, it would be possible to get to the bottom of these very disturbing occurrences. He seemed satisfied with this, and continued the interview by changing the subject from his wife to his children. His wife had disappeared from the conversation. Despite his conviction that he had an undiagnosed somatic disease, he nevertheless seemed to be interested in trying out a psychotherapeutical treatment, so we decided that he and I should follow his spasms over a period of time to see if we could find some pattern concerning when they occurred.

To make a long story short, what gradually emerged from "listening" to his back symptoms for several months (noting when they appeared) was that they served as a rudimentary expression of his fear that his wife was having an affair. He stayed home from work to keep an eye on her (she was a housewife), and every time some inkling of her possible extra-marital sexual activities managed to nudge his awareness, he had muscle spasms. He realized during the months that followed that he had suspected his wife of infidelity for some time, but had held these thoughts at bay, in the twilight of his consciousness. He was not thematically aware of these tormenting thoughts, yet whenever something triggered his vague suspicions of her, and the panic he felt about them, he expressed this through his twitching back. The symbolism of the "spasm" and the panic he felt about his sexual pantomime was not available to him until he could begin to think about unthinkable things, like the thought of his wife having sex with another man. As soon as this theme became thinkable, his muscle spasms faded away.

If we were to describe Mr. S's cure in terms of the phenomenological theory presented here, we would say that in the course of his therapy, his lower level, body meaning became higher order level signification. He could gradually tolerate the thought of his wife's infidelity, reflect upon it, and eventually confront her with it. As long as these levels of meaning were only expressed bodily, through back spasms, no such solution to this problem was possible. Because human life is intricate and complex, psychological and social, the level of the body (sensations, aches, pains) cannot help us successfully grapple with the various difficulties arising in our life situations. Low level body meaning cannot aid us in forming new structures which allow us to take in new and challenging aspects of the world. It *is* salutogenic to think and reflect, not because thoughts "bind energy" or because thinking necessarily leads to coping, but because we need higher orders of reflection and thought in order to *transform* the personal meaning of our lived situations. It is only through higher levels of signification that we can transcend towards the possible, the new and the different. When we are unable to do this, we find ourselves stagnated at lower levels, unable to come to grips with that which has thrown us into question.

In order to shed light on body expression as rudimentary speech, we need to examine what the speech of the body entails. I will in the following discussion be inspired by some of Merleau-Ponty's reflections upon speech and body expression,[2] and use them in order to develop an understanding of the body-meaning expressed in the psychosomatic symptom. It is only when we can listen carefully to the speaking body that we will be able to understand and treat psychosomatic pathology. Refining this skill is an important task for health care today.

For Merleau-Ponty, the body is itself intentional and meaning bestowing. But "bestowing meaning" should not be understood merely as an abstract process of assigning fixed meanings to referents. Expression, be it the expressing body or formal speech, is always directed towards a specific context, always immersed in a concrete situation. All expression and communication is contextual, part of a situation. Merleau-Ponty explains in *PP* that the aphasic has not lost a certain stock of words, which should be floating around in his head, but rather, he has lost a certain relationship to words. He can say "no" to the doctor's direct question, because he still finds "no" in purposeful language, but he cannot find the word "no" when asked about it abstractly, in a context which has no existential bearing for him. To speak is to activate various relations to the world. To name is to recognize, to reach the object through words. I do not first think "cup" as a concept and then subsume the object on the table under the category. Likewise, to speak to the Other is to incarnate

---

2   For Merleau-Ponty on speech and body expression, see Merleau-Ponty: 1964/1973; 1969/1973; and *PP* 174-199.

him into our field, to initiate what Merleau-Ponty calls a "dual being.[3]" It is through expression that things and Others come to be for us. Words (and gestures) place us, as psychological, social, cultural beings, in a living matrix of meanings, a communal life, wherein we orient ourselves as naturally as we "find" our body. Forms of expression (words, gestures, or, in the present case, body meaning) reveal not just themselves, but along with them an entire being-in-the-world. Our openness to the world (as transcending possibilities) encourages expression, while expression, in turn, makes possible our specific human openness to the world.

We may begin our descent from cognitive reflective thought to body meaning by looking at a level of expression which lies somewhere in-between, namely the gesture. Merleau-Ponty writes of the gesture that we must not make the mistake of confusing it with a cognitive act. The gesture *is* what it expresses, it is not an indication of something else going on behind the scenes. The clenched fist *is* the anger. Gestures are understood immediately, as I recognize in the other's body a reciprocity of my own intentions. I understand gestures of anger, seduction, love etc. by letting my own body mingle with them.[4] However, gesture is never the result of pure biology (a body devoid of meaning), it is a signification which partakes of cultural meanings. The angry Japanese smiles, while the Westerner gets red in the face, stamps his feet and hisses his words.[5] The manner of <u>living</u> anger differs, and there is thus no anger which can be once and for all defined biologically or phylogenetically. The important point is that the emotion, body expression and a specific way of being in the world are harmoniously patterned together. In gesture we find once again the ambiguous mixing together of body and signification

---

3   "...the other is for me no longer a mere bit of behavior in my transcendental field, nor I in his; we are collaborators for each other in consummate reciprocity. Our perspectives merge into each other, and we co-exist through a common world" (*PP* p. 354).

4   "It is through my body that I understand other people, just as it is through my body that I perceive 'things.' The meaning of a gesture thus 'understood' is not behind it, it is intermingled with the structure of the world outlined by the gesture, and which I take up on my own account." (ibid. p. 186).

5   In ibid. pp. 188-189.

which is characteristic for man. The way in which man transcends his given, biological nature is demonstrated at every level, from the perceptual act to the gesture and, at the highest level, the intricate world of language and thought. It is our existential power of transcendence which lends to our corporeality a signification which is unique to the human mode of existence. If we did not have this fundamental power, we would not speak, nor gesture, nor even perceive a human world.

For Merleau-Ponty, spoken expression is just the refinement of a more fundamental meaning which is based upon a bodily, perceptual meaning.[6] This prior level of meaning is more affective and direct. This could be the reason why gestures, which are perhaps closer to body meaning than spoken language, often have to do with emotions. We gesture when our relationship to the world is emotional, when we are filled with anger, desire, excitement etc. Spoken language is a super-structure which expands this body-emotion foundation, and it is no surprise that language often refines emotions and distances us from our strongest feelings. That culture tends to refine nature is a well-known phenomenon.[7] The reason that Merleau-Ponty's theory of language has been called a "gestural" theory is that he dismisses the idea that there could be a pure, finished, universal language which is expressed concretely in various languages. Language is completely contextual and cultural, it is a series of refined gestures, created and developed in the situated exchange that goes on between one embodied being and another. Language and communication have arisen from forms of behavior and conduct which were already communal, already a part of a shared world. When language evolved from gestures, it brought to light a new communality, but this does not mean that language can ever completely eradicate the basis of language (shared gestural communality), just as cognition cannot do away with its perceptual roots. To speak is not to create meaning so much as to move from an implicit to an explicit

---

6   See also Johnson, M. (1987) for an account of the bodily basis of meaning, imagination and rationality.

7   Douglas (1970/1982) has pointed out that when social reality is highly structured, body experiences tend to fade into the background.

meaning, to allow a nascent meaning to take form on a higher level of signification, to explicate something ambiguous more clearly. As soon as we exist as embodied, transcending human beings, we are in the process of enacting expression and communication, on all levels.

Let us now examine the level of body meaning found in the psychosomatic symptom as expression and rudimentary speech. The psychosomatic symptom does not possess the status of a gesture, as it is not intentionally directed towards anyone in particular. It is general and impersonal, showing up in a variety of situations which have no apparent meaning for the person in question at the time. However, the psychosomatic symptom is not a meaningless body functioning. It has a meaning, but this "meaning" can be understood in several ways. Let us first look at that which is common to all forms of psychosomatic body meaning. No matter what their specific content may be (with or without metaphorical, symbolic signification) they are always set in motion by the breakdown of higher order structures. Thus, all psychosomatic symptoms are lower level embryos of a meaning which should have emerged, more appropriately, at a higher level. Psychosomatic pathology is the patient's attempt to respond to something in the world, although the level of response is inadequate to the task. What is needed in order to resolve the "tension" and thus achieve true equilibrium is are higher order structure transformations. Because the meaning expressed in the symptom is impersonal and thematically unknown, it does not enter into the dialectical process of becoming (see chapter 7) nor does it participate in higher order levels of communication. The psychosomatic communication is always manifestly about an "it" (leg hurts, head aches, back pain etc.), never an "I". This way of living the world, which has been previously described as "being-towards-the-body", is gradually sedimented as an habitual response to an overwhelming, intolerable life situation. Lower level body responses are triggered by something in the world which the patient cannot handle with thoughts, feelings and reflection. Because we can never cut ourselves off entirely from contact with the world, and because we are always both mind and body together, when the higher order levels of signification break down for us, we will fill in with lower levels of body meaning. The body responds, in place of higher order structure transformations. The psychosomatic symptom will continue as long as the life situation which has triggered it into being remains in the field of the patient, demanding a solution on a higher level order. Let us now see what can be said more specifically about the "meaning" of the body expression in psychosomatic symptoms.

The body can be said to express meaning in a variety of ways. First of all, we have seen through some of the clinical examples presented in these chapters that the body may express meaning symbolically, or metaphorically.[8] These metaphorical symptoms manage to convey a rudimentary meaning because of the similarity between the physiognomy of the symptom and the higher order signification metaphorically expressed therein (e.g. to lie down (is) to give up; to have a back spasm (is) to have an orgasm). This category of symptoms would correspond to the Freudian "conversion symptoms", as opposed to the "vegetative neuroses" which, according to Alexander, lacked any symbolic signification. The metaphorical body symptoms, which already contain within them the seeds of a higher order signification, could be called "high level psychosomatic symptoms". They metaphorically express, through their particular symbolism, a specific meaning which we can trace out in a rudimentary form, a meaning which would be better expressed in fully developed thoughts and feelings. This body symbolism is possible because the body as embodied (the *lived* body) already partakes of a basic physiognomy which the higher level orders build upon, although the level of body meaning is general and fairly wide. To yawn, spit out, sneeze, and vomit are all expulsion actions, and they express rejection, or rather, they *are* rejection, at the body level. Precision movements, like pinching, grasping, and clasping are the opposite of rejection, they are taking possession of things on a bodily level. These meanings are completely enacted bodily, and we do not need to translate them in order to grasp

---

8 Metaphors are built perceptually around similarity or equivalence, and they are shaped culturally by specific meanings which are sedimented in a particular culture. The essence of metaphor is that we understand one thing in terms of another, like "argument is war," "love is madness," "time is money" (in Lakoff & Johnson, 1980).

their significance. They are immediate, albeit general and imprecise. Gradually, instead of spitting out food, the small child learns to say "no", and eventually as an adult she can build intricate, personal significations around rejection which she could only rudimentarily express as spitting as a baby. In the same way, there is a metaphorical similarity between having a muscle spasm and having an orgasm, having a backache and being unable to "take a stand". Whether certain body metaphors are universal (not culturally mediated) is an interesting question.[9] Medical anthropologists have shown how different cultures structure differently their understanding of bodies, minds, emotions and relationships between them.[10] What is important in light of the present discussion is to understand that high level psychosomatic symptoms express body meaning in this metaphorical way. A rudimentary speech is formed, but this "speaking" is still very far from the fully articulated, reflective, personal level of signification. Let us now look at psychosomatic symptoms which do not seem to have any metaphorical meaning, those symptoms which could be called "low level psychosomatic symptoms."

I can begin with a clinical example. I had a young woman in therapy for many years. Her flora of symptoms was impressive. She had backaches, headaches, stomach pains, and from time to time she had very bad skin rashes. Her body more or less exploded in a variety of symptoms, and it would be hard to say that there was a specific meaning (metaphorical, symbolic) expressed in each of these somatic tracks. My impression was rather that when she felt overwhelmed, one of these symptoms would come into the foreground, while the others faded into the background, and it would be hard to say that the "meaning" expressed therein was on the way towards rudimentary speech. Her body wasn't

---

9 For example, can we imagine a culture where lying down would be an expression of power, initiative and will? Or a society where limping and stuttering would be indications of social competence and leadership ability?

10 Low (1994) has concluded in his study of "nerves" across different cultures that those conditions called nerves or nervous disorders are culturally interpreted symptoms, even though there may be some commonly lived body experiences. See Csordas (1994), Jackson, M. (1989), Sachs (1996) for interesting reading on medical anthropology.

expressing rudimentary meaning so much as signaling chaos. My impression was that these symptoms were simply body turbulence, triggered by something in her world, but the turbulence itself was at a very low level of signification. The symptoms signaled that her body was out of control, and this was all the "meaning" they expressed. What has happened when someone responds to the world in this way, with such a diverse array of symptoms?

My hypothesis about low level psychosomatic symptoms is as follows. For patients with such symptoms, the structures which make up the give and take dialectic of meaning (the "in-between" of being-in-the-world) are extremely impoverished. The patients do not lack intelligence or the capacity for abstract thought, but they are lacking in some very basic comprehension of the world, which makes their understanding of various life situations full of blind spots, confusions and feelings of panic. My patient above could never explain to me what was going on in her life, nor could she ever say what she felt or thought about various situations. At first I was irritated by her incapacity, since she was obviously of normal intelligence and she should have been able to answer my questions. I was frustrated and wondered why she didn't understand what I was asking of her. She once reported, for example, that the man whom she had been dating had broken up with her. Trying to find out the course of events which led up to this event was simply impossible. I asked her to tell me what happened, but the tale which followed, although all the words were comprehensible, had nothing to do with the issue at hand. All attempts to get back onto the track floundered. This peculiar lack of communication happened so many times with her, in so many different contexts, that I began to understand that she herself did not structure her situations in the way in which one would expect. What met her in her world was a tangle of disparate facts which she could not manage to put together in any comprehensible way. The only area where she seemed to function adequately was her work, which had a technical character. She could understand numbers, but she could not make sense out of other people. Because that which presented itself to her from the "world side" was so badly organized and basically chaotic, she could not muster up a symptom which had any coherence (meaning). The difference between her symptoms and those of the previous patients presented would be that while they had a basic grasp of the world and could therefore respond with a meaningful body response (body as metaphor), this patient had no articulation on the world side which would have helped her form a symbolic symptom. Her body-answer to the world was, in fact, a mirror of her chaotic world. The long process of her recovery had to do with building up a basic understanding of herself in a comprehensible situation. The similarity between this patient's difficulties and McDougall's conceptualization of psychosomatics as an alternative to psychosis would seem to suggest that psychosomatic functioning can indeed serve as a way to structure a chaotic world, at least when we are speaking of low level psychosomatic symptoms. Following McDougall, it would seem that my patient could function in a kind of pseudo-normality (work and have a semblance of relations) as long as her body was in chaos. Without her symptoms, she may very well have become psychotic.

As clinicians, we meet patients who bring us their bodies in order to get relief from their symptoms. They have some disturbing experience of their bodies which they wish to be treated for. This is a perfectly reasonable communication. When a problem is experienced in the body, it is natural to seek a body solution. To have problems with our bodies is very disruptive, especially when, in the case of psychosomatic symptoms, the body symptoms are activated for such a long period of time. Merleau-Ponty points out that normally we do not call attention to our bodies in dealings with others, unless we wish to fascinate, awaken pity, or require physical assistance of some kind or another. Our bodies, like our speech, are not normally the focus of attention, but are passed over on the way towards their goal (movement, gesture, linguistic communication).[11] When the psychosomatic patient brings his body to the clinician, there is a deeper communication which we should hear, a communication which conveys the breakdown of higher order structures. The

---

11 For interesting reading on the *absence* of the body see Leder (1990).

persistence of the psychosomatic symptom testifies to its inadequacy as a harmonizing structure. The more the symptom gets sedimented as a response to life situations, the harder it becomes to find the *person* in their life situation. The important point to understand is that it is the *rupture* between self and world which has brought the symptom into being. Unfortunately, traditional biomedicine works through the examination and treatment of the objective body, which is precisely to focus on a body without a context. Biomedicine thus sediments the rupture instead of healing it. The only efficacious cure is to back up to the fork in the road where the patient's transforming dialectic broke down. It is from this point onward that the symptom has been trying to answer an impossible question. If we are to ever understand the message of the symptom, we need to develop our sensitivity to what the body of the patient is trying to say. Where the body has been, the self shall be, to paraphrase Freud's famous dictum.[12] Just how this dialogue between the clinician and the psychosomatic patient should be carried out is an important issue which needs to be developed in order to better understand and treat psychosomatic patients.[13]

Thus far, I have said that psychosomatic body symptoms function as expression (of the unthinkable) and rudimentary speech, in cases where this body "speaking" has a symbolic, metaphorical content. The meaning of the body is still an "it" rather than an "I", although body meaning is always contextual, it is always *about* something in the world of the patient. This is just another way of saying that the lived body participates in the "in-between" dialogue between (embodied) man and the world. The symptom comes into being because of the lack of higher order structure significations. Were the higher orders capable of transformations in the concrete problematic situation(s), there would be no need for the psychosomatic symptom. I have likened the "choice" of body meaning and expression to the Sartrian "breakdown" into emotion. We do not thematically choose to become emotional, nor do we consciously

---

12 "Where id was, there ego shall be." Freud (1933) *SE*, Vol. XXII, p. 80.
13 See Hellström (1994) for an interesting approach to this issue, which he has called "dialogue medicine."

choose to use our bodies instead of thinking and feeling in relation to various life situations. The relationship between body meaning and emotion is an interesting question. It would be tempting to place emotion and body meaning in a hierarchical relationship, with body meaning farthest down on the mind-body continuum, emotion next, and finally at the highest level thought and reflection. For example, when we are unable or unwilling to think, we react emotionally,[14] and when we cannot be emotional, we become psychosomatic. The research on alexithymia could support this idea, since it has been shown that alexithymic patients, who have "no words for feelings," often suffer from psychosomatic symptoms.[15] However, it is not entirely clear what emotion *is*, and to regard emotion as a purely negative phenomenon (a breakdown of the rational, an inferior state etc.) has been challenged by modern neurophysiological research.[16] Emotions have played an important role in traditional theories on psychosomatics, as they were often considered to be the essential link between mind and body, ultimately responsible for the formation of psychosomatic symptoms. Let us now take a brief look at emotions.

Traditional psychosomatic theories needed to find a bridge between psyche and soma. This bridge had to be something which could naturally account for both meaning and physiology, signification and materiality, motivation and causality. Emotions were a good candidate, because of their "level-ubiquity."[17] Emotions partake of both mind and body.[18] The bodily aspects of emotion help to distinguish them from other types of beliefs and judgments, while their specific psychological content dis-

---

14 This chain of reasoning is based on Sartre's (1948) theory of emotion. He reverses the everyday understanding of emotion, whereby we first become emotional and then we cannot think. Rather, according to Sartre, we are emotional *in order to not have to think.* Emotion is a magical transformation of oneself and the world, the aim of which is to avoid difficult or impossible situations.

15 See chapter 2 on alexithymia.

16 See Damasio (1994); Goleman (1995).

17 Term taken from de Sousa (1987).

18 "Emotions are like Descartes' pineal gland: the function where mind and body most closely and mysteriously interact" (Ibid. p. xvi.).

tinguishes them essentially from other kinds of physiological states of arousal.[19] Furthermore, emotions are culturally conditioned, which means that human emotions connect to all levels of our existence, from the biological to the psychological and social levels. However, for my purposes I do not need emotions to serve as a bridge between psyche and soma, since we begin with the lived body. Emotions do not connect isolated islands of psyche to segments of matter, nor do they translate brain processes into meaningful content, or vice versa (signification into physiological activity). I do not use emotions in order to account for either the formation of symptoms or the explanation of cure. Nevertheless, emotions are interesting as a particular way of being-in-the-world, a way of being in the world which could perhaps be seen as a middle position between body meaning and articulated personal signification, understood as such. By "emotion" I am referring to strong emotion, that is, disruptive states[20] involving perceptions of one's own body as explosive, intrusive, out of control, as well as thematic awareness of what the emotion is about (the object). Emotions are a way of being-in-the-world

---

19 de Sousa (ibid.) gives an interesting example from the movie *The Exorcist*. When the film was initially shown in the 1970s, people in the audience were so horrified and repulsed by certain scenes that they often threw up in the aisle. de Sousa points out that if the audience had in fact vomited because something was wrong with the popcorn, they would have indignantly demanded their money back. Getting sick because of the *film* was acceptable because experiencing emotion is one of the reasons people go to movies in the first place.

20 Buytendijk (1974) has characterized emotions as a dysregulation of normal and appropriate relations to the world. Being emotional is a disturbance of normal aspects of embodiment. The emotional experience is one of being out of control, of being bodily disorganized. Throughout the history of emotions there has been a wide variety of classifications of emotions, with various attempts to identify "primary emotions." There are as many lists of basic emotions as there are theories, although most regard emotions as having something to do with biological or psychological/social survival. Following the phenomenological work of Buytendijk, de Rivera (1977) and Sartre (1948), I mean by "emotion" those states whereby the subject's relationship to the normal flow of the world is disorganized and one's self-boundary is disturbed. Emotion is a transformation of our being-in-the-world. If our experiences of ourselves and our world are not disrupted, we are not emotional, according to my definition.

characterized by a rupture of the normal, everyday fluidity of our dealing with the world. Emotions are a way of thinking and acting which are perhaps closer to gesture than reflective thought. Emotions are being bodily engaged, but they are more articulated and personally owned than the body meaning of the psychosomatic symptoms. Let me try to illustrate the relationship between emotions and psychosomatic symptoms with a clinical example.

Mrs. P. was around 35 years old, and worked as an elementary school teacher. She had gotten married quite young, and had a turbulent relationship with her husband, a much older man who enjoyed the company of other women rather too much. They had two children of their own, while he had another child with a woman from a previous marriage. He maintained close contact with his "other family" and he often used this relationship to his ex-wife, who had not remarried, and their child in order to keep Mrs. P. in line, although Mrs. P. was not aware of this at the time of the referral. She came to our clinic because of continual, intense headaches which refused to go away. No organic cause for these headaches could be found. Mrs. P. thought that she might get some relief if she could learn some relaxation techniques. When I met her for the first time, she was quick to assure me that she had no difficulties in her life, and that the only problem she had right now was her headache. That was fine, I said, but I would still like to know a bit about her and her current life situation in order to be able to help her in the best way. She spoke very quietly, and started to tell me about her family and her work. When she spoke of her husband, she clenched her right hand into a fist and quietly drew it under her left hand, as if to hide it from view. All the while she spoke of how charming her husband was, her right hand was clenched into a very tense fist. She seemed to be completely unaware of this body language, and I did not draw attention to it. When she changed the topic to her work, she relaxed her hand and her body became less tense. She said that she had been having terrible headaches since Christmas (about 3 months earlier). Nothing particular had happened at Christmas, except perhaps that her husband had spent quite a bit of time with his ex-wife, which had "irritated" her. When I asked her to tell me more about her irritation, she looked somewhat puzzled, and said that she didn't know what to say, she had simply been irritated. Because she had initially announced that she did not have any problems she wanted to speak to me about, I did not pose any more questions. I wondered to myself if there was something about this situation at Christmas and her feelings towards her husband which could have something to do with her headaches, something which was not available to Mrs. P. at this time. She and I agreed that we would meet a number of times to see if I could help her with her headaches.

Mrs.P. was a mild and tolerant woman, according to her own testimony as well as the appraisals of her friends and family. She told me that she had been praised as a child for being so quiet and nice, and that her friends said she was the kindest, most even tempered person imaginable. What happens when such a "nice" person becomes angry, insulted, furious, enraged? Mrs. P. became, at the most, "irritated" or sometimes "annoyed" or "bothered". These states were, for her, minor occurrences, or so she thought. However, in these situations where she said that she felt "irritated," her body was mobilized into tremendous muscular tension. Her tense body seemed to live a life of its own, as she initially had no awareness at all of her body tension. She was as unaware of her body as she was of her feelings. She did not consciously experience rage and anger because she had not developed any higher order structures for these feelings, so in a sense they did not exist for her. She was thus not conscious of being "angry," yet something happened in her body at certain times in certain situations. What she was thematically aware of was an experience of minor irritation, while her body prepared itself for a major battle. We could say that she had the rudiment of very strong emotions in her body, although they were not yet conscious, directed or filled with any cognitive content. Her only contact with these unthinkable, impossible feelings was her headache, which was the result of her chronic muscular tension. During the course of her therapy, she was gradually able to feel and express anger towards her husband for his manipulation of her. As she became aware of her anger, she reported that she felt, for the first time, *her muscular tension* as well. It was as if her anger needed to be formulated and directed in order for her body experiences to have any meaning for her.[21] When Mrs. P. became aware of her anger, her muscular tension and her difficulties in expressing negative emotions, her headaches diminished in strength. After several months of treatment, she no longer suffered from headaches.

What can this clinical example tell us about emotions? The English word "emotion" derives from the Latin verb "emovere" - which means literally to move out, originally referring to getting a crowd out of a forum, forcefully removing soldiers from a private residence, moving dirt from an excavation sight, or in general authoritatively pushing a resistive mass.[22] To be emotional is to be "moved" in English, "ému" in French, "rörd" in Swedish, all of these words conveying the central idea of movement. De Rivera's[23] phenomenological theory of emotions analyzes emotions in terms of movements towards others or away from others, as well as regulating basic relations of belonging/non-belonging to the self. Regulating distance and closeness could thus be seen as one of the basic functions of emotions. In the case of Mrs. P., she wished to push her husband away from her, to place him farther away from herself. Had she allowed herself to feel angry, she might have accomplished this, first with her body (which was tensed up and ready to push) and then perhaps with words or deeds. If emotion is this basic regulation of distance and

---

[21] This patient differs from the previously presented cases in that she did not pay any particular attention to her body. Her psychosomatic symptom (the headache) was not lived with "cognitive attentionality". Perhaps this patient was actually more alexithymic than psychosomatic. Her cure was to find words for her feelings. The relationship between alexithymia and psychosomatics is not clear (see chapter 2). However, it is reasonable to assume that there is some connection between experiencing emotion and experiencing one's body. When Mrs. P. felt how angry she was, she felt her body as well. Some research on alexithymia shows that alexithymic patients do in fact have trouble differentiating between bodily experiences of hunger, sexual urges, sadness, shame and so on. In contrast, the psychosomatic patient has better access to his/her feelings in general, (as well as a hyperawareness of the body), although specific feelings need to be further articulated in terms of thematic content and directedness.

[22] In de Rivera (1977) p. 11.

[23] Ibid.

closeness, we could say that the next level, thought and reflection without body turbulence, is the refinement of closeness and distance. Anger goes over into either the work of reconciliation (close again) or separation (permanently far away), sorrow passes laboriously through mourning to acceptance and new beginnings. What does the case Mrs. P. tell us about emotion? She felt something in relation to her husband, but this something was not a thought (I am angry with you because...), a feeling (I would like to hit you....) or even a conscious body awareness that something was upsetting her. She only knew about her headache, which was the result of her chronic body tension. Her tense body was all that appeared in the place where her anger should have been. When she felt her emotion and expressed it to her husband, her tense body relaxed. Mrs. P. *was* angry with her husband, although this anger was lived in her body rather than articulated and known. The cure for her headaches was nothing more and nothing less than the discovery of this anger and her expression of it, at the level of thoughts and feelings, in the situation where it occurred, that is, together with her husband. She was cured of her headaches when she could formulate a personal meaning about how she experienced her relationship to her husband. This process I have called "transformation of structures." She was no longer "irritated" or "annoyed" with her husband, nor did her body tense up the way it did before her treatment. She learned to express verbally towards another that which had previously tormented her physically, with no viable outlet for resolution. I will wind up this chapter with another clinical example, another angry woman; however, in this case there was no cure.

A woman in her 50s (Mrs. F.) was referred to our clinic because she had chronic, persistent symptoms which could not be diagnosed in terms of any physical, somatic cause. She experienced that her arms became very hot and heavy, she became very tired, and she was forced to go to bed. She could then lie in bed for several days until she felt that her symptoms had abated. She also described that she felt paralyzed in her arms, and when she felt this way she was incapable of doing anything. She did not work outside the home, but she had charge of all of the housework responsibilities such as shopping, cooking, cleaning and washing clothes. When she was unable to do these things, because of her illness, her oldest daughter had to do them. This bothered her, since she wanted her daughter to have a normal life as a teenager. Although she was married, she could not imagine that her husband could take over any of these household responsibilities. She and her family had immigrated to Sweden from a country in the Middle East, where men were simply not expected to do housework. The metaphorical meaning of her symptoms was rather obvious, i.e. that she didn't want to do all the work at home but could not express this complaint. She became paralyzed (incapable of housework) instead of asking her husband to help her out. From my experience with other psychosomatic patients, it seems that "hot" symptoms often have to do with body expressions of anger. So, we have a woman who cannot express her anger and dissatisfaction with her husband except through her symptoms. How to start a dialogue around this?

Mrs. F. had seen many doctors, specialists and physical therapists. She felt that she had been treated badly, dismissed as a "psychosomatic" patient, and not taken seriously as a person with severely incapacitating symptoms. Her referral to a psychiatric clinic was not her own wish, although she was not as hostile to the idea as one might have imagined. She wondered, what could we do for her? To start a dialogue with someone who is focused on their body, it is a good idea to start with the body. I thought it might be appropriate to let Mrs. F. work with relaxation exercises and body awareness training in order to get in touch with her body, to realize that it was *she* who was "hot" (angry) and "paralyzed" (on strike). If she could really feel and own her body, instead of externalizing her body as and "it" or "not-me," as people with symptoms often do, perhaps she just might become interested in the messages it (she) was sending out. I explained to her that since no physical causes had been found for her symptoms, they might be caused by another kind of mechanism, a mechanism which lets our bodies react to situations when we find it too difficult to think about or cope with them at the present time. If she was interested, I could teach her how to re-route this mechanism, but the first step would be to learn how to relax her body so that she could feel calm, despite her symptoms. She looked skeptical and wondered if I didn't have any machines or medication which could help her. She had no problems in her life, and she didn't feel tense. My next sally was to try to interest her in any connections at all between her symptoms and her life situation, even if the connections made might be far from illustrating the "rupture" which had elicited the symptom in the first place. I answered her request for passive treatment by telling her that she had already tried all of the machines and medication available, and that my idea was to try a somewhat different approach. I could understand that she was skeptical, since it must be hard for her to imagine at this point exactly how this treatment was going to work. I continued by asking her if she noticed when she got her symptoms. We were able to discuss this at some length. She experienced symptoms during various weather conditions, after eating certain foods, and in connection with certain household chores. She agreed to come to a second meeting to further discuss the possibility of therapeutical treatment.

Mrs. F. came to the following meeting somewhat late, and seemed to have lost interest in the treatment. She sat passively while I asked her about her household chores. When she mentioned her daughter's work load during her illness, she started to cry, and wondered how we could let her suffer like this, and let her daughter suffer as well. It was when we were talking about how she felt about her daughter's work load that the obvious question of her husband's lack of participation arose. I asked her why he didn't help out with the chores when she couldn't do housework. Her reply was that men do not do housework, and it was out of the question for her to ask him. She laughed as she tried to imagine him doing dishes or hanging up laundry. This image was completely foreign to her, and although she was aware that Swedish men shared housework with their wives,[24] this could never be the case in her home. There was

---

[24] Had she not been aware of this, it is possible that she might not have formed her symptoms. Her husband must first of all be conceptualized as a "possible" helper, in order for her to even imagine asking him for help. An interesting question is whether or not she would have formed these symptoms in her home country, where the image

nothing here to discuss. That she might be trying to force her husband into a more helping role, by being ill, was also a completely foreign idea to her. She *wanted* to do the housework, she assured me, but she could not because there was something wrong with her arms. We met a few more times to discuss her problems/symptoms, without any openings for a dialogue between us. I could not treat her symptoms as mechanical malfunctions in an "objective" body, as she wished me to do, and she could not regard herself as a lived body, nor her symptoms as a communication, as I wished her to do.

Why do some patients enter into a dialogue and others do not? There are of course a variety of reasons, having to do with person to person "chemistry", the level of trust and interest in the clinical situation, the courage and motivation to change, the sensitivity of the clinician etc. A dialogue does not just spring from nothing, it needs a common ground upon which to begin. Mrs. F. and I never found a common place from which we could have communicated with each other. But it must be remembered that when the patient brings her aching body to the clinician, this is already an attempt to change something, although this "something" is expressed bodily. If the patient can be helped to begin to understand that the symptom is a message, and that we can hear the message together if we focus on the patient's being-in-the-world, we have the first key to beginning a dialogue. The rest of the dialogue must unfold in the concrete narrative of the patient's situation. When patients can eventually rise above low level meaning to higher order signification, their symptoms are no longer needed. The speaking body becomes the speaking subject, and the psychosomatic way of life is replaced by the experience of being once more (or for the first time) rooted in concrete situations with others. When we are able to communicate freely with others and take part in a changing, complex world, the body is background. The specific etiology of this process will be examined in the following

---

of a man in the kitchen and in the laundry room would never have even crossed her mind.

chapter, which will take stock of the phenomenological theory of psychosomatics and see what it has been able to accomplish.

.

CHAPTER 10

An examination of the phenomenological theory

"Now! Now!" cried the Queen. "Faster! Faster!" And they went so fast that at last they seemed to skim through the air, hardly touching the ground with their feet, till suddenly, just as Alice was getting quite exhausted, they stopped, and she found herself sitting on the ground, breathless and giddy. The Queen propped her up against a tree, and said kindly, "You may rest a little now." Alice looked round her in great surprise. "Why, I do believe we've been under this tree the whole time! Everything's just as it was!" "Of course it is," said the Queen: "what would you have it?" "Well, in *our* country," said Alice, still panting a little, "you'd generally get to somewhere else - if you ran very fast for a long time, as we've been doing." "A slow sort of country!" said the Queen. "Now, *here*, you see, it takes all the running *you* can do, to keep in the same place. If you want to get somewhere else, you must run at least twice as fast as that!"

Through the Looking Glass
--Lewis Caroll

It is time to examine the phenomenological theory and see if we have succeeded in presenting a fruitful alternative understanding of psychosomatic pathology. We have done a bit of running, but where have we landed? I will in this chapter be looking at the following aspects of the theory: my definition of psychosomatics, my interpretation of the clinical material, the validity of the theory (in terms of human scientific validity criteria), ontological questions, the issue of etiology and the cure. This analysis will be carried out in light of the aim of the theory, which has been to offer a holistic alternative to the dualistic, reductionistic traditional theories of psychosomatics. The phenomenological theory begins with the unity of the lived body and the person in his/her concrete life situation, and for that reason cannot be reasonably criticized for not choosing *another* starting point (like the objective body, or the functionalist conception etc.). The perspective or point of view taken is phenomenological, which means that I will not be spending time defending my theory against charges that it is not "natural scientific" or "non-falsifiable" or any other such criticism which springs from a framework outside of the phenomenological project. The aim was not to remedy traditional theories from *within* their frameworks, but to present an alternative. This does not mean that the theory cannot be examined, but it will be examined in terms which are appropriate to the approach. Let us now turn to that examination, and see what we have managed to say about psychosomatics in this second part of the dissertation.

Definition of psychosomatic pathology

I stated earlier on in chapter 1 that definition and theory are very closely tied together. To say what psychosomatic pathology *is* already implies certain presuppositions about and ways of understanding the field as it is delineated by the definition. My general definition of psychosomatic pathology is that psychosomatic symptoms/diseases are low level body responses to challenges from the world which would require higher order articulation for true resolution. Psychosomatic pathology testifies to the breakdown in the dialectical transformation of meaning. When meaning is denied higher level signification, it lives on as body in various ways (e.g. body memories, "cognitive attentionality," body expression). The implicit understanding operating in this definition is that man and the world are always in an on-going dialogue. We are never cut off from the world, and the world never ceases to challenge us to formulate meaning until our last moment. Meaning is understood in my theory as both high order as well as lower level signification, such as the intentionality of body functioning. The body referred to in this theory is the *lived* body, not an impersonal "objective" body orchestrated into activity by Mind. Because mind and body share a common life, the functioning of the body is intentional and meaning-bestowing, at various levels of signification (see chapter 9 on "high level" and "low level" psychosomatic symptoms). The "meaning" found in the body functioning of psychosomatics as described in this theory is a lived meaning, it is not translated nor derived from some meta-position outside of the lived body. Just as shaking the fist *is* anger, so is back pain the bodily expression of ambivalence. The pain does not stand for or represent ambivalence, it *is* ambivalence at the body level. According to my theory, the pain in the back is the patient *living* her inability to "take a stand" rather than reflecting upon this inability, and thereby weaving this meaning into her life narrative. The objective body is not under consideration in my theory, although it is of course possible to take that point of view, and examine this person's back and possibly find lesions which could "explain" the pain in objective, physicalistic terms (or alternatively, not find anything, and then dismiss her pain as less "real"). However, as shown in part I, physicalistic descriptions are not much help to us if we want to reach an understanding of psychosomatics. The phenomenological theory points out that back pain can be lived in different ways, and may arise according to different mechanisms, one of which is psychosomatic. There are patients who have back pains without psychosomatic etiology, as well as those who have back pains without living them in a psychosomatic way. It is the meaning of the symptom and the way it is lived which gives it the status "psychosomatic," not any pre-determined collection of signs or specific physicalistic causal mechanisms or lack thereof.[1]

According to my definition of psychosomatic pathology, we have a wide and a narrow way of understanding psychosomatics. The wide definition says that any and all parts of the body may be used to replace an utterance. In this case, even without a specific psychosomatic etiol-

---

[1] For the sake of clarity, one may distinguish cases where the symptom itself is the mechanical (physicalistic, causal) result of a process, and it is the process which is psychosomatic (meaningful/expressive), not the actual symptom. An example would be a young child who gets a rash on his bottom because he has started to defecate in his pants since the birth of a younger sister. It is the inability to regulate bowl movement which is the psychosomatic expression, not the rash itself. (Example from Hellström, personal communication.)

ogy, the body may fill in where a higher order level meaning should have been. For example, a person who breaks his leg may find that this situation provides him with a way to express dissatisfaction with his marriage, a dissatisfaction of which he may be only vaguely aware. Someone who has a satisfactory marriage, or who has the ability to speak and communicate about his/her dissatisfaction, will not be using the broken leg in this way.[2] The narrow definition concerns the specific psychosomatic initiation and maintenance of the symptom. Here, the formation of the symptom/disease is motivated by the psycho-social world of the patient. The body becomes ill or dysfunctional as a reaction to something in the life of the patient which cannot be handled by sedimented structures. This person is unable to transform his/her structures in order to accommodate the new and challenging meaning which has arisen. Because human beings live as a mind-body continuum, the meaning which cannot be taken up and transformed in higher order signification is caught up and expressed at the level of the body, forming symptoms which persist until the tension or disharmony has been resolved. This process will be examined later in the section on psychosomatic etiology.

Is this two-fold definition helpful? What are the advantages of this definition as compared to, for example, Freudian psychogenesis or Weiner's perturbed biological rhythms? Are there difficulties with my definition? If we begin with the advantages, the most important aspect of the phenomenological definition is that we have placed the person-world interaction in focus.[3] Traditional theories all agree that there is some-

---

[2] The wide definition is somewhat reminiscent of what is traditionally called "secondary gain" in psychoanalytic theory. Secondary gain refers to the interpersonal advantages of the sick role, while "primary gain" is the way in which the symptom keeps forbidden material away from consciousness. Secondary gain generally refers to a limited number of advantages such as attention and concern, and lessened responsibility if one is an adult. However, the way in which the body is used interpersonally in my theory goes far beyond traditional secondary gain, since the body is used in order to express a variety of meanings, not only those related to the advantages of the sick role.

[3] Lazarus had the intention of explicating the person-world interaction, but for theoretical reasons he could not develop this theory in a genuine way. Weiner's "integrative" theory suffers from similar problems (see chapters 4 and 5).

thing about the way in which people experience the world and constitute meaning (appraise, cope, adapt, sublimate, repress) which is responsible for both health and ill health. I have placed this insight at the center of my theory, and defined psychosomatics in terms of a disturbed relationship between the subject and his concrete life situation. The phenomenological "in-between" is where we trace out the pathology, not in the objective body nor the intrapsychical mind. The notions of lived body and structure transformation help to describe both the flow and the stagnation which account for health and ill health respectively. Although the definition presented here is limited to psychosomatics, one can also imagine that the theory presented could be used in order to investigate other types of ill health, such as obsessive compulsive behavior and depression. For example, while the psychosomatic patient uses the body in order to try to reduce the disharmony of impossible structure transformations, another person may instead choose activity in order to try to reduce tension (e.g. workaholics, manics, compulsive behavior). So, the dynamics of the theory are applicable to a wider group, although this dissertation has not included the intention to work out any further applications.

A second advantage of the definition is that I am able to address a variety of instances of symptoms and diseases which, as Weiner has pointed out, are heterogeneous in nature. We may include bacterial ulcers as psychosomatic if they are used in place of an utterance, but we may also exclude this "same" bacterial ulcer (which is not really the same) if it is lived in a non-psychosomatic way. We get beyond the either/or classifications and concentrate upon the lived signification of the symptom. In what situation has it arisen? How is it lived? The phenomenological approach has chosen to examine those aspects of the phenomenon which are relevant to a discussion of psychosomatics, the meaning and function of symptoms in the world of the patient, and disregards those questions which are unfruitful, or lead to impossible unsolvable mysteries. There is no Freudian "mysterious leap" to account for here, nor do we have to try to close the gap between experience (the "first cause" problem for Selye, Weiner and PNI) and physiological tissue alteration. The unity of the lived body and the being-in-the-world of the subject are the appropriate starting points for the study of psychosomatic pathology. The discipline of psychosomatic medicine had this initial insight, but was unable to pursue this project due to the constraints of its ontology and methodology (see chapter 3). The phenomenological theory has avoided the pitfalls of traditional theories since I have not begun with either the disembodied mind or the objective body. I have preserved meaning (psychosocial reality) without dualism, and found in the phenomenology of Merleau-Ponty a way in which to understand meaning as it is lived at the level of the body. Let us now turn to a critical examination of the definition of psychosmatics according to my theory.

Is it really possible to delineate the psychosomatic region according to the general idea that body replaces utterance? Are there not borderline cases and ambiguous symptoms which would challenge such a simple definition? We have seen such a borderline case concerning alexithymia in chapter 9, and one may also want to include other conditions such as anorexia in a psychosomatic definition. If I wish to exclude anorexia from my definition of psychosomatic pathology (which I do), what would be my argument for this exclusion? After all, the anoretic is concerned with her body, and she starves herself in order to convey something which she cannot say. According to my definition, anorexia is not psychosomatic in the wide sense, because it is not the experience of the body as an "it" which is lived with cognitive attentionality in situations where the anorectic should have developed thoughts and feelings. The anoretic has not lost contact with meaning transformation, but she has developed a delusional (psychotic) meaning rather than a bodily symptom in order to cope with an unbearable life situation. The psychotic idea (I am fat) *functions* in the same way as the psychosomatic symptom, but the pathology is the idea, not the bodily consequence of this idea (the starved body). According to the narrow definition, the anoretic has indeed been motivated by her life situation to develop her illness, but again, the pathology here is the delusional idea, not the bodily outcome of actions (dieting and hard exercise) which are performed because of this delusional idea of herself as fat. Finally, the anoretic does not wish to rid herself of her bodily experiences, but rather enjoys feeling light and euphoric. For these reasons, anorexia falls outside of the definition.

An opponent of my theory may ask, can I imagine a psychosomatic patient who did not experience her body with cognitive attentionality, who did not lack higher order signification, who could transform structures in accordance with the new and the different, but who nevertheless had a "psychosomatic" symptom? I would have to reply, if this patient can do all these things, and does not experience her body as a persistent, problematic "it" which she wishes to have fixed, what is it that makes *you* want to call her symptom "psychosomatic"? It is possible that one may wish to use the term "psychosomatic" in a very broad sense, including everything from transformations of self-world relations to short-lived psychophysical reactions such as shock or fright. I have nothing against other theorists using wide definitions, but it is up to them to elucidate their position with respect to mind/body questions, the nature of efficacious mechanisms and the meaningfulness of such a wide definition. Since I wish to reserve the term "psychosomatic" for the self-world transformations, it is not sure that my opponent and I are even referring to the same phenomena when we speak of "psychosomatic conditions." Nevertheless, there must be something about the patient's way of living/presenting her symptom which calls for the characterization "psychosomatic." I have chosen to describe this "something" in these terms, although they could be described in other terms as well.[4] This brings us to the next issues to be examined, namely the status of my interpretations and the validity of my theory.

---

[4] For example, Boss (1979) asks three basic questions in his *Daseins analytik*, namely: 1) how is a person's freedom to carry out his potentialities impaired at any given time; 2) what are these potentialities; and 3) with respect to which entities of the person's world does this impairment occur? These are interesting and legitimate questions from a Heideggerian perspective, questions which in no way contradict nor detract from my Merleau-Pontian approach. Within the human sciences we are not out to capture an objective entity, but to interpret phenomena. See the coming section on validity on this issue.

Interpretation of clinical material

All of the clinical examples used to illustrate the phenomenological theory come from my own working experiences with psychosomatic patients. Although I was a psychodynamically oriented therapist, I was equally interested in existential issues, and I did not force patients into Freudian categories. As I became familiar with the work of Merleau-Ponty, a new way of understanding these patients and their problems opened up. Because the theory I have generated is an interpretation of those encounters and processes, I am not saying that this is the only possible way to understand the clinical material presented. The phenomenological theory developed in this dissertation is the result of phenomenological reflection upon my clinical experiences in the light of Merleau-Pontian ideas. The theory is not a set of hypotheses to be verified as true or false, it is a possible way of understanding a particular way of being-in-the-world. Following Fingarette[5] we may see various interpretations as "meaning-reorganization" rather than "true" exact reproductions of some "hidden reality," illuminated definitively once and for all. Meaning-reorganization can be compared to cloud gazing. We look up at a cloud and say, "Look, it's a rabbit!", and indeed, the cloud configuration may resemble a rabbit. But then someone else looks at the same cloud and says, "I think it looks like a ship" and suddenly the figure of the ship fills out the cloud completely, and there is no shape or part of the cloud which is not meaningfully accounted for in the image of the cloud as a ship.[6] For this reason, "the ship" interpretation is better than "the rabbit," although seeing the ship does not exclude being able to see the rabbit as well. The object under study, in this case psychosomatic pathology, is subjected to various interpretations, and the different ways of trying to understand it give rise to more or less coherent, rich and detailed pictures. An *in*adequate meaning scheme is one which fragments, disorganizes and renders the material meaningless. The more ad hoc hypotheses needed in order to support the theory, the more violence done

---

[5] Fingarette (1963).
[6] In ibid. p. 20.

to the phenomena and the greater the counter-intuitivity of the ideas, the less plausible the theory. Adequate meaning schemes are ones that work, that make sense, that provide meanings which fit (like the ship) and allow us to see new aspects as well as to integrate previously disparate parts. Adequate theories have internal coherence, clear lines of reasoning and good fit with other, closely related ideas. Fingarette writes that the person who comes voluntarily to a psychotherapist is someone who is unhappy, and who finds his unhappiness *without meaning*. The therapist helps the patient understand the meaning of his suffering. In the same way, my interpretation of persistent, resistant, un-treatable body symptoms as the breakdown of higher order signification gives their intractability a meaning. That which was previously incomprehensible ("I just can't understand why Mrs. D. doesn't get any better after physical therapy!") becomes understandable. These patients cannot be cured of their symptoms by somatic treatments of the objective body because the symptoms are not the result of somatic mechanical dysfunction, they are expressions of *another lack*, a lack which my theory has brought to light.

A positivist would object, how do you know that your interpretations "fit" or are correct? You have no (objective) way of ascertaining their truth value, short of asking the patient, setting up experiments, or ruling out all other alternative interpretations as logically impossible. This view assumes that it is possible to <u>interpret</u> meaning in exactly the same way that the natural scientist <u>observes</u> facts. For the human scientist, there is no fixed (natural) reality which is just waiting to be discovered, there is no referent, like a physical object, which can be captured, reified and "explained" in this natural scientific way. We have seen in part I of this dissertation the unsatisfactory results when one insists upon applying natural scientific methodology to psychosomatic phenomena. As for asking the patient, engaging in a dialogue with one's subjects would be a perfectly acceptable human scientific avenue of evaluation, although not acceptable to natural science. The legitimacy of my clinical interpretations boils down to the following. Does my theory bring order to disparate, fragmented pieces of the patient's life? And does it do so in a better way than alternative theories? For example, at a general theoretical level, does my theory present a better picture of why it is curative to express oneself than is given by the psychodynamic "channels of discharge" theory (see chapter 2)? By "better" I do not mean explicating a more basic, reductionistic, atomistic level, but rather, does the theory give a more nuanced, detailed and connected view of the field? Does my theory do better justice to the psychosomatic phenomenon in question? This brings us to the issue of the validity of the theory presented in part II of this dissertation.

The validity of the phenomenological theory

I wrote earlier on, that we must not understand "validity" in the natural scientific sense of measuring that which one intends to measure in an experimental situation, but rather in the human scientific sense of meaningfulness and plausibility. The human sciences deal with subjective and collective experiences of meaning, constituted and lived in intersubjective psycho-social reality. The object of study is thus not a representation of some objective "state of affairs", but the on-going exploration of a reality in which the researcher him/herself is already embedded. The claims to knowledge made from within the human scientific sphere must be defensible, which is not the same thing as being verifiable by some neutral observation *outside* of the hermeneutical circle. Ricoeur has likened interpretation argumentation to the juridical procedures of a court of law. We argue for our theories and establish their validity in a dialogue with others. These "others" may be other researchers, our subjects, patients or even lay people. This does not mean that the lay person must immediately affirm the meaning which has been interpreted from the point of view of the researcher in order for the theory to be valid. However, through dialogue, new avenues of understanding may be opened up, allowing for new meanings and ideas which may be radically different from the pre-understanding of the lay person.

Whereas traditional theories of psychosomatics strive towards generalizations and law-like relationships between various factors in the formation of psychosomatic symptoms, phenomenology is content to give a rigorous description of human life (the being-in-the-world of the psychosomatic patient) as it is concretely lived. This does not mean that one may not trace out themes and patterns in phenomenological theory, but these patterns are not to be understood as laws or causal chains. The descriptions afforded by the phenomenological theory are not meant to support theoretical constructs (the unconscious, repression) nor to prove invariant relations. Sometimes, human sciences are criticized for their lack of general principles, and this is taken as proof that the human sciences are less "mature" than the natural scientific ones. However, discovering nomothetic laws is not the goal of the human sciences, because their subject matter is not nature, but man. The validity criteria for new human scientific theories are the following. Is it an interesting theory? Is it meaningful? Does it open up new perspectives? Adopting a new theory is like getting a new perspective on a perceptual object, we suddenly see aspects we have not seen before, and our perception is enriched and expanded. The phenomenological theory of psychosomatics has shifted perspective from the objective body to the lived body, and placed the subject-world dialogue in the center of the theory. I have used Merleau-Pontian ideas in order to illuminate the realm of "the in-between" where meaning emerges in dialectical transformations between man and his world. The concepts of structure transformation and body meaning have been especially helpful to our understanding of psychosomatic pathology, since meaning is lived on all levels. I have given up the impossible project of building bridges between mind and body. The freedom and transcendence of human beings are central to my theory. The notion of meaning constitution has been given a central role in understanding psychosomatic pathology. Traditional theories have vaguely understood that meaning constitution is somehow involved in the development of psychosomatic conditions, but they have not been able to do anything with this insight, due to either underlying dualism (the mind-body interaction problem) or the reductionism operating in the conceptualization of meaning as physiology. In the phenomenological theory developed here, the "speaking body" which Freud hinted at in his second theory of conversion has found its voice, the holistic mind-body unity which psycho-

311

somatic medicine tried to establish has found an appropriate ground, and the importance of the person-environment interaction suggested by stress theory (but not rigorously pursued by it) has been taken seriously and placed front center. So, the insights which have in one way or another been present (but not investigated) in the traditional theories have found proper elucidation in the phenomenological theory.

The ontological questions

I posed some questions regarding the traditional theories about ontological issues, such as the following. What *is* psychosomatic pathology and how does it differ from purely somatic disturbances (if there is such a thing)? How do theoreticians conceptualize and understand the relationship between mind and body operating in the formation of psychosomatic symptoms? My own position on these questions is the explication of the lived body[7]and the phenomenological theory of structure transformations. Because I do not begin with a dualistic conceptualization of man, I will not have to put mind and body back together. Because meaning-bestowing goes on at all levels (even lower level body signification) there is nothing especially mysterious about the speaking body. An ontological presupposition in my theory is that man always strives towards meaning and coherence. When this cannot be provided at the higher levels of psycho-social reality, the body attempts to achieve "structure harmony" by expressing low level meaning as a response to specific life situations. I have furthermore stipulated that self-becoming and transcendence belong to the human order, and that as psycho-social creatures we strive to articulate our experience of ourselves and our world at the higher levels. But because man is embodied, it is perfectly conceivable that the body may take up and express a meaning which cannot, for the time being, find expression at a higher level. The ontological position in my theory is fairly straightforward. Less clear is the issue of etiology, to which I now turn.

---

7   See especially chapter 6 on Merleau-Ponty and the mind-body problem.

The etiological questions

The traditional theories have grappled with the issue of mind-body interaction - specifically, efficacious mechanisms of influence from mind/experience to (objective) body. Freudian theory came up with cathexis (psychical energy) and repressed emotion as possible causal factors in the development of psychosomatic symptoms, while psychosomatic medicine and stress theory emphasized sustained physiological arousal as a conceivable link between meaning and somatic pathology. Weiner ultimately settled for perturbed biological rhythms, although both Weiner and Lazarus paid a certain lip service to person-environment interaction. I have criticized traditional theories either for the incomprehensibility of their "interaction" explanations or for their exclusion of meaning constitution. Proponents of these traditional theories have themselves admitted to the difficulties inherent in the "psychosomatic" subject matter. Modern Freudians seem to have given up trying to understand the "mysterious leap" from mind to body, stress theory has not yet definitively forged the link between the stress experience and ill health, and the authors within psychosomatic medicine clearly regret the lack of hard data produced in terms of verified causal mechanisms. They are all stuck because they have the objective body in focus, while at the same time they somehow realize that it is the lived body they should be studying. The objective body admits of causal chains and verifiable physical processes, while the lived body concerns the freedom, transcendence and meaning constitution of the embodied subject. To apply mechanistic, causal thinking to the lived body is doomed to fail. However, in defense of these theoreticians, the body *can* be described in objective, physicalistic terms, and it is thanks to this level of description that modern medicine has succeeded so well. While traditional theoreticians have been misled by their erroneous notions of mind and body, I have tried to present an alternative to traditional ways of thinking. However, the question becomes, can *I* say anything about etiology from within the perspective of the lived body?

The word "etiology" comes from the Greek *aitiologia*, the root *aitia* meaning "guilt" in the sense of owing someone something. In medicine, etiology has to do with the causes of diseases. The Latin term "*causa*" was originally a legal term, having to do with litigation concerning responsibility. Thus in its etymological sense, "cause" connotes something bad, or at least something which is out of the ordinary. On-going, normal events are seldom candidates for causes, although they do form the background context within which a cause may effectuate an event.[8] In natural science, causes are observable, verifiable processes or chains of events happening in the world of nature. The objective body admits of this level of causation, but not the lived embodied subject. The human scientific counterpart to causation is motivation. Merleau-Ponty points out that in order to be (causally) determined, I would have to be a thing. Even though our bodies partake of the material world, and in this sense are "thing-like", we are always free to choose how we constitute this quasi-thing which is our body. For example, Merleau-Ponty writes: "Tiredness does not halt my companion, because he likes to feel himself in the midst of things, to feel their rays converging upon him...My own fatigue brings me to a halt because I dislike it, because I have chosen differently my manner of being in the world, because, for instance, I endeavor, not to be in nature, but rather to win the recognition of others."[9] I am never completely constituted by my corporeality, nor my history. However, the freedom which I exercise is always a freedom in relation to givenness. We are thus both constrained and free.[10] This combination, which Merleau-Ponty calls "conditioned freedom," is analogous to the ambiguous nature of the lived body, as both materiality and consciousness bound up in the

---

8 The following, somewhat macabre example is given in Mackie (1974): it is the cut across the artery rather than the pumping of the heart which counts as the cause of death, although without the pumping (the standard condition) there would have been no death.

9 *PP* p. 441.

10 "What then is freedom? To be born is both to be born of the world and to be born into the world. The world is already constituted, but also never completely constituted; in the first case we are acted upon, in the second we are open to an infinite number of possibilities. But this analysis is still abstract, for we exist in both ways *at once*. There is, therefore, never determinism and never absolute choice, I am never a thing and never bare consciousness." *PP* p. 453 (italics in original).

lived unity of embodied existence. My body as an objective body may be described in causal terms, but not my lived body. But neither is the lived body some kind of tool to be wielded by an absolutely free-floating consciousness. I am, as lived body, a transcendence which is constrained by the corporeality of my body. This double nature must be kept in mind when discussing psychosomatic etiology.

The etiology discussion in relation to my phenomenological theory can be broken up into two questions: 1) how does it come about that some people use their bodies in this psychosomatic way instead of transforming structures? 2) how do I understand psychosomatic etiology in my own (narrow) definition, where I have said that were it not for the psycho-social level of meaning constitution, the patient would not break down into psychosomatic symptoms. Other questions such as, "are there certain pre-disposing factors for developing the psychosomatic way of life?" or "are there specific personality profiles or special physiological make-ups involved?" do not belong to this discussion, since the phenomenological theory has not set out to predict, explain or control this phenomenon in generalizable terms. But I will try to address the first two questions to see if I can shed some light on the issue of etiology in my theory.

The first question concerns the breakdown into psychosomatic expression. Why does structure transformation fail? In some of my clinical material (chapter 8) I found that the failure to transform structures had to do with a past experience which had never gained access to higher orders of articulation and reflection.[11] Past experiences which were disturbing, yet not thematically known, lived on as body symptoms. A well-documented clinical finding is that as soon as past lived experiences become known through reflection and thematic memories, the body

---

[11] Freudians would claim that all forms of breakdown and dysfunction have their root in past experiences. I am not in a position to say if this is so, but from my own practice I can say that I have seen psychosomatic breakdown in current life situations where past experiences did not seem to play any significant role. However, since I have not done any systematic empirical studies on this I cannot here say what the importance of the past is for psychosomatic functioning.

symptoms disappear. How is this to be understood? A phenomenological question here is, what is the motivation for using the body in this way? What motivates one person to develop higher order structures, while another does not? To take an example, let us say that we have two children growing up in a dysfunctional family, both are treated badly, but the one child gets through her childhood by gritting her teeth and waiting patiently for the day she can leave. She knows that she suffers, and she understands what makes her suffer, but she can see an end to her suffering, and consoles herself with this. She develops an inner life, she observes, she analyzes what goes on, bides her time, and tells herself that she will get by. The other child does not speak to herself (or others) about her suffering, and does not formulate what hurts her in terms of thoughts and feelings. She may or may not develop psychosomatic symptoms as a child.[12] However, as an adult, when she gets into situations which are similar to her traumatic home life (e.g. an abusive parent), she produces body symptoms. If she feels dependent upon someone who exploits her, she becomes physically ill, instead of remembering her home life. Why should the one sister be able to remain healthy, while the other one does not? A traditional attempt to answer this question would be to try to find something in the personality/biology/genetics of the sisters which would *account for* the different ways in which they have "coped" with their home life. The phenomenological answer is that they constitute the meaning of their situation differently, and they are able/willing, in different degrees, to allow their traumatic experiences to become a part of their self-becoming and life story. The first sister decided to orient herself towards her family in such a way that she allowed what was happening to become a part of her sedimented structures. She formed higher level orders of meaning and signification around these experiences. But

---

12 The relationship between developing psychosomatic symptoms as children and as adults is not taken up in this dissertation. This is another empirical question, which could be an interesting topic of investigation. All I can say at this point is that it is conceivable that children often react psychosomatically to difficulties in their lives because they have less developed higher order structure than adults. However, this group is most probably larger than those who eventually develop psychosomatic functioning as adults.

this "decision" is a tacit decision, more like a style or general attitude towards things and people in general. To attribute this ability to something other than what it is, namely a free act of transcendence and self-becoming, is to miss the point of meaning constitution. Both children were free to react to and understand their home life according to who they were and who they wished to be. There is no other cause for the one or the other orientation. The second sister had a different way of relating to the world than her sister. She developed a more passive (less controlling), yet at the same time more extroverted way of being, which precluded developing the strong inner life she would have needed in order to take in what was going on in her family and how she felt about it. Had this second sister grown up in a more normal family, she might never have become psychosomatically ill. She might have even developed another style of being in another family. We are always freely creating ourselves in a dialogue with others and our concrete life situations. This process is itself inexplicable, *that* we do this is a given. It is constitutive of our existence as free, self conscious human beings. And how it is that we are free is, of course, a mystery, just as consciousness, time and the existence of the perceptual world are irreducible mysteries.

It may seem like an evasive answer to claim that the breakdown of structure transformations has to do with tacit decisions made in concrete life situations, concerning general styles or ways of being. However, because we are always motivated (and never determined) to ascribe a particular meaning to our lives, we must look at the motivations we have for constituting the meaning of our lives the way we do. The patient who is not able or willing to transform structures in accordance with challenging life situations is not causally determined from without, he is "choosing" this solution. Sartre[13] ends his *Being and Nothingness* by introducing the idea of an existential psychoanalysis, where all tastes, inclinations and choices reveal fundamental projects and ways of being. One person enjoys eating a sugary pink piece of cake, another person finds the same dessert nauseating. The different "tastes" are not without

---

13 Sartre (1943/1956).

meaning, as they reveal how one has chosen to relate to different aspects of life. Psychosomatic patients reject thoughts, words and articulated feelings. They do not use them, they "prefer" the body. Whether this is motivated by fear, anxiety, or, more positively, an enjoyment of the passivity and diffuseness of body meaning, is impossible to say. As I see it, it is enough for the phenomenological theory to indicate the *lack* of higher order signification, and to leave the question open as to what reason the person may have for "choosing" this solution. Because we are dealing with motives instead of causes, it is possible that one person will choose this line of retreat because of fear, another because of an inclination towards irresponsibility and passivity. Further research does not exclude investigating this area, but the phenomenological theory will not be laying down generalizable hypotheses on this question.

Now on to the next question concerning etiology, namely, what is my understanding of psychosomatic etiology in the narrow sense? Without disturbances in the psycho-social world of the patient, no psychosomatic symptom. I wondered in an earlier chapter if a tumor could be psychosomatic in this narrow sense. It can obviously be *used* in place of an utterance (the wide definition), but what would it mean to say that a tumor (or any other symptom) has a psychosomatic etiology? I have criticized traditional theories for dualism and cannot myself use dualistic characterizations to account for the formation of psychosomatic symptoms. I also asked why some patients break down into psychosomatic symptoms, some become psychotic, while others develop anxiety neuroses. Is my theory capable of answering these types of questions?

To begin to try to answer these questions, it must be remembered that in the phenomenological theory we are always dealing with the lived body, which is the subjective embodied existence of some particular individual in some concrete, meaningful situation. Upon this lived body, it is possible to take the perspective of the objective body, but when we do this, we no longer refer to the lived body, but to a derived, constructed perspective upon the lived body. The risk is that as soon as we start to speak of "tumors" and "headaches" and "back pains" we switch over to the perspective of the objective body, and see in front of us various physiological processes taking place in an impersonal objective body made up of tissues and nerves and so on. This is natural, since it is within the perspective of the objective body that we have learned what a tumor *is* in the first place, but the problem becomes, how can we maintain our focus upon the lived body and at the same time discuss the etiology of conditions which we have learned to think about in terms of impersonal third-person processes? When I say that Mrs. Y. gets a migraine when she feels overburdened, this explanation is at the level of the lived body, but when I say that a migraine *is* such and such a physiological process which constricts and relaxes blood vessels in the brain, I am talking about the objective body. Would it be helpful to mix these levels and say that without the experience of being overburdened, the blood vessels of Mrs. Y will not behave in such a way as to give her a migraine? This is counterfactual causality, but do I not then have exactly the same problem as traditional theories, when I have to explain the relationship between experience (being overburdened) and physiology (blood vessel dialation)? How to get around this?

I will follow Merleau-Ponty again, and insist that physiology and psychology are not to be understood as an *in-itself* and a *for-itself* respectively. They are integrated and directed towards the world as existence, and they only are available to us as separated regions thanks to an unnatural analytic separation. Do we need to separate them in order to understand the etiology of psychosomatic pathology? Is the perspective of the objective body necessary for the understanding these conditions? If we follow conventional dualistic thinking, yes, but if we stick to the unity of experience, and the lived body, let us see if we can reason about psychosomatic etiology without separating man into mind and body, meaning and material, motivation and causality.

My body/my self is always directed towards a situation. When I wish to find my friend in a crowd, I gaze over the crowd and pick him out. I do this without conscious effort or reflective thought, yet it does not happen unless I decide to look for him (it is not a kind of reflex). I do not need to refer to the neural functioning of the optic nerve to understand that I am able to find my friend when I wish to do so. I do not need to look for my hands when I want to use them. My body, my intentions and my world are normally co-present to me in a natural flow. Because I am this unity, it will be the unity which is damaged in conditions which may arise at any of these three levels (objective body, lived body, socio-cultural life). Merleau-Ponty has examined some examples of brain-damaged patients in *PP* and concluded that the difficulties they experienced had not to do with selective inabilities (for example, the inability to point to one's nose despite the fact that one can grasp it), but rather concerned disturbances in their "motor intentionality" whereby movements naturally belong to a certain field of signification. He asks, how is it possible that these brain-damaged patients can in fact grasp their nose, but not point to it? The answer cannot be found at the level of physiological causality. The brain-damaged man who can reach towards his tool which he is about to use, but cannot extend his arm that same distance when asked to do so abstractly (pretending to pick up a tool) is not comprehensible at the atomistic level of physiology. The neural brain-circuits, muscles and vision needed to perform these two tasks cannot be intact in the one case and damaged in the other. The way to understand the true nature of the damage is to interpret it existentially, according to Merleau-Ponty. These brain-damaged patients can no longer orient themselves towards a *possible world*. Merleau-Ponty thus *interprets* brain-damage (which we automatically tend to think of in objective terms) in an existential framework of being-in-the-world. One brain-damaged man called Schneider, referred to in *PP*, could never raise himself above the concrete present. He could only comb his hair with a real comb in his hand, only knock on a real door and so on. He could not project around him a possible world. His sexuality was reduced, he could not initiate an encounter. He could no longer make conversation or have opinions, even if he would have liked to. He was disturbed in the function which would have allowed him to live as transcendence. This disturbance is not "caused" by physiology, but neither is it indifferent to physiological functioning: "After all Schneider's trouble was not initially metaphysical, for it was a shell splinter which wounded him at the back of the head. The damage to his sight was serious, but it would be ridiculous...to explain all the other deficiencies in terms of the visual ones as their cause; but no less ridiculous to think that the shell splinter struck symbolic consciousness. It was through his sight that mind in him was impaired."[14]

For Merleau-Ponty, bodily processes are not to be observed (in third-person terms) but understood. We should focus upon existence as being-in-the-world, and allow that, as human beings, we partake of both physiology and meaning. Thus, the answer to the question of etiology in psychosomatic pathology is not to isolate physiology, juxtapose upon it a psychological level, and hope that no one notices the incompatibility of these terms. The answer is to find a third term wherein we can understand both physiology and psychology simultaneously as the ambiguous embodied subjectivity of existence.[15] The psychosomatic symptom must be understood as a way of relating to the world, a way in which the whole person as corporeality and personal acts gathers together into this specific psychosomatic form of expression. Just as we do not need the neurophysiology of the optic nerve in order to understand the gaze, so may we leave the third-person descriptions of symptoms aside and focus upon the meaning, function and significance of the symptom for the concrete subject. The etiology of psychosomatic symptoms refers not the interaction of a for-itself (consciousness) and an in-itself (physiology), but rather to the integrated way in which the subject "chooses" to express

---

14 *PP* p. 126.

15 "...it is not clear how the imaginary (phantom) limb, if dependent on physiological conditions and therefore the result of a third person causality, can *in another context* arise out of the personal history of the patient, his memories, emotions and volitions. For in order that the two set of conditions might together bring about the phenomenon, as two components bring about a resultant, they would need an identical point of application or a common ground, and it is difficult to see what ground could be common to 'physiological facts' which are in space and 'psychic facts' which are nowhere...The phantom limb is not the mere outcome of objective causality; no more is it a *cogitatio*. It could be a mixture of the two only if we could find a means of linking the 'psychic' and the 'physiological', the 'for-itself' and the 'in-itself', to each other to form an articulate whole and to contrive some meeting-point for them: if the third person processes and the personal acts could be integrated into a common middle ground." (*PP* p. 77. italics in original).

her difficulties at this lower body level.[16] She is motivated into doing this by a meaning which she cannot accommodate at a higher level. If this meaning had not emerged in her world, or if she had been able to take up this meaning, reflect upon it and bring it into her life story, she would not somatize. Why some people react in this way, while others choose another line of retreat, is impossible to say at this general level. Perhaps further qualitative clinical and empirical research can shed light on the existential choices people make. However such research will not be looking for determinant causes, but possible ways of being-in-the-world, in line with Sartre's existential psychoanalysis. A phenomenology of the choices of breakdown would indeed be an interesting topic of research.

The cure

The phenomenological theory emphasizes freedom, transcendence and self becoming. We human beings use the higher orders of psycho-social reality (thought, reflection, communication) in order to develop ourselves and our understanding of the world. There is something salutogenic about thinking, speaking and reflecting. In my theory, meaning transformation at these levels is necessary for the transcendence of human self-becoming. When we are no longer capable of transforming meaning at the higher levels, we find ourselves in ill health, alienated from ourselves. Through the higher order meanings which we understand, produce and express, we unify our experience of ourselves and make sense out of our lives and our situations. We may call this coherence "the life story" or "narrative". It is possible to interpret that which is salutogenic in traditional theories as everything which tends towards coherence and unification of the self. The psychoanalyst and the analysand together unravel the tangled threads of the analysand's life story, and fill

---

[16] It must be pointed out here that the "subject" who chooses is not just the mind or consciousness of the person, but her body as well. It is the mind/body unity which chooses headaches, or ulcers or back aches. The risk of falling into objectivistic thinking is ever present in these discussions.

in the gaps where meaninglessness and confusion have prevented understanding. Meaningful connections replace senseless repetitions, and that which seemed to be isolated, disparate fragments of behavior finds a place in the whole story of the person's life. Stress can be interpreted as the breakdown of the narrative flow, when the "now" blocks out the natural movement from the present towards a future. In stress, the person has lost contact with this flow towards the future, and experiences the present as an impossible task which she can neither perform nor escape. Coping can be understood as the ability to maintain narrative coherence, despite a certain degree of indeterminacy in the situation.[17] The phenomenological theory focuses upon self-becoming as the primary salutogenic factor which keeps us in good health. According to my definition, a person may have a disease or pain or disability, but if she can continue to experience herself in her life, and form new meanings and significations, she is in good psychosomatic health.

As for the therapeutical process itself, I have interpreted the cure in terms of the reinstatement of meaning transformation at the level of psycho-social structures. When patients are able to integrate previously unthinkable meanings into their narrative, to think and reflect upon them and to take a stand towards them, their body symptoms disappear. However, as any clinician knows, some patients become cured, while others do not. I cannot say anything general about this, since I have not set out to study the patient-therapist interaction in this dissertation. However, as I mentioned in an earlier chapter, certain factors such as the quality of the communication between the therapist and the clinician, the courage and willingness to change on the part of the patient, the degree of trust between patient and therapist, the "personal chemistry" between the clinician and the patient, all seem to play a part in the eventual outcome of the treatment. But these are empirical questions which require empirical investigation. At the general theoretical level, my notion of cure is tied to what I have considered to be the reason for the development of the psy-

---

17 Thanks to Jan Willner for the suggestion that coping could be understood as increased tolerance for indeterminacy (personal communication).

chosomatic solution. Because I see psychosomatics as the breakdown of structure transformation, it will be the reinstatement of that process which is responsible for the cure. How this cure works, and what facilitates this process, are topics for further research.

Concluding remarks

The dissertation is now finished, and I hope that the readers have enjoyed the ride. Part I has shown how traditional theories of psychosomatics have collapsed due to ontological, methodological problems. Although the theories examined in the first part of the dissertation do contain some interesting ideas and basic insights, dualism and methodological reductionism have made it difficult for them to coherently deal with psychosomatic phenomena. I have presented an alternative theory based upon the perspective of phenomenology, in particular the phenomenological work of Maurice Merleau-Ponty. My phenomenological theory of psychosomatics outlined in part II provides an appropriate starting point for theorizing about psychosomatics and has generated some new categories of understanding which allow us to take "a new look" at psychosomatic pathology. The theoretical ground is now laid for further work in this field, work ranging from theoretical developments to empirical studies as well as clinical applications in health care services. Whether or not this new look bears fruit, time will tell.

> "For if I have ventured amiss -- very well, then life helps me by its punishment. But if I have not ventured at all -- who then helps me?"
> --Søren Kierkegaard

324

References

Ader, R. (1980) Psychosomatic and Psychoimmunologic Research - Presidential Address 1980, *Psychosom. Med.,* vol. 42, No. 3 (May 1980).

Ader, R & Cohen, N. (1975) Behaviorally conditioned immunosuppression, *Psychosom. Med.,* 37: 333-340.

Alexander, F. (1939) Introductory Statement to *Psychosom. Med., 1939, 1,* 1.

Alexander, F. (1948) *Studies in Psychosomatic Medicine,* Franz Alexander & Thomas Morton (eds.), New York: The Ronald Press Company.

Alexander, F. (1950) *Psychosomatic Medicine,* New York: Norton.

Amacher, P. (1965) Freud's Neurological Education and Its Influence on Psychoanalytic Theory, in *Psychological Issues,* Vol. IV, no. 4, New York: International Universities Press.

Arieti, S. (1974) *Interpretation of Schizophrenia,*London: Crosby Lockwood Staples.

Arnheim, R. (1958) Emotion and Feeling in Psychology and Art. in M. Henle (ed.) *Documents of Gestalt Psychology,* in M. Henle (ed.), Berkeley: University of California Press, pp. 301-323.

Axelrod, J. (1971) Noradrenaline: fate and control of its biosynthesis, *Science,* 173: 598-606.

Backus, F.I. & Dudley, D.L. (1977) Observations of Psychosocial Factors and Their Relationship to Organic Disease, in Z.J. Lipowsky, D. Lipsitt, & P. Whybrow (eds.), *Psychosomatic Medicine; Current Trends and Clincial Applications,* New York: Oxford University Press, pp.187-203.

Ballard, E.G. (1972) On the method of phenomenological reduction, its presuppositions, and its future, in L.E. Embree (ed.) *Life-world and Consciousness. Essays for Aaron Gurwitsch,* Evanston: Northwestern University Press, pp. 101-123.

Bastiaans, J. (1969) The Role of Aggression in the Genesis of Psychosomatic Disease, *J. of Psychosomatic Research,* 13: 307-314.

Bastiaans, J. (1977) Psychoanalytic Psychotherapy, in E.D. Wittkower & H. Warnes (eds.) *Psychosomatic Medicine: Its Clinical Applications,* New York: Harper & Row Publishers, pp.86-93.

Bernet, R. (1993) *An Introduction to Husserlian Phenomenology,* Evanston, Ill: Northwestern University Press.

Binswanger, L. (1964) *Grundformen und Erkenntnis menschlichen Daseins,* Munchen: Reinhardt.

Binswanger, L. (1975) *Being-in-the-world. Selected papers of Ludwig Binswanger*, London: Souvenir Press.

Birley, J.L.T. & Connolly, J. (1976) Life Events and Physical Illness, in O. Hill (ed) *Modern Trends in Psychosomatic Medicine 3*, London: Butterworths, pp.154-165.

Bleicher, J. (1980) *Contemporary Hermeneutics, Hermeneutics as Method, Philosophy and Critique*, London: Routledge & Kegan Paul.

Bolwig, T.G. & Trimble, M.R. (eds.): (1989) *The Clinical Relevance of Kindling*, Chichester: John Wiley & Sons.

Booth, R.J. & Ashbridge, K.R. (1992) Implications of psychoimmunology for models of the immune system, in A. J. Husband (ed.). *Behavior and Immunity*, Ann Arbor: CRC Press, pp. 13-21.

Booth, R.J. & Ashbridge, K.R. (1993) A Fresh Look at the Relationship between the Psyche and the Immune System: Teleological Coherence and Harmony of Purpose, *Advances, The Journal of Mind-Body Health*, Vol. 9, No. 2, Spring, 1993.

Boss, M. (1979) *Existential Foundations of Medicine and Psychology*, New York: Aronson.

Brenner, S. & Rosen, M. (1991) *The Rosen Method Movement*, Berkeley: North Atlantic Books.

Briner, R.B. & Reynolds, S. (1993) Bad theory and bad practice in occupational stress, *The Occupational Psychologist*, 19.

Bruhn, J.G. (1966) Social Aspects of Coronary Heart Disease in Two Adjacent, Ethnically Different Communities, *American Journal of Public Health*, 56: 1493-1506.

Bunkan, B. (1983) *Undersökelse og behanling ved muskelspenninger*, Lund: Liberförlag.

Buytendijk, F.J.J. (1974) *Prolegomena to an Anthropological Physiology*, Pittsburgh: Duquesne University Press.

Bynum W.F. & Porter, R. (eds.) (1993) The Role of Emotional Factors in Somatic Disease, in *Companion Encyclopedia of the History of Medicine*, Vol. 2 London: Routledge.

Campell, D.T. (1974) "Downward Causation" in Heirarchially Organized Biological Systems, in F.J. Ayala & T. Dobzhansky (eds.) *Studies in the philosophy of biology: reduction and related problems*, Berkeley: University of California Press, pp. 179-187.

Cannon,W. (1914) The interrelations of emotions as suggested by recent physiological researches, *Americal Journal of Psychology*, 25: 256-82.

Cannon, W. (1929) *Bodily Changes in Pain, Hunger, Fear and Rage* (2nd ed.), New York: D. Appelton.

Cannon,W. (1932) *The Wisdom of the Body*, London: Kegan Paul, Trench, Trubner.

Cannon, W. (1935) The Stresses and Strains of Homeostasis, *Amer. J. Med. Sci.*, 189:1-14.

Cheren, S. (ed). (1989) *Psychosomatic Medicine: Theory, Physiology and Practice, Vols I & II*. Madison Connecticut: International Universities Press, Inc.

Cohen, S. & Williamson, G.M. (1991) Stress and infectious disease in humans, *Psychological Bulletin*, 109: 5-24.

Csordas, T.J. (1993) Somatic Modes of Attention, *Cultural Anthropology,* Vol. 8, no. 2, May 1993.

Csordas, T.J. (ed.) (1994) *Embodiment and Experience. The existential ground of culture and self,* Cambridge: Cambridge University Press.

Cunningham, A.J. (1978) "Gestalt Immunology": A less reductionistic approach to the subject, in G.I. Bell, A. S. Perelson, G.H. Pimbley Jr. (eds.): *Theoretical Immunology,* New York: Marcel Dekker, Inc., pp. 45-61.

Damasio, A. (1994) *Descartes' Error: Emotion, Reason, and the Human Brain,* New York: Avon Books.

David-Ménard, M. (1983/1989) *Hysteria from Freud to Lacan, body and language in psychoanalysis,* Ithaca: Cornell University Press.

Davidson, D. (1968) Actions, Reason and Causes. In Care and Landesman (eds) *Readings in the Theory of Action,* Indiana.

Delbrück, M. (1970) A physicist's renewed look at biology: twenty years later, *Science* 168: 1312-1315.

Dennett, D. (1991) *Consciousness Explained,* Boston: Little, Brown and Company.

de Rivera, J. (1977) *A Structural Theory of Emotions,* New York: International Universities Press. Inc.

Derrida, J. (1967/1973) *Speech and Phenomena,* Evanston: Northwestern University Press.

de Sousa, R. (1987) *The Rationality of Emotion,* Cambridge, Mass: The MIT Press.

Deutsch, F. (1939) The Choice of Organ in Organ Neuroses, *Int. J. Psa.,* Vol. 20.

Deutsch, F. (1959) *On the Mysterious Leap from the Mind to the Body: A Workshop Study on the Theory of Conversion,* New York: International Universities Press, Inc.

de Waelhens, A. (1951) *Une Philosophie de l'ambiguité: L'existentialisme de M. Merleau-Ponty,* Louvain.

Dilthey, W. (1894/1977) Ideas concerning a descriptive and analytic psychology, in *Descriptive Psychology and Historical Understanding,* The Hague: Martinus Nijhoff.

Douglas, M. (1970/1982) *Natural Symbols,* New York: Pantheon.

Downing, G. (1980) Psychodiagnosis and the body, in G. Kogan (ed.) *Your body works,* Berkeley: Transformation Press.

Dunbar, F. (1935) *Emotions and Bodily Changes, A Survey of Literature on Psychosomatic Interrelationships,* Columbia University Press: New York.

Dunbar, F. (1943) *Psychosomatic Diagnosis,* New York: Hoeber.

Duval, S. & Wicklund, R.A. (1972) *A Theory of Objective Self-awareness,* New York: Academic Press.

Engel, G.L. (1968) A life setting conducive to Illness: The giving-up, given-up complex, *Archives of Internal Medicine,* 69: 293-300.

Engel, G.L. (1977) The Need for a New Medical Model: A Challange for Biomedicine, *Science;* 196: 129-136.

Engel, G.L. & Schmale, A.H. jr. (1967) Psychoanalytic theory of somatic disorder, *Journal of the American Psychoanalytic Association,* 15: 344-365.

327

Feigl, H. (1958) The "Mental" and the "Physical", in H. Feigl, M. Scriven & G. Maxwell (eds.) *Concepts, Theories and the Mind-Body Problem*, Minneapolis: University of Minnesota Press, pp. 370-497.

Fenichel, O. (1946) Nature and Classification of the So-Called Psychosomatic Phenomena, in Hanna Fenichel & David Rapaport (eds.) *The Collected Papers of Otto Fenichel*, London: Routledge & Kegan Paul Limited.

Fingarette, H. (1963) *The Self in Transformation: Psychoanalysis, Philosophy, and the Life of the Spirit*, New York: Basic Books Inc.

Fletcher, B. & Jones, F. (1993) A refutation of Karasek's demand-discretion model of occupational stress with a range of dependent measures, *Journal of Organizational Behavior*, 14: 319-331.

Folkman, S., Lazarus, R.S., Rand, J.G. & DeLongis, A. (1986) Appraisal, Coping, Health Status and Psychological Symptoms, *Journal of Personality & Social Psychology* 1986, Vol. 50, no. 3: 571-579.

Fox, B.H. (1981) Psychosocial Factors and the Immune System in Human Cancer, in R. Ader (ed.): *Psychoneuroimmunology*, New York: Academic Press, pp. 103-157.

Freud, S. (1893-1895) Studies on hysteria, *Standard edition of the complete works of Sigmund Freud*, Vol. II, London: The Hogarth Press.

Freud, S. (1894) The Neuro-Psychosis of Defense, *Standard edition of the complete works of Sigmund Freud*, Vol. III, London: The Hogarth Press.

Freud, S. (1895) Project for a Scientific Psychology, *Standard edition of the complete works of Sigmund Freud*, Vol. I, London: The Hogarth Press.

Freud, S. (1898) Sexuality in the aetiology of the neuroses, *Standard edition of the complete works of Sigmund Freud*, Vol. III, London: The Hogarth Press.

Freud, S. (1909) Notes upon a case of obsessional neurosis, *Standard edition of the complete works of Sigmund Freud*, Vol. X, London:The Hogarth Press.

Freud, S. (1910) Five Lectures on Psycho-Analysis, *Standard edition of the complete works of Sigmund Freud*, Vol. XI, London: The Hogarth Press.

Freud, S. (1914) On Narcissism: An Introduction, *Standard edition of the complete works of Sigmund Freud*, Vol. XIV, London: The Hogarth Press.

Freud, S. (1915) Papers on metapsychology, *Standard edition of the complete works of Sigmund Freud*, Vol. XIV, London: The Hogarth Press.

Freud, S. (1916-1917) The Common Neurotic State, *Standard edition of the complete works of Sigmund Freud*, Vol. XVI, London: The Hogarth Press.

Freud, S. (1918) An infantile neurosis, *Standard edition of the complete works of Sigmund Freud*, Vol. XVII, London: The Hogarth Press.

Freud, S. (1920) Beyond the Pleasure Principle, *Standard edition of the complete works of Sigmund Freud*, Vol. XVIII, London: The Hogarth Press.

Freud, S. (1926) Inhibitions, Symptoms and Anxiety, *Standard edition of the complete works of Sigmund Freud*,Vol. XX, London: The Hogarth Press.

Freud, S. (1933) New Introductory Lecture on Psycho-Analysis, *Standard edition of the complete works of Sigmund Freud*, Vol. XXII, London: The Hogarth Press.

Freud, S. (1938/1940) An Outline of Psycho-Analysis, *Standard edition of the complete works of Sigmund Freud*, Vol. XIII, London: The Hogarth Press.

Gatchel, R.J. (1995) Stress and Coping, in B. Parkinson & A.M. Coleman (eds.): *Emotion and Motivation*, London: Longman, pp. 76-95.

Goleman, D. (1995) *Emotional Intelligence*, Brockman, Inc.

Graham, D.T. (1967) Health, Disease, and the Mind-Body Problem: Linguistic Parallelism, *Psychomatic Medicine*, 29: 52-71.

Grinker, R. (1948) Hypothalamic Functions in Psychosomatic Interrelations, in F. Alexander & M. French (eds.) *Studies in Psychosomatic Medicine*, New York: The Ronald Press Company, pp. 46-84.

Grinker, R. (1973) *Psychosomatic Concepts*, New York: Jason Aronson.

Grunbaum, A. (1984) *The foundations of psychoanalysis: A philosophical critique*, Berkeley: University of California Press.

Habermas, J. (1972) *Knowledge and Human Interest*, Boston: Beacon Press.

Harte, J. (1992) Psychoneuroendocrine concomitants of the Emotional Experience, in A.J. Husband (ed.) *Behavior and Immunity*, Ann Arbor: CRC Press, pp. 43-53.

Haugsgjerd, S. (1986) *Den nya psykiatrin*, Stockholm: Bokförlaget Prisma.

Heidegger, M. (1927/1962) *Being and Time*, Oxford: Basil Blackwell.

Heinroth, J.C.A. (1818) *Lehrhuch der Störungen des Seelenlebens oder der Seelenstörungen und ihrer Behandlung*, Leipzig: F.C. W. Vogel.

Hellström, O. (1994) *Vad Sjukdom vill säga*, Örebro: Bokförlaget Libris.

Hellström, O., Bullington, J., Karlsson, G., Lindqvist, P., Mattsson, B. (1998a) Doctors' Attitudes to Fibromyalgia: A Phenomenological Study, *Scand J Soc Med* Vol. 26, No. 3: 232-237.

Hellström, O. Bullington, J., Karlsson, G. Lindqvist, P., Mattsson, B. (1998b) A Phenomenological Study of Fibromyalgia: Patient Perspectives, *Scandinavian J. of Primary Health Care*.

Hempel, C.G. (1965) Aspects of Scientific Explanation, in *Aspects of Scientific Explanation and other Essays in the Philosophy of Science*, New York: The Free Press.

Hench, P.S., Kendall, E.C., Slocumb, C.N. Polley, H.F. (1949) The effect of a hormone of the adrenal cortex (17-hydroxy-11-dehydrocorticosterone: Compound E) and of pituitary adrenocorticotropic hormone on rheumatoid arthritis, Proc. Staff Mtgs. Mayo Clin. 24: 181-97.

Hinkle, L.E. (1974) The Effect of Exposure to Cultural Change, Social Change, and Changes in Interpersonal Relationships on Health, in Barbara S. Dohrenwend (ed.) Conference on stressful events, New York: pp. 9-44.

Hinkle, L.E. (1977) The concept of social "stress" in the biological and social sciences, *Science, Medicine, and Man*, 1: 31-48.

Hofer, M.A. (1975) Physiological mechanisms for cardiac control by nutritional intake after maternal separation in the young rat, *Psychosom. med.*, 37:8.

Holder, A. (1990) The Genetic Point of View, in Humberto Nagera (ed.) *Basic Psychoanalytic Concepts on Metapsychology, Conflicts, Anxiety and other Subjects*, London; Karnac Books Limited, pp. 43-46.

Holmes & Rahe (1967) The Social Readjustment Rating Scale, *Journal of Psychosomatic Research,* Vol. 11: 213-218.

Hume, D. (1888/1961) *A Treatise of Human Nature,* London: Everyman's Library No 548.

Humphrey, N. (1992) *A History of the Mind,* London: Chatto & Windus.

Husserl, E. (1913/1962) *Ideas: General Introduction to Pure Phenomenology,* Vol. I. New York: Collier Books.

Husserl, E. (1954/1970) *The Crisis of European Sciences and Transcendental Phenomenology,* Evanston: Northwestern University Press.

Ingram, R.E. (1990) Self focused attention in clinical disorders: Review and a conceptual model, *Psychological Bulletin,* 107: 156-176.

Jackson, J. (1994) Chronic pain and the tension between the body as subject and object, in *Embodiment and Experience: the existential ground of culture and self,* T.J. Csordas (ed.). Cambridge: Cambridge University Press, pp. 201-228.

Jackson, M. (1989) *Paths Toward a Clearing: Radical Empiricism and Ethnographic Inquiry,* Bloomingdale: Indiana University Press.

Jensen, M.P., Turner, J.A., Romano, J.M. Karoly, P. (1991) Coping with chronic pain: a critical review of the literature, *Pain* 47: 249-83.

Jern, S. & Carlsson, S.G. (1990) Metatheory of Psychosomatic Research. *Gothenburg Psychological Reports,* No. 4, Vol. 20.

Jewson, N.D. (1975) The Disappearance of the Sick Man from Medical Cosmology, 1770-1870, *Sociology* 10.

Johnson, M. (1987) *The Body in the Mind: The Bodily Basis of Meaning, Imagination, and Reason,* Chicago: The University of Chicago Press.

Jonas, H. (1966) *The Phenomenon of Life: towards a philosophical biology,* New York: Harper & Row Publishers.

Karasek, R., Gardell, B. & Lindell, J. (1987) Work and non-work correlates of illness and behaviour in male and female Swedish white collar workers, *Journal of Occupational Behaviour,* 8: 187-207.

Kasl, S.V. (1983) Pursuing the link between stressful life experiences and disease: a time for reappraisal, in C.L. Cooper (ed.): *Stress Research: Issues for the Eighties,* Chichester: Wiley.

Kessler, R.C. (1987) The interplay of research design strategies and data analysis procedures in evaluating the effects of stress on health, in S.V. Kasl & C.L. Cooper (eds.): *Stress and Health: Issues in Research Methodology,* Chichester: Wiley, pp. 113-140.

Kiely, W.F. (1977) From the Symbolic Stimulus to the Pathophysiological Response: Neurophysiological Mechanisms, in Z.J.Lipowsky, D. Lipsitt, P. Whybrow (eds.) *Psychosomatic Medicine: Current Trends and Clinical Applications* New York: Oxford University Press, pp. 206-218.

Kimball, C.P. (1970) Conceptual Developments in Psychosomatic Medicine: 1939-1969, *Psychosom. Med.* 73: 307-316.

Kitcher, P. (1992) *Freud's Dream; A Complete Interdisciplinary Science of Mind,* Cambridge, Massachusetts: The MIT Press.

Kockelmans, J.J. (1972) Phenomenologico-psychological and transcendental reductions in Husserl's "Crisis," in A.T. Tymieniecka (ed.) *Analecta Husserliana,* Vol. II Dordrecht: Reidel, pp. 78-89.

Krakowski, A.J. (1977) Process of Consultation, in E.D. Wittkower & H. Warnes (eds.) *Psychosomatic Medicine: Its Clinical Applications,* New York: Harper and Row Publishers, pp. 26-39.

Kvale, S. (ed.) (1989) *Issues of Validity in Qualitative Research,* Lund: Student Literature.

Lakoff, G. & Johnson, M. (1980) *Metaphors We Live By,* Chicago: The University of Chicago Press.

Lazarus, R.S. (1977) Psychological stress and coping in adaption and illness, in Z.J. Lipowsky, D. Lipsitt, P. Whybrow (eds.) *Psychosomatic Medicine; Current Trends and Applications,* New York: Oxford University Press, pp. 14-26.

Lazarus, R.S. (1993) Coping Theory and Research: Past, Present and Future, *Psychosom. Med.,* 55:234-247.

Lazarus, R.S. & Folkman, S. (1984) *Stress, Appraisal, and Coping,* New York: Springer Publishing Co.

Leder, D. (1990) *The Absent Body,* Chicago: The University of Chicago Press.

Lesche, C. & Stjernholm-Madsen, E. (1976) *Psykoanalysens Videnskapsteori,* Copenhagen: Munksgaard.

Lévinas, É. (1947/1987) *Time and the Other,* Pittsburgh: Duquesne University Press.

Levine, F.M. (1991) *Mapping the Mind,* Hillsdale, NJ: The Analytic Press.

Lindahl, B.I.B. & Århem, P. (1994) Mind as a Force Field: Comments on a New Interactionist Hypothesis, *J. theor. Biol.* 171: 29-39.

Lipowsky, Z.J. (1976) Psychosomatic Medicine: An Overview, in O. W. Hill (ed.) *Modern Trends in Psychosomatic Medicine 3,* London: Butterworths, pp. 1-20.

Lipowsky, Z.J. (1984) What Does the Word "Psychosomatic" Really Mean? A Historical and Semantic Inquiry, *Psychosom. Med.* 46: 153-171.

Lolas, F. & von Rad, M. (1989) Alexithymia, in Stanley Cherin (ed.) *Psychosomatic Medicine: Theory, Physiology, and Practice,* Vol 1. Madison, Connecticut: International Universities Press, pp. 189-237.

Low, S.M. (1994) Embodied metaphors: nerves as lived experience. in T.J. Csordas (ed.) *Embodiment and Experience: The existential ground of culture and self.* Cambridge: Cambridge University Press, pp. 139-162.

Lowen, A. (1975) *Bioenergetics,* New York: Coward, McCann & Geoghegan.

Mackie, J.L. (1974) *The Cement of the Universe: a Study of Causation,* Oxford: Oxford University Press.

Madison, G.B. (1981) *The Phenomenology of Merleau-Ponty,* Ohio: Ohio University Press.

Mallin, S.B. (1979) *Merleau-Ponty's Philosophy,* New Haven: Yale University Press.

Margretts, E.L. (1950) The Early History of the Word "Psychosomatic", *Canadian Medical Association Journal,* Oct. 1950, Vol. 63: 402-404.

Magretts, E.L. (1954) Historical Notes on Psychosomatic Medicine, in Eric D. Wittkower & R. A. Cleghorn (eds.) *Recent Developments in Psychosomatic Medicine*, London: Sir Isaac Pitman & Sons, Ltd.

Marty, P.M. & de M'Uzan, M. (1963) La pensée opératoire, *Rev. Franc. Psychoanal.*, 27, (Suppl.): 1345.

Mason, J. W. (1975) Emotion as reflected in patterns of endocrine integration, in L. Levi (ed.) *Emotions: Their parameters and measurement*, New York: Raven.

Mason, J.W., Maher, J.T., Hartley, L.H., Mougey, E., Perlow, M.J. & Jones, L.G. (1976) Selectivity of corticosteroid and catecholamine response to various natural stumuli, in G. Serban (ed.) *Psychopathology of human adaption*, New York: Plenum, pp. 147-171.

Mathews, G. & Wells A. (1988) Relationships between anxiety, self-consciousness, and cognitive failure, *Cognition and Emotion*, 2: 123-132.

Mattis, I. (ed.). (1994) *På Freuds Divan*, Stockholm: Natur och Kultur.

McDougall, J. (1982/1986) *Theatres of the Mind; Illusion and Truth on the Psychoanalytic Stage*, London: Free Association Books.

McDougall, J. (1989) *Theatres of the Body*, London: W.W. Norton & Company, Ltd.

Merleau-Ponty, M. (1942/1963) *The Structure of Behavior*, Boston: Beacon Press.

Merleau-Ponty, M. (1945) *Phénoménologie de la Perception*, Éditions Gallimard.

Merleau-Ponty, M. (1945/1962) *Phenomenology of Perception*, Translation Colin Smith. London: Routledge & Kegan Paul.

Merleau-Ponty, M. (1947/1964) *The Primacy of Perception*, Evanston: Northwestern University Press.

Merleau-Ponty, (1964/1973) *Consciousness and the Acquisition of Language*, Evanston: Northwestern University Press.

Merleau-Ponty, M. (1964/1993) "Cézanne's Doubt" in *The Merleau-Ponty Aesthetics Reader: Philosophy and Painting*, Galen A. Johnson & Michael B. Smith (eds.) Evanston: Northwestern University Press, pp. 59-75.

Merleau-Ponty, M. (1964) "The Child's Relations with Others" in *The Primacy of Perception*, Evanston: Northwestern University Press, pp. 96-155.

Merleau-Ponty, M. (1964/1968) *The Visible and the Invisible*, Evanston: Northwestern University Press.

Merleau-Ponty, M. (1969/1973) *The Prose of the World*, Evanston: Northwestern University Press.

Metal'nikov, S. & Chorine, V. (1926) Rôle des réflexes conditionnels dans l'immunité. *Ann. Inst. Pasteur, Paris,* 40: 893-900.

Mirsky, I.A. (1958) Physiologic, psychologic and social determinants in the etiology of duodenal ulcer, *Amer J Dig Dis* 3: 285-314.

Moss, G. E. (1977) Biosocial Resonation: A Conceptual Model of the Links betwen Social Behavior and Physical Illness, in Z.J. Lipowsky, D. Lipsitt, P. Whybrow (eds.) *Psychosomatic Medicine: Current Trends and Clinical Applications*, New York: Oxford University Press, pp. 90-99.

Nagel, E. (1961) *The Structure of Science*, London: Routledge & Kegan Paul.

Nagel, T. (1974) What is it like to be a bat? *Phil. Rev.* 83: 435-450.

Nagel, T. (1986) *The View from Nowhere*, Oxford: Oxford University Press.

Nagel, T. (1994) Consciousness and Objective Reality, in Richard Warner & Tadeusz Szubka (eds.) *The Mind-Body Problem*, Oxford: Blackwell Publishers, pp. 63-68.

Nemiah, J.C. & Sifneos, P.E. (1970) Affect and fantasy in patients with psychosomatic disorders, in O.W. Hill (ed.) *Modern Trends in Psychosomatic Medicine*, Vol. 2, New York: Appelton-Century-Crofts, pp. 26-34.

Nemiah, J.C., Freyberger, H. & Sifneos, P. (1976) Alexithymia: A View of the Psychosomatic Process, in O. W. Hill (ed.) *Modern Trends in Psychosomatic Medicine,* Vol. 3, London: Butterworths, pp. 430-439.

Newton, T. (1995) *"Managing" Stress: Emotion and Power at Work*, London: Sage Publications.

Nordenfelt, L. (1987) *On the Nature of Health*, Dordrecht: D. Reidel Publishing Company.

Ots, T. (1994) The silenced body - the expresssive *Leib*: on the dialectic of mind and life in Chinese cathartic healing, in T.J. Csordas (ed.) *Embodiment and Experience: the existential ground of culture and self.* Cambridge: Cambridge University Press, pp. 116-136.

Palmblad, J. (1981) Stress and Immunologic Competence: Studies in Man, in R. Ader (ed.) *Psychoneuroimmunology*, New York: Academic Press, pp. 229-257.

Parkinson, B. (1995) Emotion, in B. Parkinsson & A.M. Colman (eds.) *Emotion and Motivation*, London: Longman.

Patkai, P. (1971) Catecholamine excretion in pleasant and unpleasant situations, *Acta Psychologica*, 35: 352-363.

Pearlin, L.I. & Schooler, C. (1978) The Structure of Coping, *Journal of Health and Social Behavior*, 1978, Vol. 19 (March), 2-21.

Pines, F. (1990) *Drive, Ego, Object, and Self; A Synthesis for Clinical Work*, Basic Books.

Pollio, H.R., Henley, T.B., Thompson, C.J. (eds.) (1997) *The Phenomenology of Everyday Life*, Cambridge: Cambridge University Press.

Pollock, K. (1988) On the nature of social stress: production of a modern mythology, *Social Science and Medicine*, 26: 381-92.

Popper, K.R. & Eccles, J.C. (1977) *The Self and its Brain: An Argument for Interactionism*, London/New York: Routledge.

Putnam, H. (1976) The Mental Life of Some Machines, in J. Glover (ed.) *The Philosophy of Mind. Oxford Readings in Philosophy*, Oxford University Press, pp. 84-100.

Reich, W. (1933) *Charakteranalyse*, Sexpol Verlag.

Reiser, M. (1966) Toward an Interrated Psychoanalytic-Physiological Theory of Psychosomatic Disorders, in Rudolph M. Loewenstein, Lottie M. Newman, Max Schur & Albert J. Solnit (eds.) *Psychoanalysis- A General Psychology; Essays in Honor of Heinz Hartmann*, New York: International Universitites Press, Inc., pp. 570-582.

Ricoeur, P. (1970) *Freud and Philosophy: An Essay on Interpretation*, New Haven: Yale University Press.

Ricoeur, P. (1974) *The Conflict of Interpretations: Essays in Hermeneutics,* Evanston: Northwestern University Press.

Ricoeur, P. (1981a) *Hermeneutics & Human Sciences,* Cambridge: Cambridge University Press.

Ricoeur, P. (1981b) The question of proof in Freud's psychoanalytic writings, in J.B. Thompson (ed.) *Hermeneutics and the human sciences,* Cambridge: Cambridge University Press, pp. 247-273.

Rooymans, H.G.M. (1974) Some remarks about training in psychosomatic medicine, *Psychiat Neurol Neurochir* 76: 305-307.

Rubenstein, B.B. (1965) Psychoanalytic Theory and the Mind-Body Problem, in Norman S. Greenfield & William C. Lewis (eds.) *Psychoanalysis and Current Biological Thought,* Madison: The University of Wisconson Press, pp. 35-56.

Rubenstein, B.B. (1967) Explanation and Mere Description: A Metascientific Examination of Certain Aspects of the Psychoanalytic Theory of Motivation, in R. Holt (ed.) *Motives and thought,* New York: International Universities Press, pp. 20-79.

Rudebeck, C.E. (1991) Body-as-Nature, Body-as-Self, *Scand J Prim Health Suppl 1*: 40-47.

Ruesch, J. (1948) The infantile personality, *Psychosom. Med.* 10: 134-144.

Ryle, G. (1949) *The Concept of Mind,* New York: Barnes & Noble Books.

Sachs, L. (1996) *Sjukdom som oordning,* Falun: Gedins.

Sapolsky, R.M. (1994) *Why Zebras Don't Get Ulcers,* New York: W.H. Freeman and Company.

Sartre, J-P. (1943/1956) *Being and Nothingness,* New York: Simon & Schuster.

Sartre, J-P. (1948) *The Emotions: Outline of a Theory,* New York: Philosophical Library.

Saul, L.J. (1948) The Physiological Effects of Psychoanalytic Therapy, in Franz Alexander & Thomas Morton French (eds.) *Studies in Psychosomatic Medicine,* New York: The Ronald Press Company, pp. 91-100.

Schafer, R. (1976) *A New Language for Psychoanalysis,* New Haven: Yale University Press.

Schafer, R. (1983) *The analytic attitude,* New York: Basic Books.

Schur, M. (1950) Basic Problems of Psychosomatic Medicine, in H. Herma & G.M. Kurth (eds.) *Elements of Psychoanalysis,* Cleveland: The World Publishing Company, 237-266.

Schur, M. (1955) Comments on the metapsychology of somatization, in *Psychoanalytic Study of the Child,* 10: 119-124.

Selye, H. (1937) Studies on Adaption, *Endocrinology,* 21: 168-88.

Selye, H. (1946) The general adaption syndrome and the diseases of adaption, *Journal of Clinical Endocrinology,* 6: 117-230.

Selye, H. (1950) *Stress,* Montreal: Acta.

Selye, H. (1956) *The Stress of Life,* New York: McGraw-Hill.

Selye, H. (1974) *Stress without Distress,* Philadelphia: Lippincott.

Selye, H. & Fortier C. (1950) Adaptive reactions to stress, *Res. Publ. Assoc. Nerv. Ment. Dis.* 29: 3-18.

Solomon, G.F. (1981) Emotional and Personality Factors in the Onset and Course of Autoimmune Diseases, Particularly Rheumatoid Arthritis, in R. Ader (ed.): *Psychoimmunology*, New York: Academic Press, pp. 159-182.

Speisman, J.C., Lazarus, R.S., Mordkoff, A.M., Davidson, L.A. (1964) The experimental reduction of stress based on ego-defense theory, *J Abnorm Soc Psychol* 68: 367-80.

Spence, D. (1982) *Narrative truth and historical truth,* New York: W.W. Norton & Company.

Spiegelberg, H. (1982) *The Phenomenological Movement,* The Hague: Martinus Nijhoff Publishers.

Straus, E. (1980) *Phenomenological Psychology,* New York and London: Garland Publishing Inc.

Stoutland, F. (1982) Philosophy of action: Davidson, von Wright and the debate over causation, *Comtemporary philosophy. A new survey.* Vol. 3: 45-72.

Sulloway, F. (1979) *Freud: Biologist of the Mind,* New York: Basic Books.

Taylor, C. (1989) *The Sources of the Self,* Cambridge: Cambridge University Press.

Taylor, J.T., Bagby, R.M. & Parker, J.D.A. (1991) The Alexithymia Construct: A Potential Paradigm for Psychosomatic Medicine, *The Journal of the Academy of Psychosomatic Medicine,* 32: no. 2, Spring 1991.

Toombs, K. (1992) *The Meaning of Illness, a phenomenological account of the different perspectives of physician and patient,* Dordrecht: Kluwer Academic Publishers.

Van den Berg, J.H. (1961) *The changing nature of man,* New York: W.W. Norton.

Varela, F.J., Thompson, E. & Rosch, E. (eds.) (1996) *The Embodied Mind: Cognitive Science and Human Experience,* Cambridge Mass: The MIT Press.

von Uexküll, T. (1963) *Grundfragen der psychosomatischen Medzin,* Hamburg: Rowohlt-Taschenbuchverlag.

Weiner, H. (1972) Presidential Address: some Comments on the Transduction of Experience by the Brain: Implications for our Understanding of the Relationship of Mind to Body, *Psychosom. Med.,* 34: No. 4, July-August 1972.

Weiner, H. (1977) *Psychobiology and Human Disease,* New York: Elsevier.

Weiner, H. (1979) Psychobiological Markers of Disease, *Psychiatric Clinics of North America,* Vol. 2, No. 2, August 1979: 227-242.

Weiner, H. (1984) An Integrative Model of Health, Illness, and Disease, *Health & Social Work,* National Association of Social Workers, inc. 9: 253-260.

Weiner, H. (1987) Some Unexplored Regions of Psychosomatic Medicine, *Psychotherapy and Psychosomatics,* 47: 153-159.

Weiner, H. (1989) The Dynamics of the Organism: Implications of Recent Biological Thought for Psychosomatic Theory and Research, *Psychosom. Med.,* 51: 608-635.

Weiner, H. (1992a) *Perturbing the Organism: The Biology of Stressful Experience,* Chicago: The University of Chicago Press.

Weiner, H. (1992b) Specificity and Specification: Two Continuing Problems in Psychosomatic Research, *Psychosom. Med.,* 54: 567-587.

Weiner, H. (1995) Cunningham's Cogent Points Are Too General, *ADVANCES: The Journal of Mind-Body Health,* vol. 11, No. 2, Spring 1995.

Weiner, H. & Fawzy, F.I. (1989) An Integrative Model of Health, Disease and Illness, in S. Cherin (ed.) *Psychosomatic Medicine: Theory, Physiology, and Practice*, vol. I. Madison: International Universities Press, pp. 9-44.

Weiner, H., Thaler, M., Reiser, M.F., Mirsky, A. (1957) Etiology of duodenal ulcer, *Psychosom. Med.*, 19: 1-10.

Weiss, J.H. (1977) The Current State of the Concept of a Psychosomatic Disorder, in Z.J. Lipowsky, D. Lipsitt, P. Whybrow (eds.). *Psychosomatic Medicine: Current Trends and Clinical Applications*, New York: Oxford University Press, pp.162-171.

Wittgenstein, L. (1922) *Tractatus Logico-Philosophicus*, London: Kegan Paul.

Wittkower, E.D. (1974) Historical perspective of contemporary psychosomatic medicine, *Int. J. Psychiat. Med.*, 5: 309.

Wolff, C.T., Friedman, S.B., Hofer, M.A. & Mason, J.W. (1964) Relationship between psychological defenses and mean urinary 17-hydroxycorticosteroid excretion rates: I. A Predictive study of parents with fatally ill children, *Psychosomatic Medicine*, 26: 576-591.

Wolff, H.G. (1953) *Stress and Disease*, Springfield, Ill. Charles C Thomas, Publisher

von Wright, G. H. (1971) *Explanation and Understanding*, Great Britain: Routledge & Kegan Paul.

von Wright, G.H. (1974) *Causality and Determinism*, New York: Columbia University Press.

Zaner, R. (1964) *The Problem of Embodiment: Some Contributions to a Phenomenology of the Body*, The Hague: Martinus Nijhoff.